'Nick Holdsworth's book . . . is a bird's view of a people in rapid transition. A camera's angle on subjects which, however, achieves something that cameras rarely do – a warm, compassionate and even empathic touch . . . It is an honest book by someone who is not grinding any political axes, either clean or dirty. It is a book that anyone remotely interested in Russia or just people amidst a social upheaval should read.'

Sergei Roy, editor-in-chief, *Moscow News*

'I started to read this book with suspicion. The problem was in the title. It reminded me that the author is speaking to a mass foreign readership for whom the main purpose of reading this book about our country is to look through a keyhole and see not those things which are true, but that which corresponds to the stereotypes formed in their minds by press, TV and bad journalists' books. Fortunately the pretentious title is the only thing that is pretentious about this book.

'In Nick's book there are people, many of them. I know them – not personally – I know these types from our Russian reality. He found them. He cultivated them. They opened up to him and he forced them to tell the truth.

'Each person in this book plays a role precisely devised by the author. Each comes in order to share his experience from which the truth about today's Russia is formed.'

Igor Mozheiko, historian and writer

Moscow: The Beautiful and the Damned

Moscow
The Beautiful and the Damned

LIFE IN RUSSIA IN TRANSITION

Nick Holdsworth

André Deutsch

First published in 2000
This edition published 2003
by André Deutsch
An imprint of the
Carlton Publishing Group
20 Mortimer Street
London W1T 3JW

A catalogue record for this book is available from the British Library

ISBN 0 233 00998 1

Typeset by Derek Doyle & Associates, Liverpool
Printed and bound in Great Britain by Mackays

For Irena

Contents

Preface and Acknowledgements

Since first arriving in Russia at Moscow's Byelorussky railway station on a hot May morning in 1991 my life has been inextricably bound up with this beautiful, fascinating and mysterious country. I was intoxicated by Russia's people, language, history and culture from that very first moment, and the sense of something very different and essentially unknowable has never left me.

Russia was always an enigma for me. As a child I recall being fascinated by this faraway land, shrouded in mystery and hidden behind a political Iron Curtain. We met Russians during family holidays in Eastern Europe in the 1970s. I remember watching jolly Russian women dressed in bright clothes performing impromptu traditional dances when we came across their tour bus at a picnic spot in Bulgaria – somewhere I still have the small Lenin lapel badges they gave me as souvenirs.

Images of frozen Siberian landscapes, of prison camps hidden away in the harsh wastes of a vast land, filled my boyhood imagination. The idea that one day I would be able not only to visit, but to live and work in Russia seemed incredible. At university my focus was turned westward and I spent summers working and travelling in America. Russia was still locked behind its Cold War façade and Mikhail Gorbachev was yet to enter the world stage and begin opening up this strange place.

In the summer of 1987 I visited Dresden, East Germany, part of an official exchange group from Coventry, where I was working as a reporter on the local evening newspaper. Passing through the border controls was the stuff of spy novels – sniffer dogs, barbed wire and high concrete walls everywhere. Two years later the Communist regimes of Eastern Europe started collapsing and the notion that travelling and working in Russia and other countries of the Soviet Union might be possible began to grow.

My father, Bill, had been to Russia for the 1980 Moscow Olympics. There had been talk that I would go too but school-leaving exams made this impossible. We had long talked of visiting Russia and finally, in the spring of 1991, the opportunity arose. We took the train across Europe and two days later, after passing through Berlin, Warsaw, Brest and Minsk, arrived in Moscow. The ten days we spent as guests of a business acquaintance of my father were hectic and hilarious. I had taught myself enough Russian from a BBC course to read the metro station names and engage in embarrassingly rudimentary conversation. We met dozens of people, explored scores of fascinating ideas and even managed to do some work – my first Russian story, an interview with the deputy mayor of Moscow, was published in, of all places, the *Municipal Journal*, a local government magazine, the very week of the August putsch.

After the events of August 1991 I was desperate to get back to Moscow. By this time I was freelancing for the *Sunday Express* and it was thanks to the paper that I found myself in Moscow again in January 1992, commissioned to write a piece about a village called Yeltsin. Moscow-based photographer Jeremy Nicholl had come up with the idea for the story and it was his insistence that Russia was wide open for freelances that strengthened my determination to come back and work in Moscow.

It took a while to get to the point where I felt confident

enough to move out and base myself in Moscow full-time, but between 1992 and 1995 I shuttled back and forth whenever I had enough commissions from editors to warrant the expense. In November 1995 I moved out here permanently and have spent most of my time exploring Russia and the former Soviet republics ever since.

I have been fortunate and many, many Russians have extended their hospitality to me, welcoming me into their hearts and homes.

My thanks are due to Irena Alexandrovna, my landlady for several years, for her kindness and patience, especially since my Russian language skills were so poor at first. To Inna Stam, my Russian teacher, I owe an immense debt of gratitude for her help in bringing my Russian to a reasonable level of fluency.

I have made so many good Russian friends it would be impossible to mention them all, but Marina Goon and Luba Boris have been both dear friends and gifted interpreters. Valya and Yuri Kryukov, Igor Mozheiko, Olga Borovik and Vera Obolonkina have all also been loyal, generous and supportive.

Among my friends and colleagues in the foreign press and expatriate community, I should mention Iain Law and Michael Bird of the British Council, Marcus Warren at the *Daily Telegraph*, Ben Aris, a fellow freelance writer, and Peter Ford and Edith Coron at the *Christian Science Monitor*. Russian colleagues, including Professor Svetlana Ter-Minasova and Professor Yulia Tourchaninova, have provided invaluable help and friendship over the years. Grigory Simanovitch, press secretary of Russian Public Television, was a keen advocate of this book. Thanks are also due to David Jobbins, foreign editor of *The Times Higher Education Supplement*, for his unflagging support; to Jeff Kaye, Ray Bennett and Matt King of the *Hollywood Reporter*; and to all those commissioning editors in

London and elsewhere who have ordered – and paid for – the hundreds of stories I've filed from Russia since 1991.

To all those people who agreed to open their lives to me to make this book possible I shall always be indebted. Not every one wished to be identified by their real names, but my thanks are due in equal measure to all, identified or not.

Irena Sashenkova, Inna Stam and Sergei Roy read the draft manuscript of the book and made valuable and intelligent comments and corrections. Dr Mark Galeotti, director of the Organized Russian and Eurasian Crime Research Unit at Keele University, was particularly helpful in the preparation of the chapter on the Mafia.

Thanks are due to my agent, Jonathan Harris, of Associated Publicity Holdings, for having the faith and courage to take on me and my project; to Louise Dixon, my editor at André Deutsch for her patient and good humoured guidance through the process of planning, researching and writing this book; and to Lesley Levene for her excellent and painstaking copy-editing.

My love and thanks must also go to my parents, Bill and Wyn, brother Simon and sister Claire. To my grandmother, Annie, who celebrated her hundred and first birthday in April 1999, as I was in the thick of researching the book, congratulations! Her recollection that the Bolshevik Revolution of 1917 'cost my father his job' – because my great-grandfather had been working in a munitions factory under contract to Tsar Nicholas, always caused great amusement when related to Russian friends. To my Russian family – to Irena, my wife, her mother, Vera, her father Vyacheslav, and brother Andrei – thanks for the ever open welcome into your *dur-dom* – mad house!

Nick Holdsworth
Moscow, 1999

Prologue

Moscow: The Beautiful and the Damned – Life in Russia in Transition came into focus one wintry December's night in Moscow in 1996, when I found myself drinking vodka and swapping stories with a group of Muscovites in their mid-thirties at a school reunion party. The drunken jokes, the old stories regaled to laughter and embarrassment, would have been familiar anywhere in the world. But this group of Russians, like all their 146 million compatriots, were now living lives for which little in their formal Communist-era education could have prepared them. The bland, innocent faces peering from the old class photograph of seventeen-year-old school leavers in 1979 were the source of much mirth as it was handed around the group. But the gulf between their lives then and now revealed a snapshot of the human side of a nation in transition. These Russians are the key generation in the country's chaotic emergence from a Soviet past to a more modern future. Brought up under Soviet leader Brezhnev, at university, starting families and careers during President Mikhail Gorbachev's perestroika reforms, and confronted by a society changing beyond recognition since 1991, when the Soviet Union collapsed, this generation is critical to Russia's future. Through people like this, their families and friends, the human story of Russia in transition can be told.

School Number 279 had been founded to provide an education for the children of the large numbers of Communist Party apparatchiks who were then moving into the new apartment mansions that were creeping out in Stalinist-designed fingers into what was then Moscow's rural green belt. It was now celebrating its sixtieth birthday.

The large, four-storey concrete block school, which sits on a small rise overlooking the traffic-choked four-lane Prospekt Mira (Peace Prospect), a stone's throw from Moscow's famous Kosmos monument to the Cold War space race – where a soaring Dan Dare of a rocket heads for the stars at the tip of a sweeping 200-foot arch of steel – was thronged with hundreds of former pupils, from the crowds of excited teenagers who had just started their university studies after leaving the previous summer, to the declining band of frail, elderly men and women who remembered the dark days of Stalin's purges and the Nazi invasion which followed a few years later.

I was there with my friend and a former teacher at the school, Professor Yulia Tourchaninova, intending to coax some of Stalin's schoolchildren, today's pensioners, into talking about those dreadful and bewildering times when their classmates' fathers, mothers, elder brothers or sisters started disappearing in the internecine bloodletting of the party purges of 1937 onwards. Yulia, a professor of education in her forties, and I met at the rush-hour-crowded metro station VDNKH, which once marked the site of the Soviet Union's answer to Crystal Palace – an exhibition centre and park celebrating Soviet economic achievements. Here the products of Soviet science were displayed under the watchful gaze of giant sculptures of muscular peasants and workers, hammers and sickles held high. Today, as the jumble of prefabricated kiosks on the station forecourt blaring pop music from pirated cassettes testifies, Russia's economic motor has moved on. These days VDNKH is home to a warren of small, privately owned shops. Where Soviet space modules and rockets were once displayed under heroic party slogans in hangar-sized exhibition pavilions, the latest Japanese or Korean CD players, technical gadgets and music equipment can now be bought.

Picking our way through the log jam of traffic on Prospekt Mira, through the dirty car-churned slush of snow and ice, we made our way around the corner of a building site where the pavement had been carelessly grubbed out. In the early winter darkness, flinching from the passing Volgas, Ladas, Zhigulis and massive old olive-green army trucks that are ubiquitous in Russia, Yulia and I found our way to School Number 279.

Clusters of old boys and girls were visible in the evening gloom around the poorly lit entrance to the school, the tinfoil glow of their cigarette ends bright points within the cloudy condensation of their breath. Here and there the parked cars gave a clue to the material progress some had made since leaving school: among mostly old Ladas, a Mercedes and a BMW gave a glimpse of the new Russia.

Through the heavy wooden double doors of the narrow vestibule, designed to keep the bitter cold of the Russian winter out of the warm interior, and stamping snow from our boots across the flattened cardboard boxes laid over the gritty concrete floor, we entered the cloakroom area, where a mêlée of different generations of students, plus husbands, wives and children, milled about in an excited sea of laughter and chatter.

The hubbub and the chaos, the hugs and smiles as old friends met again, cut across cultural and linguistic barriers. This could have been a school reunion anywhere in the world. Faces and eyes were marked by lives of hard work or ease; here were the careful and the careless, dress reflecting social and income divisions familiar the world over. The wide, brightly lit parquet-floored corridors were crowded with people looking at the wall displays of children's work, photographs of old theatrical productions and the eager young faces peering from the pages of yearbooks stretching back decades.

It could have been anywhere but this was Russia, where on the stone stairwell a marble memorial to the school's war dead was mute testament to the horrors of the summer of 1941, when young men and women went straight from their classes to fight Hitler's army as the might of the Nazi Third Reich was unleashed on a country still scarred by what was to become known here as the Great Patriotic War. The school's own museum records the lives lost and the on-going project to locate the battlefield graves of its former pupils, displaying the rusting, bullet-holed helmets, broken rifles, shattered canteens and other detritus of war found during the annual upper-school pilgrimages to the killing fields of Novgorod, Rzhev and other parts of the old front line.

Groups of former students were by now finding their way through the throng to the school's large gymnasium hall, where prize-giving and speeches from the head, from governors and from ancient, venerated teachers from half a century ago wove another year into the pattern of the school's history. Gone were the portraits of Lenin, along with the obligatory eulogies to the Communist Party or visiting local party chiefs, but little else in this formal part of the evening would have differed from the reunions of ten or twenty years ago.

Back upstairs, however, in the warren of large, high-ceiling classrooms still decorated in the trademark dull browns and greys of the Communist command economy, the changes wrought in people over the few short years since those momentous events of August 1991 were more obvious. The collapse into disorder of the coup so ineptly plotted against President Gorbachev by the hardliners of the Central Committee of the Communist Party gave Boris Yeltsin his historic chance to command the twentieth century's second great experiment in Russian society and economy. The ordinary people from the community of School Number 279, like millions of other Russians throughout this vast country, had already lived through the first five years of this experiment.

The questions I wanted to ask the oldest people at the reunion, about their lives in the Stalinist 1930s and the 1950s, would have been unthinkable just ten years earlier. In the late 1950s Soviet leader Nikita Khrushchev had openly criticized the cult of personality Joseph Stalin had perpetuated, but a detailed exploration of the evil done during the Georgian-born dictator's rule would come only much later, as Gorbachev's policy of glasnost began to lift the covers on so much personal and national pain and shame.

Professor Tourchaninova, a familiar figure at the school who, after teaching here for a few years early in her career, had moved on to the academic side of teacher-training and maintained close links with the school, led me through the crowded corridors to the classroom where the few remaining pre-war pupils, men and women in their seventies and eighties, were celebrating their reunion with a typical Russian buffet of fruit, sweet biscuits and small open sandwiches decorated with slices of ham, cucumber or red caviare. Her introduction of me as a British journalist interested in talking with people about life in the Soviet Union in the pre-war years seemed to excite little interest among the pensioners. As we moved from table to table, with Yulia easing communication by helping with interpretation, it became obvious that their concerns were more immediate than historic: how to survive on savings made worthless through hyper-inflation; how to get by on pensions worth about £30 a month in a city rapidly rising up the league tables as one of the most expensive in the world.

Most didn't even want to think back to the 1930s. Some tacitly admitted that although they had horrific stories to tell, having stirred them in the immediate explosion of national soul-searching that had accompanied Communism's collapse in 1991, they no longer wanted to revisit that part of their past. One white-haired old man talked briefly of his denunciation during the second wave of party purges in the early 1950s, of how he lost his privileged job in a scientific research institution and was sent to the Gulag in Siberia, emerging after Stalin's death in 1953 still tainted and unable to find any work other than as a cab driver for years afterwards. But his recollections ended abruptly as some old friends came over and he turned to us and said, 'Tonight is about happy memories, not sad. The past is gone, we have to live for today.' Another woman in her seventies promised to consider my request for an interview and said I should contact her at home, but my calls in the following weeks were never returned.

Sensing the futility of pursuing the story further and aware that Yulia was itching to join her old students I gave myself up to the evening's celebrations and we made our way downstairs to the canteen, where raucous tables of different year-groups were loudly enjoying the occasion.

So much has changed in Russia in the years since 1991 and yet so much remains familiar to anyone who knew the old Soviet Union. The condition of most public institutions, impoverished by the sharp decline in public funding heralded by the break-up of the old regime, is shocking. But even during the Soviet Union's heyday the bare adequacy of design and services was something most Russians were ashamed of.

School Number 279 is a good school by anyone's standards: renowned for its dramatic productions and academic standards. The building is of a better quality than many in Moscow and the district it serves is one of the better residential areas of the capital, barely twenty minutes by metro from the Kremlin. But to walk through the washrooms – a bare, blue-tiled area served by stands of washbasins – or as one enters the canteen to visit the toilets – brick-built open stalls containing ancient and filthy floor-level pans where, after squatting, users can only hope to find some scrap of *Pravda* or *Moskovsky Komsomolets* with which to clean themselves – this is to come face to face with a reality of Russia's transition. Russians today live in two worlds. The vast majority inhabit a world much the same as they ever did, one of shortages, poverty and grubbiness, where the cultural and social distractions so heavily subsidized in Soviet times have all but disappeared. A minority, mostly young and clustered in Moscow and other large cities, enjoy something approaching a European middle-class standard of life, where hard work, luck or less than legitimate activities enable them to *remont* – restore to European standards – their apartments, run a car and take holidays in places like Cyprus, Turkey or even London.

There are winners and losers in the Russia of transition. The older generation is disproportionately numbered among the losers, but even among the key generation which straddles the change from Communism to the free market there are wide differences. When Yulia introduced me to the class of '79, looking down the long wooden bench around which the twenty men and women were seated, the differences Russia's historic shift has made, even among this small, relatively privileged, educated urban élite, were obvious.

Sitting at the end of the table next to Andrei, an insurance company administrator, and Olga, an administrator in a state-owned company, and opposite plump, balding banker Sasha, his fur-coat-clad wife next to him, the human elements of a story I had been thinking over for some time began to come into focus. The newspapers were full of the Russia of crooked politicians, a boozing president, corrupt businessmen, the hopeless lives of poverty-stricken peasants. Books on historical, political or economic Russia abounded. But nowhere had I seen the book I wanted to read: the book, if you like, I had been seeking since I came to Russia for the first time in the spring of 1991; the book that told the story of how ordinary Russians are living through the fundamental changes imposed upon them by historical circumstances.

Drinking shots of vodka, chatting with a group of classmates who were at school during the same years I was, who started university, careers and families during the same period, and then in 1991, when they were in their late twenties and established to varying degrees in their lives, had found the rulebook torn up and thrown away, I began to wonder how I and my old British classmates would have coped in such circumstances.

When Sasha pulled out the old black and white photograph and the class yearbook of 1979, the focus was pulled even sharper. The uniform young faces peering from the neatly arranged ovals were models of Communist order. There was the young Sasha, lean-faced and keen-eyed under a thick bush of hair. Andrei and Olga were easy to spot, and Sasha's wife, the prettiest girl in the class, was there too, although perhaps not quite as glamorous as the rich fur coat, expensive hairdressing and perfectly applied make-up suggested tonight.

Here were the starters under the notional equality of the Soviet Union, poised for lives in a social system where rigid rules would dictate their paths. Looking around the canteen bench of thirty-something men and women in the new Russia, the winners, losers and strugglers of today were clear to see. These old school friends – some recently rich 'new Russians', others making their way in business or professional worlds, struggling to keep some sort of decent living standards, a few lost in badly paid, Soviet-style public sector jobs – represented a snapshot of a generation which bridged Russia's transition. Old enough to know and remember the Soviet Union; young enough to take advantages of the precarious world of the new Russia.

Through the lives of people of this generation an insight into the human consequences of Russia's shift could be told. Through their parents, colleagues, former teachers and friends a picture of the real world of Russians would be revealed.

The rest of the evening continued as these sorts of events do the world over: the vodka had its effect and we all found ourselves dancing away with the school's teenaged students in the disco which had been set up in the gym. Later someone suggested a nightclub and I decided it was time to slip away as a convoy of old school friends headed for Night Flight, one of Moscow's trendier new-Russian hang-outs where the drinks cost almost as much as the high-class whores who hang around the dance floor.

But the idea had taken hold. This, then, is a glimpse into the lives of just a couple of dozen of the millions of Russians who are daily having to reinvent their lives as society is in transit around them. Some are drawn from this group of old classmates. Others are people I have met in eight years of working visits to Russia, during the last four of which I have lived in Moscow. Through their own words and experiences, ordinary Russians talk about their lives in extraordinary times. These people struggling to find purpose, meaning – and often simply a way to survive – reveal the real Russia. The Russia of the rich and of the poor. The Russia of constant pressures and uncertain rules. The Russia of Soviet-style jobs and poverty-level wages. The Russia of crime and the Mafia. The Russia of changing values and shifting roles. The quixotic and contradictory world of Russia today, where an ageing, hard-drinking president can sack his entire Kremlin cabinet one day and then calmly force a truculent parliament to accept his choice of new prime minister the next.

1

From Failed Coup to Crony Capitalism

August is a dangerous month in Russian politics. Moscow's professional, business and social élite have all left town for their holiday dachas, the dusty, sun-baked streets of the capital and its eternal intrigues forgotten for the month. Boris Yeltsin's political good fortune was to be in Moscow in mid-August 1991, when Kremlin hardliners arrested Soviet leader Mikhail Gorbachev at his Crimean holiday home and announced a change of leadership to a stunned world.

The Kremlin coup of 19 August 1991, was a ham-fisted affair engineered by Politburo insiders who lacked the guts and military support to carry it off. Sparked by the bitter opposition of a cabal of old-style Communists to the new Union Treaty between the Soviet republics and Moscow, which had been due for signature on 20 August, the State Committee for the State of Emergency, headed by Soviet Vice-President Gennady Yanayev, a sickly-looking fifty-three-year-old committed ideologist, announced their coup in a radio broadcast stressing the 'mortal danger' that hung over the Soviet 'homeland'. 'The policy of reform initiated by Gorbachev, conceived as a means to ensure the dynamic development of the country and the democratization of the life of its society, has, for a number of reasons, come to a dead end,' they told the Soviet people.[1]

The lengthy statement read as a gloomy damnation of the failures of perestroika and glasnost. Early enthusiasm had died, to be replaced by 'apathy and despair'; the public had lost confidence in authority and 'malicious mockery' of the state was on the rise. 'Extremist forces' were taking advantage of the moves towards democracy and 'prefectures, mayoralties and other illegal structures' were replacing lawfully elected soviets. Rights to work, education, health and housing were all under threat and corruption was on the rise. 'Crime is growing quickly, becoming organized and politicized. The country is sinking into an abyss of violence and lawlessness,' the committee said. 'Never in the history of the country has the propaganda of sex and violence had such scope, threatening the life and health of the future generations.' The answer was to put a brake on Gorbachev's reforms and restore good old-fashioned law and order: 'Millions of people are demanding the adoption of measures against the octopus of crime and scandalous immorality.'

The real threat, of course, was not to the health and well-being of Soviet citizens, but to the continued grip on the levers of power of Yanayev and his henchmen, who included Soviet Prime Minister Valentin Pavlov, Defence Minister Dmitri Yazov, KGB chief Vladimir Kryuchkov and Interior Minister Boris Pugo – who committed suicide to avoid arrest after the coup collapsed.

In the interests of combating the 'growing uncertainty about tomorrow and deep alarm for the future' felt by every Soviet citizen, the committee was seizing power. 'A broad, nation-wide debate on the draft of the new Union Treaty' was promised, as was the restoration 'without delay [of] legality, law and order, an end to bloodshed and [the declaration of] a merciless war on the criminal world'.

The plotters touched on many of the raw nerves of the Gorbachev years, such as declining standards of living and shortages of basic foodstuffs, while paying lip service to the promises of greater economic freedom his rule as Soviet president had ushered in. 'The country's development must not be based on a fall in the population's standard of living . . . Developing the mixed character of the national economy, we will also support private enterprise, granting it necessary opportunities for developing production and the sphere of services.'

But the true message remained clear to those who listened carefully to the mixture of populist slogans and archaic language: 'The chaotic and uncontrolled slide towards the market has aroused the explosion of egoism – regional, departmental, group and individual . . . We call on workers, peasants, the labour intelligentsia and all Soviet people to restore labour discipline and order in the shortest period of time, raise the level of production and consequently move forward decisively.'

It ended with an appeal for national unity and for 'constructive proposals' from the public and from political and labour organizations on how to restore the 'age-old friendship in the unified family of fraternal peoples and revival of the fatherland'. It was intended to be the death knell of Gorbachev's six-year experiment in reform. Within two days it had become the funeral oration for the Soviet Union, when the fragile unity of the committee crumbled before the ambivalence of the army and the defiance of Boris Yeltsin, who had been elected president of Russia two months before in the Soviet Union's first-ever direct free elections.

Early signs of lack of resolve showed when the committee went on national television to explain their actions. Flanked by his seven co-conspirators, Yanayev –

personally appointed deputy leader by Gorbachev less than a year earlier, over the objections of the Congress of People's Deputies and in a move designed to appease Kremlin hawks – outlined the reasons for the coup. Looking grey and drawn, the hands of the acting president of the Soviet Union shook with the palsy of an alcoholic suffering the DTs. By day two of the crisis, Defence Minister Yazov had resigned from the committee and Prime Minister Pavlov had been dropped after apparently suffering a heart attack.

The army was split. Half the country's 4 million servicemen were conscripts who could not be relied upon if ordered to turn their weapons on their own people. Crack units from the élite Tamanskaya Guards tank division, based at Kubinka, forty miles outside Moscow, had crossed over to Yeltsin's side and formed a defensive ring around the Russian government's White House, on the banks of the River Moscow a couple of miles from the Kremlin. Their defection signalled deep trouble for the coup; for the Tamanskayas' duties included guarding the Kremlin. If they couldn't be relied upon to further the aims of the new leaders of Communism, who could? General Pavel Grachev's top paratroops, the Ryazan Division, had also shown their colours and come over to a defiant Yeltsin, who, along with 150,000 ordinary Russians, was standing firm against the coup.

Grachev would be well rewarded for his loyalty that day, as would others who saw which way the wind was blowing. Grachev, who later became Russian Defence Minister, before being dismissed amidst a welter of corruption allegations involving expensive German cars which earned him the nickname 'Pasha Mercedes', remained loyal two years later, when he again sided with Yeltsin the next time tanks were ringing the White House, in October 1993. This time the victor of August 1991 would turn the weapons of state on his own parliament in another battle for control of Russia.

In August 1991 the issues seemed simpler and more clear-cut: Mikhail Gorbachev, the architect of perestroika, was under house arrest in the Crimea and a strange committee of Kremlin apparatchiks and opportunists was attempting to seize power. Boris Yeltsin understood that his moment had come.

An abiding image of Moscow in August 1991 is of Yeltsin clambering aboard a tank outside the White House and appealing for his supporters to resist the oppressors. What he lacked in finesse he made up for in theatricality and an instinctive awareness of the power of good timing. He ordered all army and KGB units in Russia to follow his orders as President of the Russian Federation and any involved in the coup to stand down and take no further part. Aware that the world was watching, he warned that victory for the coup leaders would mean a wave of terror equal to any delivered by Stalin being unleashed on the Russian people.

'Soldiers, officers and generals, the clouds of terror and dictatorship are gathering over the whole country. They must not be allowed to bring eternal night,' he said. To the cheers of thousands of Muscovites who braved both scores of tanks and hundreds of soldiers to join the barricades around the White House, Yeltsin's deep booming tenor continued: 'Soldiers, I believe in this tragic hour you can make the right choice. The honour and glory of Russian men of arms shall not be stained with the blood of the people. In this tragic moment for Russia, I appeal to you – do not allow yourself to be ensnared in a net of lies and promises and demagogic calls to "military duty". Think of your loved ones, your friends, our people.'[2]

Closure or censorship of newspapers, radio and television channels loyal to Yeltsin ensured that most Russian people would not hear Yeltsin's views. But a wave of popular protests against the coup in Leningrad, where 200,000 rallied in the Winter Palace square, and regional capitals including Riga, Latvia – where Soviet troops killed one man as they stormed a radio station – signalled that wresting control from Gorbachev would not be a simple matter of issuing a statement through the TASS news agency.

Fearful of ordering troops into action against Yeltsin and his pro-democracy demonstrators manning the barricades, and uncertain of the undivided support of the army, the State Committee for the State of Emergency collapsed. Gorbachev, still dressed in his casual holiday clothes, was released from house arrest in the Crimea, where he had been held by the KGB, and flown back to Moscow. For him it was the end: Boris Yeltsin had firmly grasped the mantle of leadership in the critical hours after Monday 19 August. Although the Soviet Union as a political entity was to endure until the end of December that year, when Yeltsin and the leaders of Ukraine and Belarus signed a treaty recognizing their status as independent countries, Gorbachev's last few months at the helm of the Soviet Union were marked by a series of humiliating encounters with Yeltsin in the Congress of People's Deputies, a Soviet-era body set up to satisfy demands for a limited measure of popular representation. Yeltsin consistently outmanoeuvred and outwitted Gorbachev as the shape of Russia's future began to emerge from the wreckage of the reforms of perestroika.

The key fault of the conspirators who sought to halt the process Gorbachev had initiated was a failure to understand the depth of feelings the era of perestroika had touched in the Russian people. Although by August 1991 Gorbachev himself was deeply disliked, the hopes of a brighter, less fearful future he had given to millions of ordinary Russians went a lot deeper than the daily grumbles about rising prices, queues for milk or sausage and the incipient process of national breakdown that was gnawing at the heart of the Soviet Union.

In its twilight hour the Soviet Union was a strange mixture of the old and the new. In the spring of 1991, during my first visit to Moscow, I had experienced the odd sensation of stepping into a city in which two historic time zones coexisted, each aware of the other but mostly able to carefully step around the other's edges. The warm days of mid-May seemed to most Muscovites like any other in Soviet history. The *gazirovannaya* – fizzy water – machines on dusty street corners still functioned if you could find a couple of tiny copeck coins in your pocket, 2 for fizzy water or 3 for a dollop of sweet coloured syrup to make it a lemonade. *Pravda* and other party newspapers remained unmolested in the glass-fronted display cases on patches of uneven and sparsely grassed land between the residential tower blocks. Official black Zil limousines still commanded the central lane of the city's wide boulevards, as they had since Stalin's times.

The people looked pretty Soviet too. The men were dressed in drab suits of poorly cut cotton or woollen cloth and young women conspired to appear fashionable through the ingenuity that had seen generations of Russian women through the toughest of Soviet austerities. Shops were empty, draughty spaces where dead flies and yellowing posters of yesteryear competed for window space. But there was an energy, buzz, in the atmosphere. Steered away from official *stoloviye* – canteens – by well-meaning friends, we ate lunches about town in small basement cooperative cafés run by bright and ambitious young people trying their hand at business under Gorbachev's timid moves to open Soviet society to limited free enterprise. The atmosphere was more student union than fashionable eatery, but the menus were tasty and inexpensive. Meetings with journalists and editors from official journals began in serious Soviet style, with tea and biscuits or vodka and *zakuski* – cold snacks – according to taste and venue, but boring monologues on the official line rapidly melted away as suggestions for 'joint ventures' and other business deals were aired. Muscovites and people throughout the Soviet Union felt free in a way they never had before. Everyone everywhere was open to opportunity. At the open-air flea market in Izmailovsky Park, which bordered an ancient tsarist hunting forest in north-east Moscow, weekend traders were taking their first steps in entrepreneurial careers. When I ran out of friends to give jeans to, I sold my last pair here. Just as packets of Marlboro cigarettes had become the small change of the new Russia, Levi's were the gold standard. The Caucasian trader who snapped up my last pair kept one wary eye on a couple of bored-looking *militsia* – police – officers hovering nearby as we haggled over the price. They weren't interested. Gorbachev's six years of experimentation had sapped the zealousness of the police for pouncing on petty offences like street trading that now seemed pretty harmless.

Everywhere people spoke of Yeltsin and their hopes for the next month's election. Although his campaign for the presidency was not much in evidence on the streets – I recall none of the posters, bunting and razzmatazz that characterize Western elections – people's hopes were very much alive. Gorbachev had done his job, now let a new man take the mantle, was the mood. There was a feeling of openness that the ubiquitous Communist Party slogans and banners about the streets of Moscow belied. The new generation of bright, Western-oriented politicians who had taken advantage of the Gorbachev reforms to win election to the Congress of People's Deputies were accessible and eager to talk. Sergei Stankevich, the young deputy mayor of Moscow, reflected the hopes of many. How unlike Soviet politicians was this young, well-groomed, English-speaking thirty-something-year-old. In an interview I had with him one evening at the central television studios he was anxious to stress the importance of revitalizing city government to enable Moscow to tackle its manifest social, economic and environmental problems. It was this hope the members of the State of Committee for the State Emergency underestimated.

Writing the day after the coup was launched, one Western correspondent observed:

> It seems certain that yesterday's coup will eventually be followed by another move forward. It could be a matter of days, or months, or years. But come round it will.
>
> The changes which perestroika and its chief architect, Mr Gorbachev, have brought about are simply too enormous. First of all, fear has gone. The great weight of enforced silence which used to hang over this country has evaporated, particularly among the younger generation. Even today as the tanks rolled through the streets close to the Kremlin and then in front of the Russian parliament, young people were climbing on them, and later speaking to foreign correspondents. Most of them did not mind giving their names. Policemen on the street were openly saying they disapproved of the coup. What a change this was from the days when foreign correspondents used to get embarrassed stares and shuffles when they asked strangers about politics.[3]

The Gorbachev years had truly changed Soviet society. The people who crowded around the White House to defend democracy and show their allegiance to Boris Yeltsin and the principles he espoused – the continuation of the democratic experiment – had grown up under the stultifying stagnation of the Brezhnev years. The downfall of Nikita Khrushchev in October 1964 was too long ago to be anything but a memory for some of the older people manning the barricades. Fresh in most people's minds was the last decade, when what had seemed as set as ubiquitous Soviet concrete, the monolith of Communist power, had slowly started to open a little here and there to the fresh air of free thought, discussion and challenge. As Yelena Bonner, widow of famous Soviet dissident Andrei Sakharov said from a barricaded balcony of the White House to massive cheers from the crowd below: 'It is our country and we will not give it up to a group of bandits. Everything this coup committee has issued is written for cattle. Today, all Muscovites must show their dignity and not sell themselves for a piece of sausage.'[4]

It was a telling comment. As high as Gorbachev had climbed in international esteem for his historic triumphs in engineering massive reductions in the nuclear arsenals of the Soviet Union and America, he had plunged low for his inability to do anything other than slow production, increase prices and sow discontent among the national elements of the union. Despite a policy of *uskoreniye* – acceleration of production, using new technology to speed industrial and social development – the weight of seventy years of a command economy overseen by ambitious and egotistic incompetents was too much for him. Gorbachev's genuine desire to see a reduction in international tension and build a more open, understanding world order was one of the driving forces behind his policy of dismantling so much of the Soviet Union's nuclear arsenal. But the catalyst was an acute awareness of just how bankrupt his country was after three generations of economic experiments and the massive costs of civil war in the 1920s, enforced collectivization in the 1930s and the Nazi incursion of the 1940s. The post-war years had witnessed various attempts to beat the West at its own game – the arms race, the space race, Coca-Cola détente and five-year plans to boost consumer production. But none of it had worked and the people knew it.

A centralized economy, where different and often far-flung republics produced specific raw materials or manufactured goods according to plans drawn up in Moscow, proved unresponsive to a policy of gradual reform. Cotton from Uzbekistan and textiles from Kirghizia (Kyrgyzstan) could only be produced when the tractors and agricultural machinery arrived from Byelorussia (Belarus) or the machine tools from Ukraine. As long ago as the 1950s Soviet leader Nikita Khrushchev had boasted that Soviet ingenuity and labour would overtake the West in satisfying consumer demands, but the ridiculous claim remained as unattainable as ever in an economy that remained largely embedded in the extraction and export of raw materials, a situation unchanged since Stalin's time.

Realizing that economic reforms could not work without a measure of political liberalization, Gorbachev had coupled economic rebuilding (perestroika) with openness (glasnost). But as tinkering at the edge of the dinosaur of Soviet industry succeeded only in weakening a notoriously inefficient system of centralized production, and limited price reform led to hyper-inflation for some goods and foodstuffs while others remained low under traditional price control, workers and peasants became restive.

A disastrous attempt in March 1985, soon after he succeeded the elderly Soviet leader Konstantin Chernenko, to crack down on historically high levels of alcoholism – a key contributor to both industrial absenteeism and high mortality rates – badly backfired. Restricting sales of vodka both deprived the country of a main source of tax revenues and fuelled a rise in crime. Illicit stills, which for generations had provided peasants with cheap but frequently lethal *samogon*, were put to commercial use and a new breed of criminal emerged – the vodka millionaire. International arms accords and the reversal of earlier Soviet policies of armed intervention to shore up failing Communist systems in Warsaw Pact countries speeded the thawing of the Cold War and paved the way for 1989's domino collapse of pro-Soviet regimes in East Germany, Czechoslovakia, Hungary, Poland, Bulgaria and Rumania. Without the withdrawal of Soviet troops and elimination of the Soviet arsenal of medium- and short-range nuclear missiles in the region, Eastern Europe's emergence from forty years of Communist rule would have been unlikely. But at home glasnost had also begun to stoke up dreams of freedom in parts of the Soviet Union considered to be more critical to national unity. Simmering discontent and ethnic rivalries in Armenia, Azerbaijan, Georgia and elsewhere in the Caucasus and Central Asia spilled over into outbreaks of violence as Gorbachev's gradual moves towards constitutional reform for the Soviet Union's unwieldy collection of fifteen republics opened up age-old divisions.

Sensing the first signs of freedom in fifty years, the Baltic republics of Lithuania, Latvia and Estonia, which had been annexed by Stalin in 1940 as part of the secret Nazi-Soviet plan to carve up Eastern Europe, began to push for independence. The Soviet constitution, which paid lip service to the notion that national republics were voluntary members of a socialist union, became the legal springboard for Lithuania's declaration of independence in 1990. The spirit of freedom rapidly spread to the neighbouring republics spurred by outbreaks of violence, most notoriously the killing of fifteen civilians in Vilnius in January 1991 when Soviet troops smashed up the television station, which served only to strengthen the resolve of these republics to go their own way.

Understanding that constitutional reform was needed if the Soviet Union was to continue, that a less rigid vertical relationship between Moscow and the republics was necessary to enable the country to move forward, Gorbachev drew up plans for a new Union Treaty involving nine of the Soviet republics. Leaders of the first five, the Russian Federation, Kazakhstan, Byelorussia, Tadjikistan and Uzbekistan, were due to have signed the treaty with Gorbachev in the Kremlin's St George's Hall on Tuesday 20 August, with Ukraine, Azerbaijan, Kirghizia and Turkmenistan signing later. The agreement, which envisioned a voluntary federation of sovereign states, a Union of Soviet Sovereign Republics, conceded that the six most nationalistic, independence-minded republics, Estonia, Latvia, Lithuania, Georgia, Armenia and Moldavia, would not have to sign. The treaty would have replaced the 1922 Union of Soviet Socialist Republics, a country held together by force and the centralism of Moscow, with a looser consensual arrangement where taxes raised in the republics would be kept there with only an element being remitted to Moscow. This horrified the Kremlin old guard. In the new Union Treaty the coup plotters saw the death of all they had believed in and striven for as they climbed the ladder of party power and influence. They saw it as the death of the Soviet Union and an end to the Communist system. Ironically by seizing power and their half-hearted attempts to turn back the tide of history, the members of the State Committee for the State of Emergency accelerated the complete collapse of the USSR. Before the year was out the Soviet Union would be gone and less than a year later the Communist Party – although later resurrected – would be banned in the Russian Federation by order of Boris Yeltsin, the man on the tank in front of the White House.

Boris Yeltsin's rule began with high hopes. The torch-bearer and champion of democracy had slugged it out with Gorbachev through the years of perestroika, surviving dismissal from the Politburo for his heavy-handed criticism of top party privileges, a heart attack and the depressing humiliation of appointment to a paper-pushing job in the state construction industry, before he engineered a remarkable political comeback. In March 1989 Yeltsin won election to the Congress of People's Deputies – just set up by Gorbachev as part of his gradualist approach to political reform – with a landslide vote of 90 per cent. Moscow voters had not forgotten his reign in the early 1980s as the city's party boss and liked his rough, Urals village lad manners. Grasping the hackles of the rising tide of nationalism, in June 1991 Yeltsin had used Gorbachev's reforms against him to win election as president of the Russian Federation, the largest of the constituent parts of the Soviet Union. In August his moment arrived and he gambled all on his role as democracy's saviour.

Seven years later in Moscow another August crisis brought the Russian people out onto the streets: but 17 August 1998 didn't see Boris the Brave entreating young army officers to defy their orders. Yeltsin, plagued by illness and political intrigues, was noticeably absent from the stage when the sickly flower of Russia's free market finally wilted. The financial crisis which ripped through Russia's banks, sending one after another tumbling into collapse that August, signalled an effective end to the Yelstin era. The heady days of the early post-Soviet years, when the shocks of transition from an ailing command economy to rampant robber capitalism were cushioned by the thrill of freedom and belief that Yeltsin would deliver on his promises to bring economic and social democracy to all, were long gone.

Indeed, the honeymoon with Yeltsin had not lasted very long. On 31 December 1991, a week after the formal death of the Soviet Union, I found my way back to Moscow for the second time. Commissioned by the *Sunday Express* to report on a bizarre and colourful story, I travelled to Yeltsino, some 150 miles north of Moscow. Here, in a small village that shared its name with Russia's leader, impoverished farmers had appealed to the president for help. Starved of capital investment for years, the collective farm based around the village desperately needed cash to rebuild cowsheds and invest in new machinery. The village mayor and her husband, the farm head, had written to their namesake asking for help. Boris Yeltsin's prosaic reply, that he could not do anything and that everyone in the new Russia had to work to deserve 'his place under the sun', won little favour among the villagers. By the time I arrived his name was as filthy as the frozen mud surrounding the cowsheds. Yeltsin's promise of a new Russia swiftly ran into difficulties even greater than simmering rural discontent.

Hyper-inflation in 1992 and 1993 wiped out people's savings and the fragile unity of democratic forces that existed in the late 1980s degenerated into an unseemly struggle for power between the executive and parliament. Resurgent Communists and nationalists in the executive body of the Russian parliament, the Supreme Soviet, coalesced around arguments over the adoption of a new constitution, budget priorities and hardline opposition to economic 'shock therapy'.

Yeltsin's steady slide into rule by decree and crony-capitalism, characterized by cosy insider deals as the natural and industrial wealth of Russia was stripped through a series of rigged auctions and worthless share-certificate giveaways, fuelled opposition anger.

After October 1993, when Yeltsin's row with his vice-president, Afghan war hero Alexander Rutskoi, and parliamentary speaker Ruslan Khasbulatov, boiled over into bloodshed as tank units loyal to the Kremlin bombarded the very same White House where Yeltsin had defied the coup two years before, the new Russia rapidly took shape.

The five years between October 1993 and August 1998 were dream years for Russia's new class of profiteers, black-marketeers and unscrupulous '*biznismen*'. Russia's post-Soviet economy became not so much a free market as a wild market, where anything was possible and everything could be bought. The war in Chechnya, between December 1994 and August 1996, may have been a military disaster for Russia but it demonstrated Yeltsin's willingness to resort to force on a much larger scale when he felt his authority was threatened.

Moscow's Soviet image as a grey, soulless place inhabited by stout matrons and thin, weedy men had been replaced by that of a latter-day Sodom and Gomorrah. Moscow under Yeltsin was a party town *par excellence*, where bars, restaurants and strip clubs had mushroomed and rapacious young Western MBA types flocked to further their careers and live out their fantasies. Two bizarre icons from the city's expatriate community summed up how far Moscow had travelled since Soviet times. At the Hungry Duck, a Canadian-owned bar, closed down in early 1999 (only to reopen later under new management), young Russian college girls performed voluntary strip-teases on the bar top after being served free drinks during the regular 'ladies' nights.' *The Exile*, a tawdry biweekly rag put out by cynical young American graduates, included a regular summary of Russia's more bizarre and gruesome crimes entitled 'Death Porn'.

If Gennady Yanayev and his coup comrades of 1991 had worried about crime under Gorbachev, their worst fears were realized under Yeltsin's Russia. Vicious turf wars between Mafia gangs in Moscow and other cities broke out, with scores of high-profile murders and assassinations peppering the pages of newspapers and magazines: Sultan 'Sultan' Balashikhinsky, head of Moscow's Chechen Mafia, was gunned down March 1994; Georgian 'Otarik', Otari Kvantrishvili, and Chechin 'Khoza', Nikolai Suleimanov, were murdered in April and December.[5] Ordinary businessmen trying to find their way through the maze of legal and illicit hurdles to make a profit fell foul of the Mafia and were shot down with such frequency that their murders hardly made more than a few paragraphs in yellow papers like *Moskovsky Komsomolets*, once the paper of the city's Young Communist organization. By the summer of 1998 senior Russian officials were suggesting that as much as 40 per cent of the Russian economy was controlled by Mafia groups.

Fortunes were made and spirited out of the country. In 1997 the Russian Central Bank claimed that $1 billion was being illegally exported every month by criminal organizations. A criminally dominated economy, corruption-riddled administration – top officials including Deputy Prime Minister Anatoly Chubais who had been in charge of the privatization process, had been dismissed for alleged bribe-taking – and the legacy of the disastrous war in Chechnya left the Russian people cynical and embittered.

Hospitalized for a series of complaints that had begun with his quadruple heart bypass surgery in November 1996 and continued intermittently with pneumonia, bleeding ulcers and viral complaints, Yeltsin had become ruler in name alone. The appointment of former KGB spy master Yevgeny Primakov as prime minister in September 1998 heralded the end of the Yeltsin era and the beginning of the next stage in Russia's post-Soviet development, although the president's ability to bounce back was amply demonstrated in May 1999, when Primakov was sacked and Federal Bureau of Security boss Sergei Stepashin was appointed to replace him, only to suffer the same fate soon after when another old KGB hand, Vladimir Putin, was foisted on the nation by Yeltsin. Primakov's experiment in neutering the influence of the handful of mega-wealthy oligarchs who controlled huge sectors of the economy and his attempts to reintroduce elements of state support for industry, which had been neglected almost to the point of complete collapse, were shelved.

For many the Yeltsin years represent a lost opportunity to build the foundations for a modern state in Russia. Social and political commentator Sergei Roy, an urbane, bespectacled man in his early sixties whose scholarly manner of speaking betrays his academic past, is editor-in-chief of the weekly newspaper *Moscow News*. He characterizes those Russians who have grown to maturity during the transition from Soviet power to the quasi-anarchic mixture of corruption and autocracy which is today's Russia as a lost generation.

A linguistics professor who quit Tver State University in 1979, finding the twilight days of the Brezhnev era simply 'too suffocating', Roy spent the next twenty years working as an English-language translator for leading Soviet publishing houses, including Progress, Raduga, Planeta, the scientific publishing house Nauka and others. It was a lifestyle, he says, that gave him a unique opportunity to observe the transformation of Soviet society from Gorbachev to Yeltsin at close quarters while simultaneously feeling quite removed from the vicissitudes of the times.

Roy's distinctive memoirs of the collapse of the Soviet Union, 'The Crash of an Empire: A Colloquial Chronicle. Russia, 1985–1991', a series of columns in the *Moscow News*, records in fascinating detail the human idiosyncrasies of the time. Although his acute observations of the struggle for reform within Russia don't end in 1991 his chronicle – which he plans to publish as a book in the near future – deliberately concludes with the end of the Soviet Union in December 1991.

The promise of change that the Gorbachev reforms of perestroika and glasnost heralded dissolved so quickly into a semi-criminal economy of corruption and greed, the catch-as-catch-can version of capitalism, Roy says, that to record the history of the Yeltsin years seems simply too much of an exercise in depressing futility. 'We need to skip a generation or so. Like the biblical story of Moses going into the desert and leading the tribes of Israel hither and thither for forty years until the last born slave was dead. I would not say that the Russian people feel that they are slaves, but all these old habits and attitudes die hard. If you push a Russian hard enough politically their philosophy always comes down to, "they should know at the top – let them sort it out." And they look heavenward.'

The Gorbachev years had stoked up expectations that Boris Yeltsin simply could not fulfil. If Yeltsin's primary concern had always been to win and hold on to power, he could hardly be expected to give power away to the people to achieve what perestroika and glasnost had promised them, Roy reasons. For those who were thinking strategically in the late 1980s, it was obvious that the transition from Communism and Soviet control to democracy and capitalism was never going to be achieved overnight.

Roy remembers talking about the future shape of the

Soviet Union with the intellectuals known as the 'foremen of perestroika', men like Gennady Lisichkin, Academician Nikolai Shmelyov, and the writer Ales Adamovich. 'I just computed, so to speak, the millions of people who would lose their jobs because the military industrial complex would collapse. The Soviet system could not just evaporate overnight. We could not wake up the following morning with the manners of free people. It would all take time. There were some things that were simply pathetic. The Communists who used to gather on Manezh Square, near the Kremlin in Moscow, the things they reacted to were mostly the privileges of the Communist Party top bosses. They mostly wanted better justice in dividing up the good things of life. These people would have been better off thinking where these good things in life came from – it was the total blindness of people.'

For Roy, illusion is the key image of the Gorbachev years – the illusion that changes could come without suffering. Easing of travel restrictions to the West gave people the notion that the minute they got rid of Communist bureaucracy, the 'partocracy', Russia would, like the West, become a consumer paradise.

Coming to terms with the reality of life under a free market system, a system where the old rules have gone and the new have not yet been devised, has been a massive psychological shock for the Russian people, he contends. 'There was a lot of illusion on the part of the intelligentsia. They thought they would be able to hold on to power, to keep power, using people like Yeltsin as a familiar point . . . We never figured how he would use us.'

Those people best prepared for the shock of the new were the ones who began steadily and ruthlessly converting their political and industrial power into financial and property-based wealth during the Gorbachev years. The roots of today's new Russians are to be found in the criminal gangs, regional party structures and management levels of industry under Gorbachev. The managers of state enterprises immediately abused the legalization in the late 1980s of cooperatives – small-scale businesses where limited profits were allowed. Typically a manager would appoint his wife or son-in-law to head a cooperative allied to his plant and would then begin siphoning off money for his own personal use. 'The most familiar picture is buying oil here at 4 roubles a ton or some such ridiculous figure, getting it across the border by hook or by crook – mostly by hook – and then selling it for $150 a ton before importing computers, which were virtually impossible to find in Russia, and doubling or trebling the profit because our own industry was devoid of computers,' says Roy.

The extent to which the new Russia became a state dominated by criminal forces doesn't surprise the more perceptive members of Roy's generation of intelligentsia. Criminals were best prepared to take advantage of the lawlessness ushered in with the new era and party apparatchiks, who had lived on the proceeds of corruption for decades, were well placed to work with the new breed.

According to Roy, 'The criminals were best prepared for the catch-as-catch-can kind of capitalism. It was a golden opportunity for them, which began in about 1985 with Gorbachev's anti-alcohol campaign. I remember some alcohol king-pins promising to put up a statue of Gorbachev made out of gold because that's when their capital started accumulating in huge amounts.'

Post-Soviet Russia became a nirvana for criminals and corrupt officials. The same bureaucrats who had worked the old system moved on to serve the new apparatus, with little or no disruption to their modus operandi. As Roy puts it, there was no civil war, no 'blood-letting', like in other parts of Eastern Europe undergoing similar transformation. 'All the bad blood was left here: several hundred thousand bureaucrats in Moscow. They did not go away. Some joined the business class, but most remained bureaucrats.'

Saddled with a legacy like this it's small wonder that the Russia of the 1990s has progressed precious little down the path towards the kind of property-owning democracy cheered on by George Bush, John Major and other Western leaders in the early Yeltsin years.

The mental, psychological and emotional legacy of seventy years of Soviet Communism has left its mark too. In the Baltic states, where memories of vibrant entrepreneurial business communities and free elections remained within living memory, stable economic growth and modern pluralistic democracies swiftly emerged. Soviet economic rule was never as strictly applied to the Baltics as elsewhere and even in Communist times standards of living in the three small republics were the envy of the rest of the country. Military officers, barred from retiring to homes in Moscow because of Kremlin fears of possible coups, frequently opted for the good life in Riga, Vilnius or Tallinn. Despite a measure of nationalistic backlash against ethnic Russians, particularly in Riga, where Soviet planners had deliberately settled Russians in order to create a community outnumbering the natives, political life in the Baltics resembled Western Europe and Scandinavia more closely than the Byzantine practices common in Russia.

But, Roy says, the West should not rush to judge Russia. 'People simply weren't ready to swap one set of hardships for another. They were not prepared to endure these hardships. The trouble is that no one was truly prepared to accept that seventy years of socialism could not disappear without leaving a mark. These years have left a very deep imprint on the people: the mentality of state dependence.'

As editor of a well-known and respected newspaper with offices facing the city-centre Pushkin Square, Roy is used to receiving unannounced visitors. All sorts of people turn up at the *Moscow News* with complaints of injustice and official neglect. Pensioners, war veterans, people who were forced to work in Germany during the war – the Ost Arbeiters, who remain entitled to compensation payments but are not getting them because of red tape – all of them wash up at Roy's door.

'The lowest bureaucrat wants these poor people to come up with some sort of *spravka* documentation [a document certifying eligibility for a payment or other right], as if the German Nazis were expected to hand out these documents,' he says with incredulity. 'I ask these people: do you know your deputy in the State Duma? [the lower house of the Russian parliament] Your local member of the Moscow Duma? Not one of them knows! The state is far removed from the Russian people. The bureaucracy has always been hostile to the masses and this attitude persists. On the one hand, the masses expect to be fed, especially the old age pensioners. And on the other hand, nobody wants to do anything to improve his situation.'

Roy remains bleak about the future for Russia. His personal chronicle of the collapse of the empire ends in December 1991 because he can find nothing positive to write about the period since then. 'There's very little that one can console oneself with. Philosophers like Abe Lincoln and Leo Tolstoy had the keenest sense of the differences between two sorts of time: the time in which the individual lives and the time in which the group, the mass of individuals, live – societies, political systems. This is exactly the situation we are in now. We can take the long- or the short-term view. What's my concern? Twenty or thirty years? I'm sure that nothing good is going to happen in these twenty or thirty years, not because it is predestined, but simply because there is too long a way to go to the simplest things like democracy. Democracy is not simply a case of putting up the structures, it's an attitude in the people.'

If he has any faith in the future it is based on those Russians who 'from time to time, here and there' make the economy work – the entrepreneurs who build factories, pay wages and contribute roubles to the tax budgets of regional governors. Not many Russians are entrepreneurs and the emergent middle class that fuelled the boom in Moscow's expensive shops, boutiques, night-life and service industries – legal or otherwise – was badly hit by the financial crisis of August 1998, with the collapse of the rouble and the nosedive in salary levels.

That the financial crisis brought Moscow's consumer boom of the mid-1990s to an end is amply illustrated by statistics concerning post-August 1998 incomes. The average Moscow family's income fell 75 per cent between the summer and winter. Pre-crisis most families survived on just under $400 a month; by November 1998 they were getting by on $100. A quarter of the city's workforce were laid off or fired; more than half had their salaries cut; a third didn't get paid on time; and a quarter lost savings in the banking crash.[6]

But marketing analysts in Moscow scoff at notions that the financial crisis means an end to Russia's transition from Communism to capitalism and the beginning of a slide back to the past. Masha Vakatova of ComCon2, one of a rash of Russian-owned and operated market research companies which sprang up as the country's new economy emerged after 1991, says consumerism is so deeply embedded in the Russian's devil-may-care attitude that a return to the grey days of Communism is now unthinkable. 'Russians are born splurgers and love buying the newest gadgets, whether it is a new type of kettle or car.

When I was in my twenties my brother and I went on holiday in the Crimea. He had just inherited an apartment in Moscow from our grandmother, who, as a noted doctor, had been rewarded with property by the party. He sold the apartment for something like 8,000 roubles [then equivalent to £8,000] and blew the lot within a month. I remember a Yugoslav man who observed some of this splurging remarking that my brother's actions would make an interesting case study for a psychologist.'

Vakatova, whose relatively privileged upbringing and marriage to a career diplomat gave her access to the good life in Soviet times, recalls the shock of returning to Boris Yeltsin's Russia in 1991 after a diplomatic posting to Mexico and Nicaragua to discover that the new Russia cared little about Soviet diplomats and the way inflation had eaten into the value of their wages.

The move from high-living diplomat's wife to part-time university lecturer at Moscow State University, where her wages had to support the family, was swift and abrupt. But despite the shocks of the Yeltsin years, she, like most Russians, would not swap today's Russia's for the Soviet past. Market surveys show that although the financial crisis hit people in the pocket – baskets of basic foodstuffs increased in price in rouble terms by between 180 and 210 per cent after August 1998, at the same time costs in US dollars dropped by up to half. With $40 billion in cash circulating within the Russian economy, those with dollars in post-crisis Russia are better off than ever before.

Russians have switched to cheaper brands for most foodstuffs, cut down on imported luxuries such as coffee and wine, but made no changes in the amount of money they spend on their children, leisure activities and vodka consumption, research shows. Gross domestic product in Russia has dropped from $6,000 at the beginning of the Yeltsin era to $4,000 in 1998. Half the population lives below the poverty line and two-thirds feel 'lost and abandoned' in the new Russia, but people still found the money to pay for the 4 billion litres of vodka, 3 billion of beer and nearly a billion of wine drunk in 1998.

'Russians today consume like crazy. They consume everything new or different. They have longed for this consumerism for such a long time. I didn't consume like this myself, because in Soviet times I had access to the West, to Latin America, but I know my friends could spend everything just to get this feeling that you can buy something, that you can buy whatever you want to,' Vakatova says.

The Yeltsin years most conspicuously benefited the president himself, his Kremlin cronies and industrial moguls like Boris Berezovsky, Vladimir Potanin and Alexander Smolensky, who got rich by creating empires out of state assets bought at bargain-basement prices and selling their products or capital at world values. But at the same time fully a fifth of the Russian population created businesses, found jobs or set up trading enterprises that qualified them to be statistically counted as middle class. The banking crisis of 1998 may have pitched 16 million of them back into a lower income bracket, but *Izvestiya* reported in November 1998 that before the crisis nearly 48 million Russians earned between $150 and $800 a month, classifying them as middle class by national standards.

Lower-middle-class Russians, those earning between $150 and $400 a month pre-crisis and between $150 and $200 post-crisis, include street salesmen and *chelnoki* – shuttle traders who buy cheap goods in Turkey, China or Poland and sell them at a small profit in the markets of Moscow and other Russian cities.

Slightly better off are the owners of small shops and cafés, professional white-collar workers and criminals, according to the newspaper, who typically had incomes of

$400 to $800 a month before the crisis and $200 and $500 after.

The upper middle class – higher-paid professionals and owners of larger companies and enterprises, earned between $800 and $1,500 a month before the rouble collapse whittled that down to $500 to $1,000.

The statistics show that despite the blow suffered by the Russian economy and the consequent political trade-off that saw significant power and influence transferred from Yeltsin to Prime Minister Yevgeny Primakov, Russia's cash economy remains strong enough, particularly in Moscow, where wealth and incomes are concentrated, to continue feeding a consumer wave.

The archetypes of today's Russia – the new Russians, those young, vulgar, cash-rich, partially or wholly criminal people who crowd Moscow's central boulevards with their late-registration BMWs and Mercedes, are only the most visible sign that Russia's society and way of life are in transition.

A generation that matured as the Soviet Union slid into chaos and disorder, and who used their wits to find a way forward into the uncharted waters of Boris Yeltsin's world, invested heavily in the cult of consumerism. Unlike in the West, where large parts of most family incomes are eaten up by rental or mortgage costs, the legacy of the Soviet Union means that accommodation costs are the least of an average Russian's expenses. Widespread tax evasion and under-declaration of earnings leave Russia a country where disposable incomes for those within the cash economy are among the highest in the world. Travel by train or car to virtually any city in Russia, particularly Moscow and St Petersburg, and you will move through mile after mile of countryside dotted with new, red-brick dachas or country cottages.

Sergei Adamov, director of research at ComCon2, says

Russia should not be underestimated. The creation of wealth may remain patchy and disproportionately concentrated in Moscow and St Petersburg – 90 per cent of consumers live in large cities and Moscow commands half the entire Russian market of mobile telephones, for example – but these areas also represent the centres of political decision-making. 'They say the financial crisis hurt mostly the middle classes. I would disagree. It's true that many people lost their jobs in banks and financial companies and consultancy firms. But still they are very well off. If you lose your job in any foreign company you get a severance package, including as much as six months' salary. That's enough time to find another job. I know quite a few people who lost their jobs and now they have found even better employment. I would say that poor people suffered most in the crisis, because of the rise in prices and decrease in salaries. Teachers and doctors live at a much worse level.'

Adamov remains positive about Russia's future, both from a market point of view and from personal conviction. A mathematician at the Russian Academy of Sciences during Soviet times, he recalls the reception he met with when he returned from his first overseas trip, to France in 1990: 'I was summoned to the Hotel Intourist in Moscow where I met two KGB officers. They questioned me on whom I met in France, their attitude to the Soviet Union, things like that. I was scared. I had three or four other meetings – they wanted to recruit me. My error was that I didn't tell anyone that I had this meeting, so at the final meeting, when I refused to work for them and asked them why they had chosen me – I was just a mathematician – they said, "Oh, you're such a good person, we can rely on you, you didn't tell anyone." These few months I lived under great pressure and anxiety. I was scared to say no, and at the same time I couldn't say yes. And I was an ordinary research associate, not much of a scientist.'

Adamov finally managed to refuse the security service's offer of employment by checking what he should do with a friend of his, a KGB major. The advice was that politically the atmosphere was such that he could refuse without it harming his career. Adamov escaped the clutches of the KGB with nothing more than a tart remark about the 'decline of patriotism' in Russia.

It's recollections like these, which most Russians can trawl up from their own or family's experience, that convince him that the new Russia is not one most would swap for the old. 'There's no way back today. Even if Communists come to power again, they are not like the old Communists. These people are now directors of enterprises, they are already relatively rich and they will never let go of their standards of living for some ideology. We won't move back to Communism or forward to true capitalism. Probably what the immediate future holds in store for Russia is this crony capitalism which they have in Latin America, where all the power and money are concentrated in the hands of several politicians, financial tycoons and the Mafia, but combined with freedom of speech and travel.'

True change in Russia still needs 'several generations', Adamov believes, but that the change will come he does not doubt: 'There was a Turkish hairdresser at the court of Tsar Alexander and he was the most hated person. He generated intrigues and was most repulsive. But his son was a general and hero of the war with Napoleon and his grandson was a well-known scientist. I hope that something like this will happen in Russia.'

Boris Kargalitsky is another close observer of Russia's transition, but one who does not share such a hopeful vision of the future. A dissident and political activist who spent thirteen months in Moscow's notorious Lefortovo jail in the early 1980s for distributing samizdat political tracts, he later emerged as one of the leading members of the left-wing 'Young Socialists' group of intellectuals. In the late 1980s, as a member of the Congress of People's Deputies, he was involved in setting up the Inter-Regional Group of Deputies, which included a deputy named Boris Yeltsin among its number. Later he became a member of the Moscow city council and was briefly arrested again during the events of October 1993, because he had a reputation as a critic of the Yeltsin regime.

A strong advocate of perestroika and popular political participation as a means of extending social justice, Kagarlitsky, now forty, works as a researcher for the Russian Academy of Science's Institute of Comparative Political Studies and contributes to a wide range of international publications.

After the political ferment of the perestroika years, the Yeltsin era has ushered in a time of political inactivity, he says. 'It's ironic that the tools for democracy were more freely available in Soviet times than today, when society has become atomized and everyone is too busy trying to survive – to feed their families – to have any time for politics.'

Despite the censorship and political pressures of the past, political space and the means to spread information were very cheap. Halls could be hired for a token payment; mass circulation newspapers could be used by relatively small groups of people to spread their message far and wide. The system of social security meant that many people enjoyed far more free time than they do today and those who wished to be politically active could take undemanding, low-paid jobs secure in the knowledge that they would not starve.

'Now nothing is free and we have a political system that is closer to that of eighteenth-century England, in which politics is the preserve of the gentleman. The only difference is that the people are expected to vote now,' Kagarlitsky says. But the economic shocks, the way people have been cheated during the Yeltsin years, have left a reservoir of frustration that could make for unpredictable events in the future, he thinks. 'People have not only been impoverished; they have been forced to move to another type of life. Now they have to care about daily survival and have less time for political action.'

Political power in the years since 1991 has to a large extent been centred in Moscow and revolves around money and connections, he observes. The financial crisis of 1998 proved how important connections were in Russian life, as those business people who lost money but lacked contacts in the right places found to their cost as their power disappeared with their money.

How Russia will develop as it enters the twenty-first century must remain an open question, but Kagarlitsky considers that a move towards a more diversified, regionally based system of power bases and alliances is likely. 'People always concentrate on Moscow and underestimate movements in the regions, but if you look at Russian history you will see that Russia has a tendency to change its political centre. Power has moved from Kiev, to Moscow, to St Petersburg and back to Moscow with spells of influence for Novgorod and other cities throughout our history,' he says. The industrial cities of the central Volga River region – Saratov, Samara and Voronezh – are worth close attention, he believes.

The explosion of popular anger in Russia at the launch of the NATO bombing campaign against Yugoslavia in March 1999 also demonstrated another feature of the political shape of today's Russia, its essential mystery, Kagarlitsky feels. 'I'm sure that there are hidden resources in Russia today that we just don't see – moral, political resources. We don't see certain things because they are not visible with the kind of methodology we have now. It is possible that some new forces will be freed by the further development of crisis in Russia.'

Russia's future today may not look at all bright. The country could become 'a Third World state with snow', says Kagarlitsky. It could become a small-time player on the international stage that exploits power through alliances. Then again, things could be very different. 'A miracle in Russia is not impossible. A miracle is something that happens but we don't understand how it happens. I think a miracle is possible because there are things we don't understand about Russia today. I don't pretend to understand everything and I don't trust people who claim to. Russia has always been in transition. Russia would never even have become a country if it had not served as a trade route between the Baltics and Byzantium.'

2

The Beautiful and the Damned

Yevgeny Kiselyov's face is familiar to millions of Russians. The vice-president of NTV, the country's largest independent television station, he presents Russia's most respected news and current affairs show, *Itogi* (meaning 'results', 'summary', or 'sum total'), on Sunday nights. The programme, a Russian equivalent of the BBC's *Newsnight*, is essential viewing for politicians, business people, the media and all Russians seriously interested in their country's social, political and economic life. Yevgeny can pick and choose his studio guests from the élite of Russian society. Politicians, cruelly lampooned in the channel's satirical *Spitting Image*-like puppet show, *Kukly*, later the same evening, are always keen to enter *Itogi*'s limelight.

Maxim, who does not like to give his last name, has a face millions of Russians would prefer not to see. An assistant at a Moscow feeding and clothing centre for the homeless, Maxim lived rough for nearly a year after his marriage, business and life fell apart in a sequence of treachery and deceit unchecked by the police or legal authorities. The only people who queue at Maxim's door are the ill-fed, poorly clothed and unclean *bomzhi* – the Russian acronym for homeless people – who come every day for lunch and help with their problems to the Centre for Humanitarian Aid, which is hidden away behind an old church near one of the city's main railway termini.

The Yeltsin years have been kind to Yevgeny Kiselyov. His programme, which started soon after President Yeltsin oversaw the dismantling of the Soviet Union, has been the vehicle for his success, as week in and week out he has charted the course of the new Russia. As its face, Yevgeny, a graduate of one of Moscow's most prestigious universities and fluent in English, Farsi and other languages, represents the buoyant modern image of a country determined to throw off the heavy weight of its past.

Maxim's story of rapid descent into poverty and the underclass after a university education and promising start in business reflects the more capricious side of life under the new order. If life during Soviet times gave a common, if meagre measure of security to all, affording every Russian an education, employment, access to healthcare and a sense of belonging within the larger commune, life in the Yeltsin era has been much more of a lottery.

Igor Gorin is another one of those touched by the finger of fortune since the Soviet Union disappeared into the history books. From pop group promotion during his Komsomol (Young Communists) days in what was then Leningrad to advertising and media marketing in Moscow today, Igor has amassed a fortune through luck and wit. With offices and homes in both cities, foreign holidays four times a year and a comfortable future ahead of him whatever the roller-coaster of the Russian economy throws up, Igor's life is typical of a 'new Russian'.

Maria Fedulova has never been homeless and always worked to earn enough to keep herself and her family. She can afford to pay for the small luxuries of life even though she would never consider herself well off. The tragedy of the Yeltsin years for her has not been economic, but emotional. When, during the Russian assault on Grozny in February 1995, the Chechens took her soldier son prisoner she was pitched headfirst into confronting the uglier side of reality in the new Russia. Maria became one of the hundreds of soldiers' mothers who travelled to Chechnya to seek the release of their sons. She met Chechen leaders reviled by the Russians as terrorists. She witnessed the indiscriminate brutality with which the Russian military treated the people of Chechnya, not to mention its own conscripts. She lived through the terror of coming under sniper fire from 'her' side. And she survived to rescue her son and become implacably bitter about Boris Yeltsin and all those around him.

Yevgeny Kiselyov acknowledges that without Boris Yeltsin he would never have achieved the position he enjoys today. He began his career in journalism just as the first breeze of freedom began to blow through the world of the Soviet media in the mid-1980s. But it was Yeltsin's bold actions during the putsch of August 1991 and subsequently in championing democracy as he oversaw the destruction of the Soviet Union that really opened up his horizons.

Yevgeny was already a television journalist of some standing when the Soviet regime faltered and fell. Although he had avoided joining the Communist Party as a full member, his education at the élite School of Asian and African Studies in Moscow, service as a military interpreter in Afghanistan and a stint teaching Farsi at the KGB High School helped his entry into journalism. A three-year grounding in broadcasting as a reporter for the Iranian and Afghan sections of Radio Moscow International gave him the leverage to move into television in 1987, just as the theories of glasnost were beginning to be translated into reality. His job as a member of the production team of *Vremya*, the flagship evening news programme produced by the state television and radio broadcasting authority, Gosteleradio, put him at the centre of an institution on the verge of profound changes.

Although Soviet national – or, as it was known, 'central' – television was divided into three channels appealing to different audiences, *Vremya* was shown across the wavelengths at the same time every evening. If the Politburo or party ever wished to get its message directly across to the public, *Vremya* was the medium it chose. Everything about the programme reflected the regime. The newsreaders were not journalists picked for their current affairs knowledge and professional skills, but actors chosen for their looks, voices and obedience.

'There was a popular joke in Soviet times where a worker, seeing that *Vremya* is screening pictures of Brezhnev delivering one of his long, rambling speeches in his typical slurred way, twiddles with the TV knob, only to find him on every channel. Suddenly he finds a wavelength without a picture of the general secretary and up pops a KGB colonel, finger wagging, saying, "What are you doing? Stop doing that!" ' Yevgeny says with a laugh.

Those days were numbered and, after glasnost received a boost from the January 1987 plenary session of the Communist Party's Central Committee, journalists found that pushing at the boundaries of the acceptable was much easier than before. News programmes became much more professional, with journalists allowed to report on camera, anchor news shows and present their own programmes. The apparatus of censorship remained in place – *Vremya* had its own official, to whom sensitive stories were supposed to be shown – but by this time his enthusiasm for the job was waning, Yevgeny recalls. 'There was this guy who sat in some other office, in a different corner of the building, who was supposed to act as censor, but during my years at *Vremya* I remember only one time when I was editor on duty that I was asked to clear a story about some military-industrial installation. When I found this shabby guy sitting there, he didn't even want to view the tape. He glanced over the script, tossed it back to me and shuffled off, saying it was time for his lunch break.'

If formal censorship, under the aegis of the Committee for the Protection of State Secrets in the Media, was waning, direct interference in the news agenda remained a feature until the end of the Soviet regime – and in certain cases beyond it. Key news and current affairs programmes were connected to the Kremlin and central party offices by closed-circuit scrambled phone lines. These *vertushki* (a word based on the Russian verb *vertet* – to turn, revolve, spin) were used by Central Committee figures such as Yegor Ligachev, the party's ideology tsar, and other powerful figures to manipulate the news agenda. These Soviet spin doctors could reach a programme editor-in-chief simply by picking up a *vertushka* and recommending the journalist to 'pay attention' to a particular issue.

This was how censorship was applied in those final years, through 'recommendations' to 'pay attention' to this or that, Yevgeny says. In this way news items the party didn't want screened would be dropped from the schedule. Years later, when NTV (Nezavisimoye Televideniye) Independent Television was set up by the banker and property magnate Vladimir Gusinsky, an attempt was made by the authorities to install a *vertushka* system there too. Boris Yeltsin wanted to keep a close eye on a potentially powerful organ, Yevgeny says, remarking that despite the benefits the new era has brought, the station's relationship with the president has not always been a smooth one. NTV resisted the pressures from Yeltsin which rumbled on through the period of the war in Chechnya, before rallying, along with other media, to oppose the Communists during the 1996 presidential election campaign. But back in the late 1980s the idea that journalists would soon be in a position to pit their power against that of the president was as unthinkable as the death of the Soviet empire.

What was evident from the moment of Yevgeny's arrival on the national television scene was the speed with which new opportunities were opening up. 'I came to work at the central television in January 1987 and by September I was presenting my own programme, the morning news. Opportunities were coming up not just week by week but practically day by day. Before this time there had been a long list of themes, topics and people about which we could not report.'

The relaxation of the taboos led to an explosion of journalistic energy as new programmes emerged to lift the lid on subjects long unexamined in Soviet society. Vladimir Molchanov's monthly magazine programme *Do i Posle Polunochi*, (*Before and After Midnight*) made its reputation by sticking to one simple rule: every person and topic featured had to be new to television. The first-ever televised report from a Soviet prison, interviews with Russian orthodox nuns, studio interviews with the British spy Kim Philby, new celebrities such as Valery Korotich, the editor of *Ogonyok*, a weekly political magazine, thrilled audiences and stirred Soviet television out of decades of torpor.

Stories untold for half a century were suddenly open to journalistic investigation as the appetite for raking over the recent past gripped the country. Yevgeny remembers the sense of awe and power as he researched a story about a pre-war society of former revolutionaries who had been among the very earliest members of the Bolsheviks.

Through the recollections of their children and grandchildren he was able to tell the story of a remarkable group of several thousand men and women who had shared the privations and suffering of tsarist oppression and internal exile to Siberia. In the 1930s the group, Obshchestvo Politkatorzhan i Ssyilnoposelentsev (The Association of Political Convicts and Exile Settlers), published a monthly magazine, *Vospominasiya o Revolutsii, Revolutionary Memoirs*, from a building in Moscow opposite the famous Theatre of Cinema Actors' Restaurant. 'Almost all these old Bolsheviks were arrested and executed during the pre-war purges for the simple reason they understood the real story of the Revolution and knew that Stalin had played a very minor role. This knowledge sealed their fate,' Yevgeny reflects.

Sitting in his cluttered office in Moscow's Ostankino television complex surrounded by the trappings of success – here a signed photograph of President Yeltsin playing tennis, there the Committee to Protect Journalists' International Press Freedom Award of 1995 – Yevgeny still marvels at the rapid pace of change. But the new freedoms under Gorbachev were not extended to a tolerance of political criticism, although live coverage of the opening sessions of the first Congress of People's Deputies in 1989 began to soften even that edict. 'After two weeks of live broadcasts during which every day a number of speakers were sharply and bitterly attacking the Communist Party leadership, including Gorbachev himself, it became clear that there were limits to Gorbachev's policies.'

Despite the experience of other Communist countries across Europe, where regime after regime fell during that year, Yevgeny and most journalists and observers in Russia doubted the Soviet Union would follow suit. 'Today many people say they believed the Soviet Union would break up and were waiting for the fall of the Communist system, but I remember it quite differently,' Yevgeny says. Top media commentators of the day, such as the late Vladimir Tsvetov, a long-serving foreign correspondent for Soviet television, were convinced that only the Baltic states would go their own way and that such bastions of the Warsaw Pact as East Germany would never allow democracy to prevail. The speed with which the regimes fell – a week in East Germany, a few weeks in Czechoslovakia, a couple of weeks in Rumania – left Yevgeny and his fellow journalists 'pulling their ears' in disbelief. Yevgeny had been in Bucharest in the July of 1989 for what was to be the last meeting of the Warsaw Pact leaders. A total news blackout left the journalists with little to report, but when it subsequently emerged that the meeting's key feature had been that none of the leaders could agree on a single point, one reason for the speed with which democracy swept Eastern Europe became clear.

For Yevgeny memories of pure comedy characterize the August putsch of 1991, when the democratic revolution finally caught up with the Soviet Union. Oleg Dobrodeyev, now president of NTV but then chief editor at Russian Television's *Vesti* news show, where Yevgeny was then working, habitually telephoned him at home in the morning to discuss the previous evening's programme. When the call came on the morning of 19 August at an unusually early hour, Yevgeny sleepily asked his boss to call back later, only to be told, 'There's been a coup! Get up, switch the television on and you'll understand everything!'

Yevgeny lived a few minutes' walk from the central offices and studios of Gosteleradio near Moscow's Byelorussky railway station. Fearing that the KGB or special forces would seize broadcasting facilities – as they had in Vilnius, Lithuania, and Riga, Latvia in the January of that year – he phoned colleagues and asked them to come to his flat rather than go into work.

'After a couple of hours my apartment was full of journalists from *Vesti*, all trying to decide what we should do. Then the phone rang and Dobrodeyev's secretary was on the line asking what was going on. Why was no one in the office? Where was Oleg Borisovich? She had been at her dacha and had driven into Moscow completely ignorant of the day's events.'

It soon dawned on the *Vesti* team that any coup as ham-fisted as this one could not last long and they rushed to the office to get on with covering the story. The arrest of the coup plotters and the televised clashes between Yeltsin and Gorbachev as the dying days of Soviet control were played out heralded a new Russia radically different from the old. Against this background Yevgeny devised the concept for *Itogi* as a weekly programme of news analysis. Oleg Dobrodeyev had been appointed head of news at Ostankino, the new headquarters for Russia's relaunched Channel One state broadcaster ORT (Russian Public Television), and Yevgeny and colleagues from *Vesti* had followed him.

In January 1992, just days after President Yeltsin had formally agreed the dissolution of the Soviet Union with his counterparts from Byelorussia and Ukraine, *Itogi* appeared on air for the first time. A product of the earliest days of the new post-Soviet Russia, it got a good press and was an immediate success. The format, combining award-winning investigative reporting with studio interviews of the week's newsmakers, was closely connected to Yevgeny's personality from the start. Less combative than many hard-hitters of Western TV channels, sometimes prone to a measure of pomposity, he has carved out a critically authoritative role in a country where politicians continue to regard television as a tool of state propaganda.

'On the one hand, we had all the possibilities journalistically, but on the other television in this country has always been viewed by the political and opposition leaders as a propaganda tool. This is why we are always in a state of war or truce with the political élite. We always have some sort of relationship with the power élite,' Yevgeny says, glancing around at the photographs and memorabilia that decorate his office. 'Every time we started to get critical, even if we are telling 100 per cent-proof information, not a single word of speculation – just things that we know for sure, where we are responsible for every bit of information – for the mere fact that it is not favourable to the government, a ministry, the Kremlin or whatever, they will try to create certain difficulties for us.'

The tools those in power in today's Russia use tend not to be quite so blunt as in Soviet times, but the Kremlin's clash in the mid-1990s with *Itogi* and NTV's owner, Vladimir Gusinsky, is illustrative of the uneasy relationship between television and the state in Russia today. *Itogi* moved from Channel One to NTV when the new private station was set up in 1993, aiming both to capture a younger, more influential audience and to ring the changes in the new Russia. The station made it a point of principle that no *vertushki* phone lines would be allowed in its studios. Yevgeny had already had a run-in at *Itogi* the year before when 'a group of serious-looking lads appeared at the door of [his] office saying they had orders to install a *vertushka*.' But despite 'training the Kremlin' to speak to them on ordinary telephone lines, NTV's journalists and executives frequently clashed with Yeltsin's administration.

In December 1994, shortly before the war in Chechnya began, members of Yeltsin's security service ambushed Vladimir Gusinsky's bodyguards and drivers, forcing them to lie face down in the snow and beating several of them.

Fearing arrest, Gusinsky fled abroad for a few months until the heat was off. Media-Most, the parent company of NTV, has been subject to frequent inspections by the tax police and other arms of the state ever since.

NTV's coverage of the war in Chechnya attracted consistent complaints from the Kremlin, unhappy with the frank approach the station, and *Itogi* in particular, took to an ill-conceived and disastrously incompetent campaign. The station's unflinching criticism of the war and stark reporting of the brutal and deeply flawed behaviour of the Russian army did much to fuel the popular condemnation of the conflict.

Despite threats to revoke NTV's licence, constant harassment by the tax authorities and exclusion from Kremlin briefings, the station and *Itogi* emerged with increased ratings and a hard-won reputation for objectivity and integrity. 'For many reasons, not only Chechnya, Yeltsin was very displeased with NTV,' says Yevgeny, 'because he is very keen on power and he always reacted very negatively and aggressively when a new centre of power independent of him appeared anywhere.'

NTV's 'active defence' has paid off for the station and today it commands a market share of nearly a third and is highly popular among young, well-educated and relatively well-off Russians.

The station's rift with Yeltsin was repaired in 1996 when, along with other television channels and the vast majority of the media, it supported the president's re-election campaign. The station launched a series of aggressive attacks on the Communist Party of the Russian Federation, led by Gennady Zyuganov, who threatened to top the polls and end Russia's experiment with democracy and the free market.

Yevgeny defends the station's switch from pariah to player on the presidential team on the grounds that a combative democracy where the media's relationship to power is always fluid is immeasurably preferable to a return to Communist dictatorship. His attitude towards Yeltsin's bloody clash with the parliament in October 1993 reflects his belief that vigilance and vigour must still be maintained against the threat of resurgent Communists. 'Yeltsin was right to resort to sheer power because he was faced with a rebellion. There were hundreds of armed people full of hatred towards not only the president but everything in the new Russia. They wanted to reinstate party rule and end the reforms.'

The bloodletting at Ostankino on the night of 3 October, when scores of mostly innocent people died, was regrettable, Yevgeny says. But as one who was there, he is adamant that the shooting started only when Yeltsin's forces inside the television complex were attacked and he refutes any suggestion that journalists and TV crews were especially targeted. 'At the risk of sounding cynical, however regrettable the deaths of those journalists were, these were professional risks they were taking,' he says, sitting in an office in the very building where the fighting took place. 'Let's not forget that it was these guys, [Alexander] Rutskoi and [Ruslan] Khasbulatov, with bloodshot eyes and minds full of revenge, who incited the crowds to storm Ostankino,' he says, referring to the then vice-president and speaker of the Russian parliament, who led the rebellion. 'Yeltsin took the necessary action to protect democracy in Russia.'

Relations may not always have been smooth with President Yeltsin, but as one whose career could not have thrived as it has in a Russia under Communist rule, Yevgeny is clear which he prefers. Proud of his achievements in helping to create NTV and forge a new culture of television journalism, he considers that at the very least he has helped ensure that NTV's 1,000 employees and their families will never vote for the Communists again. The station has been the consistent target of attack by left-wing elements in the State Duma and Yevgeny feels that the threat of a return to Communism in Russia still exists. His frequent professional contact with Communist leader Gennady Zyuganov gives him great cause for concern. 'I don't like him, I really don't like him,' he says in a hushed tone, after relating a story about a recent incident when he bumped into Zyuganov at a British Embassy reception in Moscow. The Communist leader told Yevgeny that his coverage of the Duma's bid to impeach President Yeltsin was 'unsatisfactory'. 'He told me the Communists felt that my programmes could be used in evidence against me at a trial. I asked, "Are your threatening me?" And he walked away.' He believes that if the Communists were to seize power again, they would immediately set about staging a series of show trials for all those associated with the Yeltsin administration. For this reason Yevgeny says he would leave Russia without a moment's hesitation.

Asked to predict the future political development of Russia, Yevgeny is uncharacteristically tongue-tied. Eventually he says, 'Of course Yeltsin will try to find a way to stay in power.' The Russian constitution limits him to two terms of office, which are due to expire in June 2000. But rumours of some kind of political fix – a union treaty with Belarus, a shake-up of the Russian Federation – suggest that Boris Nikolaievich will not go quietly, Yevgeny says.

'One idea is to make his daughter, Tanya Dyachenko, president!' he says, before musing that the de facto creation of a constitutional monarchy based on the Yeltsin dynasty would not be so bad provided the monarch's powers were limited.

A more likely scenario for Russia is that increasingly

restive regions – the far east, Siberia, the south, Moscow and the central region – will just go their own ways. 'It would not mean the Balkanization of Russia – we're a different people. The Serbs are genetic warriors. It's in their blood – they love to fight and they know how to.'

Maxim does not have the luxury of pondering the future political shape of Russia; he is too busy rebuilding his own life after months living rough on the streets.

A Ukrainian by birth, the twenty-four-year-old son of an Afghan war hero had every reason to believe his future was bright until a couple of years ago. Married with a young daughter and living in Moscow, his electrical appliance business was doing well and life was good. His fall into poverty and homelessness came literally overnight. Relations between him and his wife had soured to the extent that she left him and behind his back conspired with his business partners to sell the firm.

Depressed by her betrayal, Maxim decided to let her keep the money for the sake of their daughter and go to work as a lumberjack in the far north for several months while he tried to make up his mind about what to do next. He knew his wife planned to divorce him, but was not prepared for what he found on his return to Moscow on a bitterly cold day in February 1998. 'There were strangers living in my apartment in Sokolniki,' Maxim says, referring to the residential suburb of Moscow where he had lived. 'During my absence my wife had unregistered my name from the apartment's documents and sold it. The family I found had already been there for nearly three months and knew nothing about me.'

In the face of such treachery, Maxim's feelings today towards his wife are surprisingly free of bitterness. 'I didn't feel anything at that moment. Perhaps just disappointment that the person I had been sharing my life with could do this,' he says. As we talk in a cramped office of the Moscow Centre for Humanitarian Aid – a charity supported by Western sponsors – there are constant interruptions from homeless people coming to pick up copies of the newspaper *Yest Vykhod* (*There is a Way Out*), the Moscow equivalent of the *Big Issue*.

When Maxim left Moscow for the forests of the north, he transferred his resident permit out of the capital as a condition of the contract. In Russia every citizen must be registered to live in a particular town, city or region and this *propiska* – permit – is an essential document without which a person has no legal right of residence. Observant visitors to Moscow who stay for any length of time in the city cannot fail to notice the frequency with which police officers stop men and women on the streets and metro, particularly those from the Caucasus, to check their papers. Maxim, of course, still had his *propiska* from the far north – along with some $1,500 in cash, all his savings. Not knowing what to do and in a state of shock, he headed back to the railway station to collect his thoughts. 'I didn't know where my wife and daughter were and could only think of going to the railway station. I found somewhere to sleep and when I woke up the next morning all my cash and documents were gone.'

Overnight Maxim had become a *bomzh* – *bez opredeliennogo mesta zhitelstva* – the Russian acronym for a homeless person. Without papers, money or a place to live, he found himself at the very bottom of Russian society, practically without any rights and subject to the unwelcome attentions of predatory police officers, officials and other inhabitants of the subculture of the streets.

'I couldn't turn to friends for help,' Maxim says, looking pained. 'It's difficult to talk about friendship. When I had money I had plenty of friends, but as soon as I lost my money I lost my friends too.'

His parents were living in a distant region of Siberia. Those who had known him as a younger man were far away in western Ukraine. Maxim knew that if he 'had started weeping' all would be lost. There was nothing to do other than try to work his way back up.

His upbringing in the Ukrainian city of Lutsk had taught him some tough lessons. His father, an officer in the Soviet army, spent years away from home serving in Afghanistan – where his part in the rescue of passengers from a cargo plane shot down by rebels earned him the Order of the Red Star. Money was tight while his father was away from home and the young Maxim worked as a porter in the market after school hours to help make ends meet. A bright student, he won a place at the local teacher training university, where he combined his maths and physics studies with outside business interests. A video-salon he set up in a hired room at the railway station gave him the profits to open three cosmetic shops and by the time he graduated from the Kiev branch of the university to which he had transferred, he was already well off.

Ambitious and hard-working, Maxim took evening courses in wholesale and retail management and advertising during his first year after graduating, when he was on placement in a Kiev school. His move to Moscow was prompted by a steep decline in business in his cosmetic shops as the economic crisis in Ukraine deepened. He sold his shops and used the money to buy an apartment in Moscow and set up a new business.

'We lived at a good level – we could afford everything we wanted, the flat, a car, eating out. I was never greedy for money, earning money wasn't my goal. I earned money to live, understanding that right now in Russia money was the means of existence,' Maxim says.

Suddenly homeless and alone on that winter's day in 1998, Maxim returned to what he knew and trusted. 'I decided that I was young and fit and could earn a living. I went to the bazaar and got a job sweeping floors and unloading lorries.'

Moscow offered a multitude of different ways to make a living without questions being asked, Maxim found. He soon worked out that the safest and most secure place to sleep at night was a suburban railway station an hour and a half outside Moscow. The waiting-room seats were comfortable, the building warm and dry. The local police took a relatively benign attitude to those *bomzhi* like Maxim who did not drink, kept themselves clean and were trying to earn an honest living.

His days soon settled into a regular if demanding routine. At five in the morning he would get up and, after a wash in the station toilets, take the *elektrichka* – the suburban electric train service, where ticket inspectors are rarely seen – into Moscow's Kursk railway station. After a busy morning at the market, he would head for one of Moscow's busy mainline railway stations to earn tips carrying bags. Most days he would make around 150 roubles – worth $25 at 1998 exchange rates. The money was enough to cover food, bribes to police looking for any excuse to expel those without *propiska* from the city, and weekly visits to a public *banya* – the Russian version of a sauna. Ironically Maxim was making as much money as many Russians do in a month, but because of the residency permit laws – condemned by Western human rights organizations – getting a flat presented huge obstacles.

The mental and physical discipline he had learned as a younger man, when he took part in martial arts contests in Ukraine, helped Maxim cope. But still being homeless was a 'truly horrible' experience, he says. 'I saw things I had never seen before and to a certain degree had to change my mentality. I had never thought about the way life may knock you down, but once it happened to me I learned a lot. I made many friends among the homeless and won their respect.'

The people he encountered, as everywhere in life, had many different stories to explain their predicament. Maxim had little patience for those he considered had only themselves to blame for becoming a *bomzh* – the addicts and alcoholics who lost their jobs and sold their apartments because of drink or drugs. But the weak, vulnerable and naïve who found themselves on the streets were a testament to the grimmer side of life in Yeltsin's Russia.

'I remember an old lady of seventy-five I met at a railway station who had lost her apartment after she allowed two gypsy women to stay with her. They cheated her out of her apartment by tricking her into signing it over to them. She was kicked out but came back with the police. The trouble was the gypsies were clever – they claimed to have paid the old lady the full amount in cash and demanded she turn out her pockets and there was a pile of notes, about $200,' Maxim says. When the police demanded to know where the rest of the money was, the fraudsters simply shrugged, pointed to the signed contract and said it was not their concern.

Maxim always kept a minimum of 50 roubles on him to buy his way out of problems with the police but did not try to save money for fear of theft. His worst experience paradoxically opened the door to his way out of his situation. Hearing that there was work to be had in Vladimir, a town to the north-east of Moscow, Maxim and some acquaintances took the train there. Others had evidently also heard the rumour and on arrival teams of police were waiting to round them up. They were arrested for not having their *propiskas* and flung into a special detention centre for the homeless, a *spetz priyomnik*. It was October, the weather was already turning cold and the old lock-up next door to the town's OMON (special police) headquarters was unheated and primitive.

'There were bare concrete walls and barred windows. We were stripped to our underwear and given a tin of watery soup, *kasha* [porridge] so cold you couldn't hammer a nail into it, half a loaf of black bread and a little tea and sugar just once a day. The OMON officers came to beat us when we kept on asking them to turn on the heat. They beat me on the heels of my feet so there would be no bruises. When we became ill with fevers they delayed sending a doctor to us and when he arrived he gave just four pills between the eight of us,' Maxim remembers.

In the middle of this hell hole one of his cellmates told him about the Centre for Humanitarian Aid and the newspaper *Yest Vykhod*. When he was released after two weeks, Maxim made straight for the centre, housed in a dilapidated old wooden house behind a church in the centre of Moscow.

'On the way to the centre I earned 10 roubles and when I got there I picked up the ten free copies of the newspaper first-time vendors are allowed and spent the rest of the money on a pile of others,' Maxim says. The paper was sold to homeless people for 20 copecks a copy, who could then hawk it around the streets for whatever people were willing to give.

Within three days Maxim had made enough money to buy a decent pair of winter boots and with the centre's help he found a room to rent for 20 roubles a night. When he was not working, Maxim helped out at the centre, which runs a daily feeding programme for more than 200 homeless children and adults and helps support people trying to find a way off the streets.

Maxim later found a way to regain his residency status in Moscow when an old friend allowed him to register at an apartment he owned. A few months later Maxim was taken on as staff at the centre. Today he lives in his friend's apartment on the outskirts of Moscow and has even managed to buy a small, inexpensive plot of land where he plans to grow vegetables and build 'some kind of small dacha'.

Maxim's experience has changed his life for ever, he says, breaking off our conversation from time to time as the phone rings or a newspaper vendor knocks at the side window of his office to collect copies of *Yest Vykhod* from those stacked on shelves behind him. He finds happiness in more simple pleasures and is grateful that he has a regular job and a place in society again. He does not look too far ahead, but hopes to raise the profile of the newspaper and increase awareness of the plight of the homeless in Russia. The paper offers a way for people who are 'fighters' to progress with dignity and purpose. The general attitude towards the homeless, particularly on the part of the authorities, is that they are a problem best swept away out of sight. 'Nobody cares about the homeless. When there is some special event in Moscow the mayor orders the police to round the homeless up and dump them 160 miles away,' he observes.

He saw some terrible things during his time on the streets – people freezing to death, fainting from hunger, young girls forced into prostitution – which have left him with an enduring understanding of one face of the new Russia. 'It's too easy to lose everything in Russia today. People are not protected. Elementary human rights are ignored. Here if you don't have money you have no protection,' he says quietly. 'It couldn't have happened in Soviet times. Then if a person did not work he would be made to work and he could get a *propiska* and find somewhere to live.'

Maxim kept the truth of his life on the streets from his parents, mentioning nothing of the loss of his business and his wife's betrayal in his occasional letters home. He is unlikely ever to see his daughter again after learning that his wife has remarried and left for America. He bears his wife no ill will, remarking in a quiet voice, 'I wish her well. Let everything be all right with her. I hope she never experiences what it is like to be hungry and cold and living on the streets.' He tries not to think too much about the future. His experience of the immediate past has persuaded him that Russia today lives according to the selfish dictates of the old proverb, 'Your own clothes are much closer to your body than anything else in the world.' In conclusion, he says, 'It's difficult to think about the future. This country has betrayed its own people so many times, nobody knows what tomorrow may bring. Of course I have certain plans – I think about going back into business one day but I'm apprehensive talking about details.'

Igor Gorin could not have chosen a better business to be in when the Soviet Union collapsed. His background in rock music promotion and video distribution during the Gorbachev years put him in a prime position to take advantage of the information and entertainment explosion the new free market would bring. He had already made a lot of money in the few years since perestroika had allowed limited commercial freedom and he was confident he would make a lot more in the new Russia.

A decade after Igor, now thirty-six, tasted the thrill of making his first pile of money through organizing a national rock club tour, his film distribution, licensing and media planning businesses employ more than 100 people in Moscow and St Petersburg and turn over several million dollars a year. The collapse of the Soviet Union heralded the end of media censorship and opened a huge market to Western and domestic commercial interests. Capitalizing on the demand by those companies for agencies able to help plan advertising campaigns gave Igor a strong and expanding market.

Today he owns a large flat in a sought-after Moscow city-centre location and a newly built luxury family home in St Petersburg, drives a top model Saab and takes four foreign holidays a year. A tall, well-built man who likes to wear silk shirts, he looks a little offended when asked if he considers himself a 'new Russian'. Smiling, he replies, 'It's a very poorly defined term, but if it means one who is an entrepreneur, then yes, I'm a new Russian. But since I haven't yet married my secretary, then perhaps I'm not typical.'

His media planning and product placement company, TVIN Media, was one of the first in Russia to offer regional advertising services throughout the country and the boom in political advertising witnessed in election campaigns since 1993 offered lucrative opportunities. Igor's contacts with hundreds of local television stations and good connections in the bureaucracy of film and television secured him the contract to organize the regional distribution of Boris Yeltsin's campaign message in the 1996 presidential election. A brief spell working under the head of Goskomkino, the state film committee, where he concentrated on anti-piracy and licensing issues, helped raise his profile further. One function of his company is to act as a watchdog for the licence holders of film and television rights, using a database of regional television schedules to keep track of piracy. When a television station in the central Russian city of Izhevsk lost its licence after TVIN prosecuted it for breach of copyright laws in 1997, the company's reputation as a cost-effective tool against broadcasting piracy was established.

Unlike many of those who have become wealthy in the new Russia by exploiting the party positions and contacts they had in the old, Igor's fortune has been won through a combination of sheer good luck and astute business sense.

Born in St Petersburg, Igor spent a year at a technical college training to be a sound engineer before he dropped out to enter the Leningrad Theatre Institute where he studied the business side of stage and film. A serious car crash when he was twenty nearly cost him the sight in one eye and he spent two years recuperating after the famous Soviet eye surgeon Svyatoslav Fyodorov operated to replace his retina with a transplant. He worked as an ice-cream salesman and then later, when his sight returned to normal, he began working as a freelance journalist, selling his articles to local newspapers.

In 1985 a chance came up to work at the Leningrad Palace of Youth, one of the thousands of such Communist Party approved youth clubs which were then found throughout the Soviet world. As a non-party member his was a junior role, helping to organize events and concerts, but he learned a lot, and when Gorbachev allowed cooperatives to be set up in 1987 he and a group of friends went into the rock promotion business.

'We spent two years on the road, taking the show to clubs, cinemas and halls throughout the country. We made a pile of money and went crazy spending it. We were all young and felt the need to get rid of our complexes about never having had money,' Igor says with more than a whiff of nostalgia.

After two years of living the high life, Igor saw the need to pull himself together and moved into video distribution and documentary film-making. Western interest in Russia's political developments was at fever pitch and invitations to show the documentaries at Cannes and other festivals flooded in. Television and film projects – including working with Viktor Sergeyev, now director of Lenfilm studios in St Petersburg – replaced the capital Igor had spent on living it up and in 1992 he set up TVIN to distribute film and documentaries to Russian stations and those in the former Soviet republics. The monolithic Soviet television industry rapidly gave way to a chaotic array of local stations – some 900 different channels now broadcast throughout Russia. From film to advertising distribution was a simple and profitable move, and Igor's companies were soon turning over more than $500,000 a month.

Igor's lifestyle during the last decade has been a world away from that a man of his background could have expected in Soviet times. His mother, an Estonian who spent the war years as an exile in Siberia, is an engineer and his father managed a fleet of delivery trucks for a dairy. Both are now pensioners and, although he helps support them, Igor admits to sometimes feeling a tinge of guilt when he spends as much on a salad at a good restaurant as they get each month for their pension.

The economic crisis of August 1998 hit his business hard – advertising spending on Russia's national and regional channels dropped by as much as 80 per cent during the autumn of that year. Igor struggled for six months, spending reserves he had built up to keep his staff on and the companies going. By mid-1999 the economy had stabilized, despite the continuing political uncertainty – President Yeltsin had just survived a parliamentary attempt to impeach him over his record and Yevgeny Primakov, an old KGB hand who had served as prime minister for eight months, had been sacked.

It was a difficult time for Igor, although what he classes as troubled times would be the envy of many Russians. 'The part of TVIN that works on regional advertising was closed down for several months and I put off a move to new offices. Holidays were out of the question during this time,' Igor says. In the last few years he, his wife, Natasha, and seven-year-old daughter had become accustomed to winter trips to Florida or the Bahamas, summer holidays on the Mediterranean, a spring driving tour in Europe and autumn visits to Israel. A business trip to the Russian Kinotavr film festival in the Black Sea resort of Sochi in June 1999 was the first such break he and Natasha had allowed themselves since the crisis, he remarks.

The instability of life in Russia causes Igor little trouble. Like many Russians, he laments the loss of the Soviet Union as a geographic entity – in his teens he used to hitchhike into the Pamir Mountains in Central Asia or down to the Black Sea coast in the Crimea, regions now divided into different countries – but he has no regrets about the demise of Communism. 'Both my parents suffered during Soviet times and I even went so far as to pay for 10,000 anti-Communist handbills distributed in St Petersburg during the parliamentary elections of 1995,' Igor says, as we talk in his office in a nineteenth-century building in the centre of Moscow. However, nor does he fear the prospect, remote as it may be, of a political comeback by the Communists. 'I'm sure that I could do business under any regime. I'm against the Communists and would not take on the distribution of their political advertising, but if they got back into power I don't think censorship would affect me. We're in the business of getting time and arranging distribution of films and advertisements. What those products contain is of no consequence.'

His latest venture is the creation of a market for product placement in Russian movies. The practice, which involves the payment of fees by companies for the discrete use of their products in film plots, is already well established in the West. The idea is catching on slowly in Russia, as producers see it as a source of additional finance, and so far Igor has woven off-road cars, brand name cigarettes and well-known mobile phones into eight films.

His success has never attracted particular trouble from

competitors or the Mafia, he says. Like most businessmen in Russia, he pays for protection, in his case between $3,000 and $4,000 a year to members of an élite police unit in St Petersburg, where his head office is situated. The only time he needed to call on their services, when some competitors began threatening his staff, his *krysha* – the Russian word for roof – sent two busloads of OMON special police to his rivals' offices. 'They made a big show and worked off all that money [that had been paid] just to prove they hadn't got it for nothing,' Igor jokes. 'It certainly made an impression on those who were bothering us, but it was the first and last time,' he adds, spitting three times and knocking on the wooden table top so as not to tempt fate.

The world that Igor inhabits – television, film and show business – remains one of the most cushioned from the violent shocks the transition from Soviet society continues to deliver to the Russian people. He is confident that the economy will pick up and the long-term investments he has made in the rights to feature films and cartoon characters will provide for a secure financial future. 'I'm pretty happy with Yeltsin, although of course everyone is worried about what may happen after he goes. I don't see anyone who could replace him, although [Sergei] Stepashin [appointed prime minister in May 1999] is the first politician I've seen in eight years who I think could make a good president,' he says.

President Yeltsin's name is anathema to Maria Fedulova. The forty-nine-year-old activist, who works as a volunteer at the Moscow headquarters for the Soldiers' Mothers' Committee, loathes Yeltsin and the political apparatus around him with a bitter passion born of her experiences and those of her son during the war in Chechnya.

Until the Russian assault on Grozny in January 1995,

Maria had been no different from millions of working-class women throughout the country. Brought up in the post-war years not to question the motives and decisions of those in authority, the transition from Communist regime to nascent democracy barely impinged on her life and that of her family.

She knew something of military attitudes and culture before her son was drafted into the army early in 1994. During Soviet times she had brushed up against military structures when she was employed as a civilian worker in an anti-aircraft defence unit. President Yeltsin had yet to order troops into Chechnya to crush the increasing calls to break away from the Russian Federation when her son Denis was called up, but Maria felt uneasy and begged him not to go. 'There were certain family problems at the time, but he preferred to go to the army and left for training first in Moscow and then in Kursk,' Maria says.

She saw him once in the year before he was sent to Chechnya, in the October, when he had home leave to Moscow. They made arrangements for Maria to take the train down to Kursk in December to join Denis for his nineteenth birthday celebrations. The town, some 400 miles south of Moscow, is famed in Russia as the site of the world's biggest tank battle in 1943 and remains a major military base.

On the day Maria was supposed to leave for Kursk she received a telephone call from members of her son's squad telling her that Denis was 'away on military exercises'. The war in Chechnya was barely a week old and Maria had been told her first lie. 'The moment I heard this I knew what had happened. The war was already in full progress and Denis was away on military games? No. I knew that no military exercises, which are extremely costly, would be going on at this time. I understood that my son was in trouble.'

What happened next was the beginning of a process unprecedented in the history of modern warfare and was to change Maria's life for ever, making a radical activist out of a Moscow housewife. She packed her bags and took the train to Kursk. At her son's military base she besieged staff officers with demands to know where Denis had been sent. The military men did not know what to do with this angry and unhappy woman, but refused to tell her anything. Eventually after three days, as she was preparing to leave, one officer took her aside and whispered that all her recent letters to Denis had been sent on to Chechnya.

Beside herself with worry, she returned to Moscow and, after some asking around, was directed to the Soldiers' Mothers' Committee. The organization had already been working for some years as a pressure group lobbying for the adoption of a professional army in Russia. As the nightly news began broadcasting stark and horrific images of the war in Chechnya into Russian living rooms, it soon became the focus for even more radical demands.

Maria joined dozens of other women desperate to find a way to get their sons away from a war considered unjust and unnecessary. 'When I came to the committee there were already a number of women determined to go to Chechnya. With the help of some people in the Duma, we got tickets and left for the south,' Maria says with the air of one who has since learned a lot about fighting for what she believes in.

Her three weeks in Chechnya were to prove a baptism of fire. The woman who went down to the Dagestan border town of Khosav-Yurt in January 1995 was very different from the one who returned in February. She was to learn that Denis had been taken prisoner by the Chechens within ten days of arriving in Grozny, where he took part in the New Year assault on the city during which the

Russians suffered massive casualties against a skilled and tenacious guerrilla army.[1] She was to witness a brutality by Russian officers towards their own men matched only by that towards the Chechens. And she was to develop a respect and admiration for the Chechen fighters rivalled only by her disgust with her own nation's political leaders and military culture.

'It was really frightening. People were dying and we were there trying to find our children. In the history of warfare this hadn't happened before. There we were, mothers in the middle of a war zone, trying to drag our children out of the enemy's prisons.'

A strong and determined-looking woman, Maria is sometimes overcome with emotion as we talk in one of the warren of rooms which house the Soldiers' Mothers' Committee in Moscow, not far from Old Square, where the Communist Party's Central Committee officers were once based.

Early attempts to seek Russian military help in freeing her son soon failed and Maria realized that she had only herself to rely upon. Remarkably, she and other women desperate to rescue their sons were allowed into Chechnya and the ruins of Grozny even as the Russian military continued to press their attacks.

Maria fiddles nervously with a set of keys and smokes steadily as she remembers images of horror that will never fade. Chechen leader General Dzhokhar Dudayev's presidential palace in Grozny had been heavily bombed when 'the Chechens came and asked [the Russians] to stop firing to allow them to carry out their dead. For every dead Chechen collected they offered to release three or four Russian prisoners. We mothers lobbied the local [Russian] military commander to agree to this, but he refused,' Maria recalls.

Undeterred, the Chechens took their dead out under

fire and then got a message through to the mothers, suggesting they collect the Russians. The women were ready to do so, desperate to know one way or another if their sons were lying there or had been taken prisoner. 'But the Russian military would not let us go, saying that the dead are the dead and do not matter any more.'

It was only when Maria managed to make contact with the Chechen side through a local legal official in Grozny that she was offered the chance to help organize a prisoner exchange. It was then that she came face to face with Chechen guerrilla leader Shamil Basayev, a man reviled by many in Russia as a terrorist but celebrated in Chechnya as a national hero. (Basayev later gained notoriety when, in June 1995, he and a gang of armed men raided the southern Russian town of Budennovsk to seize hundreds of hostages in a hospital as bargaining chips to negotiate a cease-fire. A number of hostages died during two unsuccessful attempts to storm the hospital and Basayev and his men were eventually able to make their way back to Grozny.)

She was to meet Basayev many times during the process of negotiating her son's release and later, during subsequent missions to Grozny on behalf of the Soldiers' Mothers' Committee. Suggesting that her contact with Basayev was compromised by his reputation elicits an angry and indignant response from Maria: 'Excuse me, but it wasn't Shamil who was attacking Russia, it was Russia attacking his country. To me he is a trustworthy person who helped me get my son out of prison. Thanks to Shamil my son is still alive.'

Maria's disgust with her own country for the way it prosecuted a war against the Chechen people – not to mention the thousands of Russian civilian residents of Grozny caught up in the fighting – dates to her contacts with people like Basayev. 'It was quite possible to understand what Shamil and all Chechens felt. The Russians were carrying out genocide. Everything we saw in Grozny made this clear,' Maria says emphatically.

Much media coverage of the war at that time portrayed the Chechens as beasts who tortured and murdered their prisoners. But Maria's experience suggests this was Kremlin-inspired propaganda. During the negotiations for the release of her son she met many Russian soldiers who told of how the Chechens shared everything with them and treated them well. When Denis was finally released, on 1 February 1995, a day the family still celebrate as his 'second birthday', he corroborated these stories.

'When a journalist later asked my son what had been his best experience in the army, he said the nineteen days he spent in a Chechen prison,' Maria says, tears welling up in her eyes.

Denis, who had been a driver and was captured when he was sent to tow back disabled Russian armoured vehicles from the battle zone, was adamant he would not return to the army even though officially he had another six months to serve. Maria took him home to Moscow and successfully resisted army attempts to send him back to the front. Denis had been wounded during his capture and although the Chechens had tried to treat him he still had shell splinters in his legs. Despite threats from the commander of his army group, Maria and the Soldiers' Mothers' Committee successfully applied for Denis to be sent to a military hospital where he was eventually given a medical discharge from the army.

Denis, who is now married with a small daughter and working in a sawmill, survived the war but remains deeply scarred by his experience, Maria says. A 'normal, kind and good-humoured' boy before being sent to Chechnya, he has been hardened by an experience about which he prefers not to talk. Nearly five years after the battle for Grozny he continues to have nightmares about 'driving over the corpses of his comrades' and the death and destruction he witnessed.

Denis never returned to Chechnya and has tried to block the experience out of his life, but for Maria rescuing her son was not enough. Radicalized and horrified by what she had seen, she went back to Grozny several more times and has worked for the Soldiers' Mothers' Committee ever since.

Shaken by the brutality and indifference to suffering displayed by the Russian military command, Maria feels lasting shame. She recalls the first big prisoner exchange announced by General Dudayev a few days before Denis was released. The Chechens arrived with a bus full of Russian prisoners and were then kept waiting for nearly three hours before the Russians came. A local cease-fire was broken during the wait and artillery shells were dropping in the area by the time the exchange finally went ahead.

'The Chechens released their prisoners first. They were all well fed, well washed and in good shape,' Maria says. She shifts uncomfortably, fiddling with her cigarette lighter before continuing: 'Then the Russians let their Chechens out. A number of them had been beaten so badly they could hardly walk and most were hardly dressed, even though it was January and the weather was cold. It was after this that Dudayev said there would be no more prisoner swaps until the war was over.'

The Russian military's indifference to the presence of Maria and other mothers searching for their sons allowed her freedom of movement, but also put her in considerable danger. No one could guarantee her safety and she had to rely upon the kindness and hospitality of ordinary Chechens to keep her out of harm's way.

'One of the biggest shocks I had was the attitude of the

Chechens to us. They took us Russian mothers into their homes, gave us food and shelter. We were the mothers of soldiers who may well have killed their own children. They say that the Russians are hospitable, but I cannot imagine a Russian family allowing Chechens into their home.'

On one occasion Maria came under fire from a Russian sniper. The Chechen fighters escorting her and another woman could not believe the sniper did not know these were Russian women and shielded them with their bodies. Months later, in an uncanny encounter in Moscow at the Soldiers' Mothers' Committee, Maria met a young Russian soldier who had served in Chechnya and was seeking help for treatment to wounds he received there. Talking with him, it became obvious that he had been the sniper. His orders had to been to shoot at anything that moved – men, women or children. Seeing that there were Russian women picking their way through the ruins of Grozny he had aimed high.

'How did I feel? He was a child, a baby who needed help,' Maria says when asked what effect the encounter had on her.

Maria has turned her anger and bitterness at the casual way the Russian state sent its young men to their deaths in Chechnya into activism. Her days are spent working to help those injured or otherwise affected by the war to seek help. More than 700 Russian soldiers remained missing in action three years after the war ended in August 1996; and 400 unidentified bodies of Russian solders killed in Chechnya still lay in a Rostov-on-Don mortuary.

The Soldiers' Mothers' Committee continues to lobby for a change in the law to establish a professional army in Russia and to combat brutality within the armed forces, where 4,000 servicemen die in accidents every year.

Maria curses the acquiescence of the Russian people that allows its young men to be fed into a brutal and uncaring military machine, and she feels shame at a culture that supports this. 'Russians are extremely aggressive, and all the time Russia has been taking part in some kind of military activity, ever since 1914. Russia is fighting, fighting, fighting. The Russians don't live in peace. We have a massive army and always feel the need to use it.'

She blames not only Yeltsin for continuing this militaristic tradition, but all Russian politicians, observing that many of those MPs who wanted to impeach the president in May 1999 for his record in office, including the war in Chechnya, had 'voted for war in the first place'.

'During my trips to Chechnya I understood one thing: the politicians we have here are entirely untrustworthy. All of them are liars; the whole system is based on lies.' Maria's experience of the Yeltsin years has left her a woman with a mission. 'I don't want any woman to have to experience the horror that I did. No mother should be put through that.'

3

Winners

Life in Russia today is lived in a permanent crisis, says Andrei Pedorenko, a thirty-six-year-old information technology manager with the insurance department of leading Russian financial group Renaissance Capital. Andrei, an applied mathematics graduate of Moscow State University and father of two teenaged children, wasn't groomed for a job where life-changing decisions have to be taken virtually every day just to stay on top in the shark-infested waters of Moscow's modern-day marketplace.

The product of a classically stable Soviet family – both parents in the military, a leader of the Komsomol at school and college, early candidature and then membership of the Communist Party – Andrei's path was mapped out long ago. But the crisis in his country, which he first felt palpably, like a nervous tugging at the gut, back in 1982, when Leonid Brezhnev died, has not prevented him from surviving and thriving in the rudderless world of the post-Soviet era.

According to the dictates of the world he grew up in, Andrei should by now be a comfortably tenured junior professor in the applied mathematics faculty of Moscow State. The fact that he holds down a part-time teaching job there in addition to his demanding duties as head of IT at Renaissance Insurance, reflects two key factors in today's Russia. An insecure economic situation forces many professional people to have more than one job to ensure a steady income. And despite the huge changes in Russian society in the last eight years it demonstrates the strength of a social and behavioural continuity that transcends Communism and the nascent market economy.

Andrei is one of the 'winners' of today's Russia not because he has accumulated vast wealth, several homes, flashy cars and strings of stick-thin, bored and blonde girlfriends – the image of the new Russian popularized by the western press. Andrei is a winner because he has successfully welded the values of his conformist Communist upbringing and early development to the needs and character of a world which owes more to themes and trends from those times than many a Harvard-educated champion of the free market would like to admit.

Andrei's family moved to Moscow in the early 1960s when his father, a colonel in the Soviet army, was posted from the Urals to the capital. Andrei entered School Number 279 in the fourth grade, when he was eleven, and became an active member of the youth organizations there: first the Young Pioneers and later the Komsomol. There was nothing ideological about it; as a child of a military family, involvement in the youth organs of the Communist Party was as natural a choice as membership of the Cubs, Scouts or Guides is for the offspring of middle-class, suburban Britain. But it instilled patterns of both leadership and communal co-operation that were as essential to advancement in Soviet society as they are in Russia today. Andrei also headed the school's 'Poisk' – Search – society, an unusual because unofficial organization dedicated to tracing, marking and commemorating the grave of every former pupil who fought and died defending the motherland during the Great Patriotic War of 1941–5. The concept and activities of the group, first set up in the late 1960s by teachers as a way of keeping alive the memory of the school's sacrifice and teaching children about the terrible realities of war, went against official Soviet attitudes, which regarded commemoration of the war as a political task exclusively under the control of the party. The authorities didn't look kindly on groups of teenagers who set out every summer on field trips to scour the old battlefields. Around Leningrad, in the forests and swamps of Bryansk, the outskirts of Volgograd (Stalingrad) and further afield, in Belarus and Latvia, Andrei and his friends found, marked and mapped the last resting place of a generation of schoolchildren who had barely reached eighteen when they were sent to fight the Nazis.

Identifying the individual sacrifice of Russian soldiers wasn't a major consideration for authorities that preferred to use the annual 9 May Victory Day events as a means of pressing home propaganda priorities of the moment. Of course, towns and villages in Russia to this day have their own small memorials, surmounted by the five-pointed red Soviet star and displaying the sad lists of local boys who fell for their country. They're little different from those found on every village green in Britain. But I've yet to see a war memorial in Russia that doesn't have a small iron or concrete podium standing nearby from where local party dignitaries would orchestrate events every Victory Day. The Politburo's preference in the past was for the massive impersonal memorials of the sort found in Kiev or Volgograd, where gigantic stainless-steel figures of Mother Russia, sword in hand, tower above museums and mass graves.

School Number 279's small marble plinth, discretely positioned on a staircase, remembers each old boy or girl traced by Poisk in bold gold letters. The emphasis is on the individual. Nearby a large map of the territory fought over from the day Hitler's armies launched Operation Barbarossa displays contemporary photographs of the school's war dead near the cities, towns and villages where they died. Andrei's socialization at school was about membership of a Communist society trying to live up to the socialist slogans of the Kremlin and learning the bonds of sacrifice made by the Russian people only a generation before.

When Andrei talks about 'living in permanent crisis', he means the unmapped outside world of the modern Russia where all blueprints have been discarded and a multitude of new choices, options and decisions are thrust at you every day. But his inner world is one where a core of stability was planted many years ago.

A serious and intelligent man, Andrei thinks quickly and talks fluidly, switching from Russian to fluent, vernacular English as is convenient. 'It's well known that human beings experience crises from time to time. In life you have your white and your black periods and these are always changing. We call this the white/black line,' he says, sitting in the habitual location for any serious conversation in Russia – the small kitchen of a central Moscow flat. 'I have the feeling that our life has become such that the lines have grown very narrow. If in the past you could say that you had lived for a couple of years without any major problems, today it is impossible to say that. Today problems of such magnitude may arise every day, hour or second. In the past you could say, this was a good time and that was bad. Today it's impossible. Every day may hold both good and dreadful experiences and there is nothing you can do about this.' He defines a crisis as 'being torn between two options where you have to make a choice'.

For Andrei and millions of other Russians, the shock

waves of a new life of turmoil, unpredictability and anxiety began early in the new Russia. After the failed coup of the Gosudarstvenniye Komitet Po Chresvichainomu Polozheniyu, the State Committee for the State Emergency (GKCHP) hardline plotters of August 1991, the Soviet Union formally remained in existence until 8 December, when Boris Yeltsin and the presidents of neighbouring Ukraine and Belarus (then Byelorussia) met to pull the plug on it. Soviet President Mikhail Gorbachev bowed to the inevitable and resigned on 25 December, telling the Russian people in a ten minute televised address that they had 'lost their citizenship in a great country'.

Muscovites and Russians throughout the country were just recovering from their New Year's Eve hangovers and preparing to celebrate Christmas – which falls in the first week of January under the Orthodox calendar – when Yeltsin, who had demanded of and been given by parliament emergency powers to rule by decree following the coup, announced that Soviet-era price controls would be lifted.

Western free market economists who were advising the Russian government at the time, including Anders Aslund of the Stockholm Institute and Jeffrey Sachs of Harvard,[1] had urged that 'shock therapy' was the best way to rapidly shift Russia's economy from the heavy hand of state control to the fluidity of a *laissez-faire* capitalist system. Yeltsin followed their advice, telling the Russian people that decisive reforms were needed, particularly an end to government price-fixing in a 'one-time changeover to market prices'.

Prices for all commodities except energy and natural resources – metals, timber, minerals – were freed on 2 January 1992. Retaining state control of prices in these lucrative sectors opened the way for vast fortunes to be made by a select group of businessmen and advisers close to Yeltsin and the core of political power, who swiftly seized the opportunity to buy at local prices in Russia and sell at world rates overseas. The seeds were sown for the development of Russia's political-commercial oligarchy, a group of latter-day robber barons who from that point on consistently acted to keep their main benefactor, Boris Nikolaievich Yeltsin, in power.

Ordinary Russians were not so fortunate. Yeltsin and his economics tsar, the neo-liberal economist prime minister Yegor Gaidar, one of a small group of university intellectuals who had gained the president's confidence, told the Russian people that prices would increase threefold before stabilizing. What actually happened is still regarded by many Russians as the greatest crime of the Yeltsin years and one which decisively killed off any ability of ordinary people to actively take part in the desperately needed process of political reform in their country. Prices shot up twentyfold within twelve months and the word hyper-inflation entered the Russian vocabulary. In January 1992 10,000 roubles would have bought a Lada or a Zhiguli – popular brands of Russian cars. Less than a year later you would have been lucky to find a spare tyre for the same price. The life savings of an entire nation were wiped out in under a year.

As journalists Matt Biven and Jonas Bernstein noted in an article tracing the economic insults to the Russian people of the Yeltsin years:

> Shock therapy had an important side effect. Rampant inflation was the blow that smacked down Russian civil society just as it was showing faint signs of trying to rise, tottering, out of Communism's sickbed. Slowly and tentatively, ordinary Russians had been taking an interest in how their country was run. They

Above: Boris Kagarlitsky, a former dissident and left wing political activist who believes a miracle may yet save Russia from a dire fate.

Left: The changing century: a statue of Lenin remains in place alongside a pre-revolutionary building now returned to its former function as a bank.

Below: Eternal Russia: St Basil's Cathedral, Red Square, on a late-winter afternoon.

The collapse of Communism, August 1991, as seen by the British press.

Critical clash, October 1993. The White House, Moscow, following the bombardment of rebel nationalists by tanks loyal to Yeltsin.
(BEN ARIS)

Everyday life: millions rely on the Moscow metro.

Muscovites relax in the summer sunshine, Manezh Square beside the Kremlin, June 1999.

Above: Igor Gorin, made wealthy by Communism's collapse.

Right: Yevgeny Kiselyov, with President Boris Yeltsin.

Orthodoxy remains a powerful presence in Russian life and allows artists the opportunity to create marketable works.

The Eternal Flame: the Great Patriotic War continues to exert a powerful influence more than half a century later.

Old soldiers – male and female – remember Russia's sacrifice. Victory Day, 9 May 1995.

Above: A mother's duty: Maria Fedulova's life changed after she rescued her soldier son from a Chechen prison.

Left: A Russian conscript, on leave from the war in Chechnya, dancing with his girlfriend in Gorky Park.

Below: Today's Russia is politically divided. Members of the Union of Soviet Officers demonstrate against Yeltsin, Moscow, October 1998.

The placards of these anti-government protesters demand Yeltsin's resignation, Moscow, October 1998.

Young and old frequently take to the streets to protest Russia's chronically divisive political rule.

> had been debating the future and demanding changes. Then, suddenly, they were financially wiped out, their savings gone, their buying power shrinking by the hour. Any energy left over went into moonlighting at second jobs, driving gypsy cabs in the cities, for example, and tending their own garden plots, either at dachas or in apartment window boxes. Life expectancies plummeted, particularly for men, thanks mostly to an increase in violent or stress-related deaths: suicides, murders, heart failures, and alcohol-related incidents.[2]

The shock of hyper-inflation remained so powerful that subsequent crises have been taken almost stoically by a people more intent on surviving day by day than forming coherent collective actions against the body blows of an economy characterized by unpredictability, racketeering and rampant political corruption. When the banking crisis of August 1998 sent Russia's economy once more into turmoil after the government declared it would default on servicing its Gosudarstvenniye Kratkosochniye Obyazatelstva (GKO) debts – high-yielding short-term bonds in which financial groups had heavily invested – and devalued the rouble, a wave of bankruptcies swept through the country's leading savings banks. Once again hundreds of thousands of people saw their life savings disappear into a black hole. Young professionals in Moscow who had managed to save considerable sums through hard work and thrift during the boom times of the previous two years lost tens of thousands of dollars. And yet apart from television news images of groups of aggrieved savers banging on the doors of locked and empty banks in Moscow that dusty August, the nation took it with barely a protest.

When a retired Soviet army colonel held up a branch of

the state savings bank, Sberbank, in February 1999 to demand his $20,000 savings, it made headlines precisely because it was such an unusual incident. Seven years after the first cold shock of the new Russia, most people shrugged their shoulders, tightened their belts, and putting one foot in front of the other, tried to get on with their lives as best they could.

The thousand natural shocks of life in the new Russia have led to resignation, depression and a hardening of personal attitudes. Andrei believes that moral values have also been eroded by the constant alarms of an economy and society run with hardly any rules. Inner values and relationships with others come under intense pressure and the tempo of change forced by Russia's transition from a monolithic society to a fractionalized world drives the process ever more inexorably.

'Take for example the moral exhortation, don't steal,' Andrei says, toying with a teaspoon at the small table in the old-fashioned, Soviet-era kitchen where we are talking. 'When we see what is going on everywhere in Russia, when we see what those at the very top of the political level are doing, their economic crimes, the question is, why should one restrain oneself?'

Andrei's strong inner map remains a firm guide in this world, but he sees the effect on others around him. 'Morality is somehow migrating to a point that I, personally, find unacceptable. Although I feel that even within me some things are changing – for example, I'll jump red lights when I'm driving without even thinking about it,' he says, laughing to hide his embarrassment. 'If in the past this was strictly taboo, right now it's not a problem for me.'

Russians have become less sensitive as the moral coordinates of their world have drifted apart. 'Every day we see so many horrid things that we develop an immunity, become hardened to it. If in the past you saw an old woman on the street begging, everybody's attitude was clear: she had got to the point where it was so bad she had nothing else to do. People would help. Today – OK, she's begging, but that's life.'

His words are reflected in the frequent newspaper reports that can be read every winter in Moscow and other towns and cities about the drunks and homeless people found frozen to death in the streets. Most deaths hardly make more than a paragraph and such is the indifference of the public to bodies in the streets that stories only ever command more serious treatment in unusual circumstances. But public indifference always masks private grief. I recall the shock and disgust of a close friend, a professor at a Moscow institute, when he learned of the death of a close friend who had been struck down by a heart attack as he made his way through woods to the local railway station, heading home from his dacha one freezing winter Sunday. Nobody came to his aid and no one called the police. Footprints in the snow around his friend's corpse and the theft of his wallet, watch and passport were mute witnesses to an incident that has become a commonplace in today's Russia.

In Minsk, the capital of Belarus, I once passed a curious and idle group of people waiting for a bus. Lying in the gutter was the body of a tramp who had just been run over by a carelessly manoeuvred bus. The man's death seemed to occasion little reaction, other than the irritated gestures of people worried that their bus might be late.

As if to underline the casual disregard for human life that has always been, and remains, a feature of Russian culture, I came across the corpse of a homeless woman the very week I began work on this chapter.

It was early spring in Saratov, a Volga River city in central Russia, where a long icy winter was only reluctantly letting go its grasp. Having gone with a friend to collect a package from a regional train at Saratov railway station late one night, we were waiting for the approaching train in the dim light of the far side of the railway tracks. A dreary drizzle gradually turning to snow was falling on our shoulders. A rubbish-strewn embankment, covered with patches of grubby snow and grey ice, rose up from the uneven tarmac platform. A pale yellowish light weakly emitted from the windows of a nearby apartment block cast a ghoulish glow over the scene. It could have been Dickensian London. The train pulled in and we collected the package from the conductor who occupies a small cubicle on every carriage, taking care of bedding and linen for sleeping compartments, providing tea and procuring vodka. Turning to go, I noticed a body sprawled across the long metal hot-water pipes running along the side of the embankment. Lying on her back, one dirty bootless foot protruding from an ancient pair of trousers, the old woman excited little interest. The crumpled bodies of drunks lying in snow, rain or the beating heat of summer are part of the Russian scene. I long ago found myself unconsciously adopting the habits of locals and usually step around the foul-smelling forms with barely a second glance. But something was different about this old woman and I walked over to look intently into her apparently sleeping face. Dressed in navy blue tracksuit trousers, a rough green-canvas jerkin over a dun-coloured woollen vest, she looked poor and forsaken. A cheap mauve coat was gathered around her and the orange henna in her hair was already separated from her scalp by more than an inch of grey roots. Filthy fingers and misshapen, muck-encrusted fingernails like claws were clutched to her breast. Her eyes were tightly shut, a nasty vermilion bruise spread over her cheek and dried mucus clung to her nose. Her thin mouth was clasped closed and the deep wrinkles around her face seemed to speak of years of suffering. She was very still and not a trace of cloudy breath escaped her nose or mouth. That she was dead was obvious, but she wasn't long dead, as the colour in her cheeks was still that of flesh and blood. I'd seen dozens of corpses years before, working on an assignment about the murder rate in St Petersburg, and remembered the changes time marks on a corpse.

We went to find the station police and one officer rather reluctantly followed us through the cold green-glazed labyrinth of passageways beneath the platforms. On the way he muttered, '*Naverno, ona – bomzh*' – 'S'pose she's a *bomzh*'. On the platform he glanced at her, then immediately disappeared, saying he'd better find a stretcher. Fifteen minutes later he and a couple of colleagues reappeared, without the stretcher, poked the woman a few times here and there, checked her pulse at the wrist and jugular, and finally opened one eye and pushed a finger deeply into it. Her dark blue glass-like eye stared back, but there was no reaction. Where the officer's finger had pushed at her flesh a flush of red flowed back into the white marks. He could find no pulse, but she can't have been dead very long. Doctors were called for but were unlikely to hurry to collect yet another dead *bomzh*, the officers said. The indignity of the old woman's death made me linger, wanting to be sure that medical opinion coincided with common sense, that she was indeed beyond human help. It was cold and damp, with a chill wind blowing small flurries of sharp points of snow around us. A dark, oil-faced drunk joined the police, peered at the woman and took her wrist. 'Dead! She's dead!' he shouted, and laughed like a maniac. The policemen guffawed. 'Well, if this stinking bum says she's dead, that's it. Might as well pack up and go home. Why wait for the doctors?' The futility and shame of her lonely death in a dirty corner of a grubby station caught me feeling the pathos of this side of Russian life and we left.

Confronting the harshness and casual indifference of society in today's Russia is just one of the daily crises people like Andrei have to endure. Even for those like him who can be considered relatively well off, winners in a lottery that cares little for human dignity and rights, unpleasant choices have become a way of life.

Andrei feared he would have a heart attack the day his boss told him he had to fire three people from his staff of ten. As a manager for a large and successful company, Andrei isn't shy of cutting out the dead wood. But in the aftermath of Russia's financial crisis of August 1998, when the rouble more than halved in value on the foreign exchange, banks went bust and hundreds of thousands of ordinary Russians lost their life savings, downsizing became a brutal reality in Moscow.

'I was asked to get rid of three people. These were not bad workers. These were good people, members of staff without whom I was going to have problems in my department. But I had to fire them and do it there and then. Management had made a decision: out go those who were least valuable to the business. I had to make a choice. The difference was so little between those who were fired and those who stayed, it was virtually by chance I made the decision. I didn't have a heart attack when I told them, but felt very close to it. It's clear to me that we are gradually moving to a world absolutely different from that which we were brought up in.'

It's a world far removed from the party slogans of yesteryear, where all citizens were exhorted to strive to demonstrate the very best social values in their individual behaviour and attitudes, but paradoxically it is one where the gilded youth of Communism are better equipped to cope than many.

Andrei hasn't been as materially successful as some of his old friends from the Komsomol, but as head of the

Young Communists in Moscow State University's Applied Mathematics and Cybernetics faculty and later a professional Komsomol organizer in the early 1980s, his credentials and contacts have served him well. One of his colleagues, Konstantin Zatulin, who worked in the Komsomol alongside him at university and also led the small KGB section there, is now a member of the Duma's Committee for National Questions. Another, Maxim Sotnikov, is head of a big concrete-producing company. Top Moscow Komsomol leaders of the 1970s and 1980s are to be found in key positions throughout the new Russia: Sergei Kiriyenko, the thirty-five-year-old banker and technocrat appointed prime minister for a few short months in 1998, before the August financial crisis signalled his swift exit from the Kremlin, was a regional Komsomol leader. Financier and one-time deputy prime minister for economic affairs, Vladimir Potanin, is another ex-Communist Youth League member. And Sergei Lisovsky, head of Premier SV, one of Russia's leading advertising agencies, a man who infamously was caught emerging from the Russian government White House during President Yeltsin's successful election campaign in 1996 with a box containing $500,000 in cash, was one of the young high-fliers of Moscow's Komsomol committee in the 1980s. As head of the IT department at Renaissance Insurance, Andrei earns $2,000 a month. His part-time lecturing job at Moscow State University brings in extra income and he also earns 1,000 roubles from other sources. His route to a comfortable middle-class life, where he owns his three-room apartment in the popular residential district near Prospekt Mira and runs a Lada saloon, is firmly based on decisions taken more than twenty years ago – decisions designed to prepare him for a life as a member of the Communist Party nomenklatura.

'The future seemed more or less clear. I was always

research-oriented. It was going to be either maths or physics. I knew I would go either to a military academy or to university. It wasn't exactly that my life was predetermined, but there was a certain framework within which decisions would be made.' Enthusiastic participation in the state-sponsored organizations designed to channel youthful exuberance to the ends of the party, the Young Pioneers and the Komsomol, was wise for those who wanted a smooth path in Soviet society, Andrei recalls.

'Being a member of different committees and groups was to some extent a guarantee of success. Being active sent out the right signals. It was for this reason that I joined the Komsomol when I was fourteen and the Communist Party as soon as I got to university. By then this was really a smooth ride, it was what everybody wanted of me. To talk about it in ideological terms is ridiculous. It was a path, not a calling. Once you made one step you were expected to take another. Not to have taken those steps would have seemed strange, not only to others but to yourself too at the time.'

The easy transition from the red neckerchiefs and jaunty little blue side caps of the Young Pioneers, through the discrete Lenin lapel badges of the Komsomol, to the scientific materialism of the CP afforded security and a sense of purpose. Andrei makes no apologies for taking this path at a time when dissidents were struggling to be heard and the brutal practices of the KGB, although a less vicious force than earlier, remained a tool of state repression. 'We were very young. For us it was somehow natural. If I knew that I was going to get a Masters of Science degree, then I knew I would teach at MGU,' Andrei said, using the Russian acronym for Moscow State University. 'I would take my PhD there and become a professor. The next thing I would know, I would be a grandfather!'

The certainty that this received faith gave bright young

men and women began to loosen in the final years of Soviet power. Mikhail Gorbachev's top-down liberalization of the iron grip of ideology, driven by a realization that the rigidity of the command economy was killing the country's creativity and its ability to meet the people's needs, began to open up opportunities and release people from the old psychology. Then change was welcome and the chaos bequeathed to today's Russia by Gorbachev's policies – or rather his inability to single-mindedly pursue them over the objections of the hardliners in the Kremlin – was a nightmare yet to come.

Andrei remembers the years of perestroika as ones when a sense of freedom began to emerge from the heavy weight of the stagnation policies of the past. The Komsomol, a key focus for non-dissident opinion, adopted a motto from the successful student footlights comedy movement the KVN (Klub Veselykh i Nakhodchivykh), '*Partya dai porulit*' – Party, give us the steering wheel! The 'fresh breeze' of glasnost and perestroika began subtly to suggest new opportunities and a more spontaneous approach to life. 'I cannot express exactly what it really felt like because this sense of freedom emerged so gradually, but life became much easier,' Andrei remarks.

Speeches made in the Supreme Soviet made references to matters never mentioned before. Created along with the Congress of People's Deputies by President Mikhail Gorbachev as a means of clipping the wings of hardliners in the Politburo, the body soon found a voice of its own. The independent spirit of members of the Congress of People's Deputies was demonstrated during its first session, in June 1989, when one deputy asked for a minute's silence to be observed for people who had died during street clashes with troops in Tbilisi, Georgia, the month before, taking a startled Politburo by surprise. 'Things were said from the podium that we have never heard before, or which had been hidden in secret papers. Jokes that would have landed you in prison in the past became the currency of the day. There were those years in the early 1980s when party general secretaries kept on dying, first Yuri Andropov, then Konstantin Chernenko. In one anecdote one man says to another, "You won't believe it but Gensek [general secretary of the Communist Party] died again yesterday." '

Andrei spent the 1980s at Moscow State University, first as an undergraduate, then as a postgraduate and later as an official in charge of the pastoral care of a year group of mathematics students. These were heady days in Russia and students rushed to embrace the limited new freedoms allowed.

But it was not all sweetness and light. Gorbachev's reforms moved slowly and the sense of living in an interregnum between the old system and the as yet unformed new sometimes caused conflict and anxiety. Boris Yeltsin, who was then head of the Moscow Community Party apparatus, clashed with Gorbachev over the pace of the perestroika reforms and later, in October 1987, apparently aware that there was little he could do personally to change the Moscow party from within, in an unprecedented move he resigned his post. The incident sent shock waves through the Politburo and later Yeltsin was dragged by Gorbachev from his hospital bed – where he had been sent after collapsing with acute chest pains – to face the wrath of the Central Committee. It's an episode that Yeltsin later described as his darkest hour, when he suffered a mental breakdown and contemplated leaving politics.

Andrei remembers the tremors it sent through the Moscow party apparatus. 'When Yeltsin resigned no one was given an explanation, although we later found out the truth. It was a chilling moment, when we felt as if all the moves forward had suddenly stopped and the country was again marching to the beat of the old drum. All the Komsomol faculty secretaries at the university were called together by the university party committee. We were told that Yeltsin had been sacked and we needed to communicate and clarify this to the young people, the students, in our charge. The party leaders knew Yeltsin's move would drive the students out on strike. The Komsomol was planning to support these demonstrations – at the time, Yeltsin's departure seemed to us an utter crime. Something was going on in the country and nothing was being explained. A few years before, of course, this would have been quite normal, but now it was unthinkable.'

Andrei and the other Komsomol organizers turned on the greybeards of the Lenin Hills party committee, as the university branch was known, and demanded to know why they should pour oil on troubled waters about an episode of which they themselves knew nothing. A furious shouting match erupted which ended unresolved as the meeting broke up.

The continuity of Andrei's career at Moscow State University, starting in the dying days of the Brezhnev era as a student and continuing through Gorbachev's reforms and into the Yeltsin era, affords him a rare understanding of the effect of the shifting currents of those years on Russia's most idealistic generation. Andrei's upbringing and grooming for life as a smooth cog in the Communist machine propelled him through fifteen years at the university until the financial pressures of the new Russia pushed him into the private sector, where pay and conditions make college life seem as outmoded as a Soviet-era textbook. As a student, a Komsomol leader – both voluntarily and for a couple of years as a paid official – and then assistant professor in the IT department of the Applied

Mathematics and Cybernetics faculty, Andrei was closely involved in the life of the university and the student community.

As a *nachalnik kyursa* – student year head – he cared for the personal and academic concerns of a cohort of 300 students for five years between 1990 and 1995. The idealistic fervour of his generation, the hopes and dreams that finally began to crystallize in the early 1990s, seemed lost on those who freely accepted the fruits of these years. Asked about the effect on young people of Russia's lurching steps into the promised land of democracy, Andrei, whose maturity seems years in advance of his age, snorts derisively. 'Of course it had an immediate impact: the students began to study worse!' The social masks behind which people had hidden for so many long and dreadful decades fell away and people, especially the young, felt free to do whatever they wished.

The explosion of energy that began building in the late 1980s burst out in a spontaneous outpouring of liberty glimpsed only rarely in Russia's long history of social oppression. Art exhibitions, literary gatherings and impromptu street theatre flourished. An experimental student drama group shocked and bewildered Moscow metro commuters on the circle line one summer when, testing the new freedom to its limits, a young man and woman stripped naked and made love on the floor at the feet of startled old ladies and incredulous office workers. Russia resisted the purgative national cleansing of Soviet client states like East Germany, where people stormed the Stasi secret police headquarters and flung open the files of millions of citizens. But to be in Russia in 1991 or 1992 seeking access to information from officialdom was like a dream come true. The KGB openly admitted that the new American embassy being completed in Moscow had been extensively wired with listening devices, and dark secrets from Stalin's times emerged into the light of day.

The changes manifested themselves in the personal attitudes of young people as impertinence and a disregard for convention or obligations. Seeing the first flush of a market economy, tens of thousands of young people dropped out or chose not to go to university as small fortunes from trading beckoned.

As individualism began to spread after a century of social conformity, public standards declined. The aggressive 'me first' psychology of today's wealthy new Russians first became visible in the carelessness exhibited towards community values and practices. At a basic level, the lack of concern for others, for the social, was displayed physically in a rapid decline in interest in the maintenance of public buildings and spaces – rapidly exacerbated by a collapse in state funding for the upkeep of such places.

'When there are no set rules and the rules you make for yourself are not there either, then you have difficulties,' Andrei says. 'I noticed that the university immediately became much more dirty, not just physically but in the language spoken by students – this quickly degenerated into garbage too.' That this was a passing phenomenon, a symptom of change, has become evident in the last couple of years, he reckons. It seems curious, he says, but students today – a generation which has matured in a decade where all the rules were torn up and thrown away – have much greater respect for others and for their surroundings. As if the chaos of the Yeltsin years has forced people to devise their own internal rules for negotiating the rapids of everyday life, studying is back in fashion, working hard to hone intellectual skills and care in personal presentation are again seen as the keys to a more secure future. 'I'm able to see how public standards descended to a certain level and how they have risen again. Today young people are totally different from those of five or six years ago. But they are also totally different from how we were at that age too,' Andrei says, reflecting the popular notion that the boiler-house changes Russia is enduring concentrate and accelerate social changes long held back by the dead weight of Soviet Communism.

For Andrei, like millions of other Russians, the freedoms conferred through transition from a one-party state to nascent democracy have not translated into a yearning for public service or political activity. The Yeltsin years have been a period of retreat from social and community work for Andrei – although he has retained close links with his old school, where his wife works as an accountant and his children study. His weariness from years of community involvement through the Communist Party and university faculty coincided with the collapse and disappearance of the organs that coordinated social activity. You would look in vain today for any kind of nationally organized youth group or political party in Russia beyond the unpalatable choices of the Communist Party of the Russian Federation, a nationalistic successor to the old CP, and Vladimir Zhirinovsky's bizarre right-wing Liberal Democratic Party of Russia.

The key political turning points of the Yeltsin era have cast Andrei, and the vast majority of Russians, as powerless observers. Like an unwilling audience at a dangerous circus, the Russian people have been forced to watch as the critical milestones of the new Russia – the failed coup of August 1991, the White House bombardment during the showdown between the Kremlin and parliament in October 1993, the disastrous war in Chechnya, launched in December 1994 – unfolded before their eyes. The coup of 1991 caught most Russians napping, as it was designed to. Hardliners in the Kremlin seized control at the height of the August holiday season, putting Mikhail Gorbachev under house arrest at his government dacha in the Crimea. The ill-organized, ageing Politburo plotters appeared on television to announce their coup, with Soviet Vice-President Gennady Yanayev's hands famously shaking with nerves, or the palsy of a serious vodka drinker whose resolve to take another 100 grams is stronger than his political will. State television and radio were forbidden to report anything other than the plotters' statement and the first most Russians knew or guessed of events that Sunday, 19 August, was when they tuned in their radio sets or switched on their TV sets to hear only martial music or see only a blank screen.

Andrei, his wife and kids were returning from their dacha, not far from Vnukovo domestic airfield to the south of Moscow on the afternoon of Monday 20 August. The main highway to Kiev passes near the dacha and this was the road the family took as they drove home to Moscow. The Kiev highway was also the most direct route to the city for the tank corps of the Kantemirovskaya military base, called to the centre on the order of the coup leaders.

The family had enjoyed a long weekend in perfect isolation from the outside world: no radio to disturb the peace, just a normal Russian weekend at the dacha, tending vegetable gardens, chatting to neighbours, carrying out minor repairs, playing the guitar, drinking vodka. On the way home Andrei noticed the surface of the highway had been churned by the caterpillar tracks of tanks. Then they passed a column of olive-green tanks. One or two had slipped off the highway (when tanks are driven fast along concrete roads the surface becomes as slippery as ice, causing drivers to lose control).

'It was obvious to me that the column had been going very fast. The road surface was all broken up. It was not really scary, but it was the first time I had seen this. It was confusing and difficult to understand and it was so unusual. I remember being told that in 1953, when Lavrenti Beria, Stalin's secret police chief, was assassinated, tanks had shown up on the streets of Moscow, but this was the first time I had ever seen such a sight,' Andrei remembers.

The news blackout ordered by the coup leaders was effective and Moscow was characterized by an unusual silence. Objective information was all but impossible to come by. People resorted to the old samizdat habits of the past, passing out quickly printed handbills on the metro, swapping word-of-mouth rumours with friends. People knew that something was going on at the White House, but on the first day or so did not quite know what, or why. 'We knew that people were headed down there, to the White House, to stand against something and that there were people in the streets, but nothing was really clear. Nobody in Moscow really had any details at first,' he recalls.

Thinking back, Andrei finds it hard to convey clearly what happened. He was not among those people who felt impelled to defend perestroika and rush to the White House, and despite the worldwide attention, the headlines and on-the-hour TV news beamed across the globe, to be in the city during those days, you would hardly have been aware of the epoch-changing events taking place on the banks of the River Moscow, unless you were standing outside the White House itself, alongside Yeltsin and his flak-jacketed young bodyguards, holding up bullet proof briefcases to protect him against snipers.

'There has been so much worse in Russia's recent history than the events of August 1991 that I find it hard to remember,' says Andrei, going back over his theme of life as chaos in today's Russia. What does stand out much more vividly in the years of repeated shocks are the bloodshed and violence of October 1993, when after weeks of mounting tension and impasse between the Kremlin and State Duma, Yeltsin dissolved parliament by decree and ordered the army to shell the White House, where his rebellious vice-president, Alexander Rutskoi, and parliamentary speaker Ruslan Khasbulatov were holed up with an eclectic assortment of Nationalist and Communist supporters. Official figures claimed that 147 died in the fighting, but, with most deaths caused by government snipers, the clash left a deeply negative image. 'August 1991 was a mute crisis. In 1993 CNN reports were broadcast across the channels and we could see each bullet as it was fired. It was much more scary and depressing.'

The strange trail of events that led to a mysterious decision to allow pro-parliament demonstrators to leave the security ring within which they had been pinned at the White House, go on a rampage at the nearby Moscow mayor's office and then set off to try to storm the television centre at Ostankino in the city's northern suburbs brought the violence very close to home for Andrei.

From his apartment near Prospekt Mira, the sounds of shooting at Ostankino on the night of 3 October were clearly audible. Andrei's father was among those who had joined the demonstrators, so Andrei's fears for Russia's future were compounded with stronger emotions.

'In 1991 there was a feeling of high spirits, as if you'd been able to drop a heavy load after carrying it for years. In 1993 if felt as if a knot was being tied very tightly and it could be cut only by war. When the tanks came onto the streets and began firing, that felt like the beginning of the war. Students from my group at the university were down there at the White House and it was a very worrying time.'

But despite the horror of those few, violent days in October and the unpalatable pictures of the war in Chechnya, which, like Americans during the Vietnam years, Russians watched at home every evening on the television a couple of years later, Andrei marks the economic crisis of today as worst of the chaotic political events of the Yeltsin years.

The responsibility of providing for his family falls on Andrei's shoulders and with Yeltsin's succession far from clear the tug of different powerful vested interests within the Russian political economy threatens to undermine many of the achievements of the new era, whoever eventually wins control of the Kremlin, he fears. 'But as Gorbachev said when he came to power and introduced his new policies: the process has started. That process is still going on. From the death of Gensek Brezhnev to the present day, change has been my companion whether I've liked it or not.'

Emma Gushina's road to relative riches has followed a more idiosyncratic path than her old classmate Andrei's. She too was once a member of the Komsomol. She too was proposed as a candidate for the oft-coveted Communist Party card. She didn't take up the chance – the thought of all those boring party meetings seemed too much of a waste of time for a bright young woman whose scientific work at a military machine-tool designing institute was far more interesting. Had Mikhail Gorbachev's gradualist approach to reform and evolution of the Soviet dinosaur been successful she, like Andrei, would probably have stayed on the academic track, rising through the technical ranks in the ordered and steady way dictated by party ideology. But the thaw in Cold War rhetoric set off by glasnost and perestroika broke up the ice-bound aims of the Moscow Aviation Technological University well before Boris Yeltsin took to the top of a tank to challenge Russia to seize the democratic moment. As military-industrial orders fell away, the need for technical research into tool-making for the aerospace industry disappeared and in 1989 Emma, then an engineer programme-maker (a computer programmer for automated tool-making devices) on a monthly salary of 140 roubles, left to find her own way in life.

Ten years later she fits easily into the image of a modestly well-off new Russian. Elegantly dressed in a designer sweater, graceful shoes and smart jeans, her bright brown eyes reflecting the humour in her personality, she sips at a cappuccino in a French delicatessen and café housed inside the foyer of the Tchaikovsky Concert Hall on Moscow's Triumfalnaya Ploshad (Triumphal Square). Café Delifrance is just one of the scores of Western-style bistros, restaurants, diners and clubs to have opened in the capital in the last five or six years.

When Emma left the crumbling structure of her state institute to begin dabbling in business, visitors to Moscow city centre would have been better advised to take sandwiches for lunch than to expect to find a good spot for a decent cup of coffee. You might have found a basement snack bar selling greasy *gorshochki* – bowls of thick meat and vegetable stew served with doorsteps of black bread – where customers ate standing at grubby Formica counters. You could even have been lucky enough to come across one of the early 'cooperatives' – small businesses allowed to practice a limited degree of free enterprise under state supervision, where standards were, hopefully, a bit better. But an elegant, sunny, relaxed and clean modern café where well-dressed, sophisticated and cheerful young businesspeople, students and professionals drop by for a bite to eat, a cup of coffee and a cigarette? Hardly.

In 1991, during my first visit to Moscow, I took a Russian friend who had said she wanted to drink champagne to the Hotel Peking restaurant, just across the square from the Tchaikovsky Concert Hall. The food was more Comintern than Cantonese, the sweet Soviet champagne was served warm by sullen waiters in grease-spattered grubby shirts and the bill came to more than the average monthly wage of a university professor.

The fact that today in Moscow you can enjoy standards of service and catering common to any European capital in the company of similar sorts of educated, middle-class and vivacious people is in large measure thanks to the enterprise, initiative and verve of people like Emma, who took charge of their lives when the opportunity arose and single-handedly created a service industry where none had existed for more than seventy years.

In cultural centres, residential streets and the vaulted basements of old university buildings, restaurants, shops and businesses selling all manner of goods, foods and services can be found throughout Moscow and other large cities like St Petersburg today. At the Tchaikovsky, located in the heart of the city on the corner of Tverskaya Ulitsa – famed in Soviet times as Gorky Street – a luxury hairdressing saloon and beauty parlour, Häagen-Dazs ice-cream bar and Japanese sushi counter are all close neighbours of the French café. Passing trade from the thousands who flock to the daily recitals and concerts is only a small part of available custom. The exit from Mayakovskaya metro station is only yards away from the Tchaikovsky's brass-handled solid oak doors. Where once Muscovites could meet only on draughty station platforms, or hang around empty theatre vestibules, now the habitual comforts of Western urban life beckon as ideal venues to rendezvous.

As Emma can confirm, no one was available to teach the beginners in Russia's business world the rules for providing service and customer satisfaction. Her career as a clothing retailer began by chance and her lessons came not from economics textbooks or business primers, but from the school of hard knocks. From Gorbachev 'cooperative' member to self-made businesswoman via shuttle trading in cheap skirts between Moscow and Istanbul, Emma has learned all her lessons from life.

'When I started cooperatives were the fashion. Small enterprises were supposed to replace the role served by the large ailing producers and manufacturers. Small cooperatives of two or three people were very popular at the time and my friends and I decided to set up a clothing firm. The only problem was that we really didn't have the necessary skills and knowledge to organize and manage such a business. We simply had never been taught how to do this,' said Emma, who was sitting with her six-year-old daughter, Alexandra, fashionably dressed in dungarees, next to her.

Attempts to rent a tailoring workshop, set up production lines, make and sell clothes for a market hungry for new fashions after decades of dreary outfits and drab fabrics foundered. But Emma, who had never evinced any interest in fashion or creating her own business before, persevered.

She finds it hard to explain exactly what drove her. There was nothing in her upbringing that could explain her wish to carve out her own path. Her father, an industrial designer with a state firm, was the sort of man who was happy provided he had a job he could go to that he enjoyed. There was a great-grandfather, an artist and successful trader in church icons in the late nineteenth century who owned a large factory in the Oka River region near Moscow, but most Russians who are not of peasant stock can identify such entrepreneurs in their family trees. Perhaps because she had had to work a bit harder than some of her classmates to succeed, she had an edge of drive and determination. When Emma left school in 1979, she failed by half a point in her matriculation exams to reach the benchmark for entering a full-time course at the Moscow Aviation Technological University. Instead she was told to join the evening classes in 'complex project-making for automatic systems of flying apparatus', as the diploma course was called. For five years she combined evening study with daytime work – at the same institute, where she was technical secretary to the party committee. After a year she was promoted and took a job with the Sverdlovsky district committee, an area that covered the central region of Moscow around Petrovka Ulitsa. Others in the party regarded her as an ideal candidate, as a young woman who deserved the support the party could give, and she was proposed as a candidate for membership of the CP. Emma was no great believer in ideology, but nor was she insincere – she'd been in the Komsomol as a teenager and hadn't seriously questioned the political tenets of her society.

'I believed that membership of the Communist Party would help me in my future. In order to work in the institute, especially in some departments where I was studying, it helped if the person was a party member,' she says, but adds that career wasn't the sole reason she was interested. 'Maybe at some subconscious level everyone believed that such moves were right. For many people it was quite a necessary decision.'

But like many people of her generation Emma is keen to draw atttention to a distinction that clearly existed at this time – the late 1970s and early 1980s. Most youngsters joined the Komsomol at fourteen with a 'simple-hearted and sincere belief' in the organization. To become a full member of the Communist Party was an altogether different step, one which was taken either out of a firm ideological belief or, more likely, because it was seen as a useful addition to the curriculum vitae.

In the end Emma decided against joining the party.

Running her fingers through her short, stylishly cut dark hair, she laughs when I asked why. 'I grew up and became a more adult person, and it was more important for me to work in science and not to go wasting time at party meetings. It's always better to do what you want to do, what you like to do.'

By doing what she wants to do, Emma has ridden the switchback dips and arcs of economic transformation in Russia. Life wasn't bad when she started out. She graduated, after years of combining study with party work – for eighteen months she was the paid secretary to the Komsomol committee and she had stints working with the CP – and took a job as an engineer programme maker at the institute. She enjoyed the work and her monthly salary was supplemented by bonuses from helping with the contract work professors and other researchers undertook. She was living at home but did not need to rely on her parents in any way. She could afford summer holidays at resorts away from Moscow and considered her standard of living as *sredny* – middle class. The disintegration of the institute, from the beginning of rot to a full rout of staff, took just two years. 'A fish starts to rot from the head,' she remarks, as she relates how the brightest and best researchers left in droves for totally unrelated jobs in the fast-developing world of commerce. Eventually only those tutors and heads of department who, like fish out of water, were unable to survive in any world beyond the grey stolid walls of academia were left.' Emma saw the writing on the wall. There was no point in her staying any longer and she left, with little idea of what she would do next.

Dabbling in business with a few friends, she began to take the steps that would transform her life and, multiplied through others like her across the country, transform the face of the Soviet Union.

Dismissing their miserable efforts at fashion tailoring

as a learning experience, Emma's group of young entrepreneurs unconsciously adopted E. F. Schumacher's dictum, 'Small is beautiful,' and made their first small fortune by producing lapel badges to commemorate the thousandth anniversary of Christianity in Russia. She can't remember how much they made, but to young women in their twenties accustomed to seeing only a trickle of roubles and copecks drip through to their family budgets, it seemed like a lot of money. 'We four girls immediately invested the money into denim fabric to make jeans and jackets, which we wanted to sell at Rizhsky metro, where there was a big market at the time,' Emma says, adding that capital accumulated by selling badges to the devout was the breath of life to their dreams of becoming rag-trade magnates.

Their firm, ITD – Individyalniaya Tryudovaya Deyatelnost – Nadezhda (Individual Labour Activity Hope) began to see results on the very cusp of Russia's transition. It was 1991 and Emma had been married a year, to Andrzej, a Polish student at Moscow Communications Systems Institute she had met in 1987. ITD Nadezhda had a professional tailor on board who designed fashionable jeans and jackets using patterns from European magazines like *Burda* and *Moda* as a guide. Clothes cut to a European line met the demands of a hungry market at a time when a second-hand pair of Levi's could change hands for 250 roubles – at the time £6 – on Moscow's black market.

It was an optimistic time, which Emma remembers as having something of the atmosphere of a gambling den. 'Everyone was buying, selling, trying to make their way. We felt we could be part of this too.'

Busy with her own concerns, Emma barely noticed the events of August 1991. Unimpressed by the much-heralded benefits of perestroika, she was sanguine about the fall of Gorbachev and the collapse of the Soviet Union. The drama which unfolded around the Russian government White House excited her curiosity and she went down to see for herself the tanks, the barricades and the demonstrators. 'You know, we had some hopes in our hearts and souls but – this is a very personal opinion – probably the perestroika that was before 1991 no one got a lot from this. On the whole, me and a lot of my friends had lots of hopes about this change of power and maybe we supported the younger, the newer wing of power. It was a time of illusions and expectations. We were hoping that there would be real perestroika, not the old party functionaries, but someone new and democratic.'

Life soon became much too demanding to dwell on politics. By the summer of 1992 Emma's husband, Andrzej, had graduated and the couple had a baby. Hyper-inflation was wrecking the dreams of millions and destroying the chances of many talented young people and their businesses, including ITD Nadezhda. It was a hard time to be young, in business and a new mother. The couple were faced with tough choices. Their daughter barely four months old, Andrzej left to look for work in his native Poland and Emma became a shuttle-trader.

Shuttle-trading is a phenomenon as old as commerce itself. The Silk Routes which traverse Central Asia developed to serve Europe's desire for silks, spices and precious stones. Adventurers of all nations exploited the discrepancies of cost and value caused by availability that existed between the cultures. The collapse of Communism in Eastern Europe and then Russia combined to rob millions of their livelihoods, while at the same time offering chances to travel and trade for the first time in generations. What had been exotic tales from Emma's Soviet history books, stories of the traditions and past of republics like Uzbekistan, Tadjikistan and Turkmenistan, suddenly became a pressing economic necessity for tens of thousands of Russians learning to swim in the conflicting new currents of the post-Soviet world.

'My mother had just retired on a pension, so I gave her the baby to look after and went to Turkey. I had some friends who were already making a living from shuttle-trading and I saw this as a means to provide for me and the baby.'

Though Emma makes light of the decision, it was not an easy choice. Shuttle-trading remains a difficult way of making a living for many in Russia and former Soviet states to this day and can be seen in many manifestations, from the mobs of plaintive old women who tout dried fish, fresh fruit or goods from local factories at every station stop across the nation's railways, to the poor peasants of Belarus who take the overnight train to Moscow to sell cheap milk, vegetables and home baked produce for profits of a few dollars per trip. The dangers inherent in shuttle-trading – the risk of exploitation, theft, pressure on women far from home to become prostitutes – didn't deter Emma, who went with friends and followed advice from those more experienced with a keen ear and eye.

In November 1992 she took a charter flight to Turkey from Moscow's old regional airport of Vnukovo with $600 in her pocket. The return flight and three days' accommodation in a three-star hotel in Istanbul cost $140. The rest of the money she spent on cloth covers for three-piece suites, items much in demand at the time. Two weeks later, having sold her stock at Moscow's open-air markets at a profit of $150 she would be back, ready to buy more. Her shuttle-trading days lasted a year and the learning curve was steep but swift. Travel agents – another new feature of commercial activity in Moscow – were briefed to make the best arrangements for each trip and Emma soon learned to find cheaper sources for the goods she wanted. From small stores and wholesalers at first, she was soon buying up stock direct from manufacturers and diversifying into the latest hot items for the Moscow market: fashionably short *yubki* – skirts – for girls and young women. Cheap, mass-produced clothing from Turkey was ideal for the unsophisticated provincial market in Russia, where anything other than a home-made or locally produced frock was highly desirable. Reasonable quality and low prices were the secret to making money and Emma proudly claims she and her friends were among the first to stumble upon the principle of 'stack 'em high and price 'em low'.

'Girls' skirts were all the rage for about eighteen months and we were some of the first traders to profit, not with the help of high prices, but from taking small profits from a high turnover.' Skirts bought in Turkey for $2 each sold in Moscow at a mark-up of just 50 cents. Customs clearance and overheads took 30 cents a dress, leaving a profit for the shuttle-traders of around 20 cents a dress. The secret to making money this way was to retire from retail and move into wholesale. Soon Emma and a group of friends she worked with had stopped taking the regular bimonthly charter to Istanbul, had secured supply lines and were shipping in containers of inexpensive fashion items worth $80,000 a consignment. Deliveries of stocks were made to warehouses at Moscow's big retail markets, Cherkizovskaya and Luzhniki, situated on a stretch of tarmac alongside one of the city's most popular sports stadiums across the river from Moscow State University.

The women were not preyed on by the Mafia – this aspect of modern Russian society was also in its early stages and the markets at that time were relatively free trading zones where petty theft was the key concern. But backhanders were needed to bribe customs officials who were always inclined to overestimate the value – and therefore the duty payable – on consignments.

'We quickly picked up the idea of doing business. The main Mafia at this time was the customs, who always expected bribes. They would leaf through an Italian fashion catalogue and see skirts similar to ours priced at $10. Then they would demand to know why we were declaring ours at five time less than the apparent customs value,' Emma recalls with laugh.

The rules of the game were by this time quite clear. Spend days or weeks haggling with officials while your stock lingered in a bonded warehouse and end up paying the full duty, or save yourself the time, trouble and a lot of money by bribing the *tamozhenniki* – customs officers – to stamp the paperwork and release the goods. 'We were finally able to get to the point where we dealt only with one individual and waited until he telephoned us before we went down to pick up our merchandise.' For this service the customs agent took $500, a small price to pay for the traders, who were dealing in tens of thousands of dollars' worth of goods, Emma remarks, but noting that the practice was not without cost to the nerves.

Eventually shuttle-trading became boring, says Emma, who by this time – the mid-1990s – was enjoying the fruits of a business that had a healthy turnover, affording her an income that paid for a middle-class lifestyle the equal of any in Europe, something of which many Muscovites, let along Russians from the vast regions of the interior, could only dream.

Seeing a gap in the market for children's clothes, something which every parent needs and frequently has to buy, Emma and some business associates looked west to Poland to find a supplier who could design and make clothes to order. 'It struck me that selling children's clothes was much more profitable and if I could find a source of good-quality clothing I could develop a new business direction.' With the help of her husband, contracts were signed with a Warsaw factory with an established reputation for quality and service, and Emma quickly established a sales network in Moscow. But by the summer of 1997, acting on her belief in the need to follow her own path, she resigned from the company to spend more time with her small daughter and nurse her mother, who was seriously ill. OOO Round Ltd (Obshestvo s Ogranichennoi Otvetstvennostyu Round) was wound down to the point where it exists in name only.

The flexibility being in business has given Emma during the turbulent early years of Russia's transition to a market economy has been helped by the fact that her husband, having had to leave the family at one point in search of work, finally landed a well-paid and secure job with a Polish energy company employed on construction projects for the Russian state gas monopoly, Gasprom.

Following the death of her mother in November 1998, Emma, whose business curiosity has now become a way of life, began looking around for new projects. Currently she is setting up a high-quality second-hand clothes retailing company as part of a Moscow-city backed scheme to help poor people buy affordable clothing.

Emma has been a winner in the new Russia because she took risks and didn't let setbacks deter her from her path. She's taken advantage of opportunities and not been afraid to change direction when she felt the time was right. From the moment she decided not to take up membership of the Communist Party, because she wanted to be 'sincere' with herself and it didn't feel like the right step, Emma has danced to the beat of her own drum.

'There was nothing in my upbringing that could have taught me to cope with these times. My parents belonged to that category of people who were simply happy to do a job of work. Enterprise and initiative are things experience gave me. Every person may find this: life made me survive.'

If she is personally happy and fulfilled, Emma remains politically disappointed in the new Russia. She laments the collapse of manufacturing industry in Russia, even as she hastens to explain that had she been able to source the quality production for her children's clothing locally she would have done so. 'Speaking about hopes for Russia, right now I am completely disappointed. All the hopes I had have been dead for some time now. The reality I see about myself is bleak. I often go to the provinces and I see that there is no manufacturing, no production. Moscow is not Russia. You should go deep into Russia to see what is going on. Healthy people who are ready to work are practically dying of starvation. God gave me this chance. I live in Moscow and the first wave of the new Russia carried me to the top of trade, but in the provinces it's very hard to start anything. They are plagued by inertia. Huge industrial complexes are literally being destroyed. I went to Pereslavl recently and when you talk to people there you get the creeps. There was a man of thirty-five, a chemical factory worker, who was telling me he was young and fit and prepared to work, but he's not receiving his wages and cannot provide for his family. He was ready to do anything, but what chances does he have?'

Emma says she is an optimist, but despair is not far from the surface when she looks into Russia's political future. Certainly the distribution of wealth in the new Russia can give her little cause for optimism. A rare study of income distribution ordered by the central bank and conducted by the Russian Academy of Sciences in 1996 found that winners like Emma remained a tiny minority. Russians had $140 billion in personal savings, but barely 3 per cent of that money was held by the poorer 71 per cent of the population, while 72 per cent of it belonged to the richest 5 per cent. Over half of all savings in Russia were held by 2 per cent of the population.

'I see no way out for Russia. There's no way out because, unless there is industry working and a solution to this crisis of power that is getting deeper and deeper, what can we do? I see no person who can find a solution to this.'

Looking back over the Yeltsin years, an epoch which began with such promise and opportunities, she says it's difficult to judge who was to blame for the failure to deliver. 'I'm no economist, but for me one of the most painful things has been the way our natural resources have been sold off and wasted. But probably Yeltsin is not to blame alone; no person can save a sinking ship on his own.'

And then she laughs, insisting that she remains an incorrigible optimist and that these depressing thoughts are purely the result of having seen the poverty and despair of provincial Russia just a few days before.

4

Losers

The metro line from Moscow's Kievsky railway station straggles out into the untidy scatter of suburban apartment blocks, wastelands of jerry-built garages and stretches of scruffy scrubland. Villages of old log cottages once nestled here before Soviet planning logic swept them aside to replace them with 'modern' brick and concrete constructions put up cheaply by army conscripts.

The light-blue line of Moscow's metro map, the Filevskaya, quickly surfaces beyond the nineteenth-century edifice of the old railway station, where huge bronze eagles perch, wings swept out in imperial splendour, above the Roman numerals of the clocks mounted on the sides of the front portico towers.

The line serves the suburban clusters of ugly, uniform apartment blocks that huddle in isolated patches beyond the older, lower-rise residential districts of Moscow's inner suburbs. Built in the 1970s, these are mostly working-class neighbourhoods, and in the crowded carriages of the metro it's standing room only in the mornings and afternoons as the legions of office staff, market traders and bargain-hunting shoppers pour into and out of the centre from their dormitory communities.

Muscovites without the money or connections to live nearer the centre find themselves in these characterless suburbs, so far out that from Krylatskoye station, the end of the line, Moscow's skyline is a canvas of prickly Stalin-era towers, belching power station smokestacks and glinting spires and golden onion domes of cathedrals and monasteries.

It's not fair to say that the losers of Moscow's transition from the heart of Soviet empire to today's bizarre capital of crypto-capitalism are to be found exclusively in such places. Tatiana Vasieleva, a chemistry teacher who holds down two jobs as well as taking in private students to help make ends meet, admits she's poor but doesn't consider herself a loser. She likes the panoramic view from the kitchen window of her twentieth floor flat, where she, her husband, Alexei, and teenaged children, Ivan and Olga, share a spacious three-room apartment. She and Alexei waited a long time to get the flat, spending the early years of their married life living with his parents in the centre of Moscow before their names reached the top of the city housing list. Tatiana, a tired-looking woman of thirty-seven, doesn't begrudge the hour-long metro journey into the city centre where she works. She doesn't complain about the cold, draughty journey in the winter; the hot sweaty, humanity-scented trawl back home on hot summer afternoons. All things considered, her and Alexei's lot isn't such a bad one in today's Russia, she reckons. And yet with a combined income of less than the equivalent of £100 a month – 3,500 roubles as at August 1999 rates –she and her husband are hardly wealthy even by Russian standards, with median monthly household income calculated in March 1999 at around £130 by Russian social surveys.

Everything about the neighbourhood Tatiana lives in reflects the division in Moscow between the city centre of postcard views of ancient churches and broad boulevards and the scruffy neglect of the outskirts. It's only a twenty-five-minute journey by metro from Kievsky station, but the two districts are worlds apart. Kievsky station is situated on the banks of the River Moscow in a district noted for its splendid old apartment blocks, diplomatic compounds and offices of international media and foreign wire agencies. Krylatskoye is so far out that it's practically in the countryside, in an area divided by poorly made roads and half-completed rubble-strewn factory complexes.

During eight years of visiting and living in Moscow I've rarely had cause to step into a carriage from the Filevskaya metro line, unless it was for the short hop the other way from Kievsky station two stops to the arty central shopping district of the Arbat. Rattling out through the midwinter landscape of mountains of grubby roadside snow, bleak parks and the tangled hot-water pipes of the above-ground district heating grids which criss-cross suburban Moscow was like stepping back in time. The line is one of the more modern and austere, unlike the central circle line and fabulous architecture of chandelier-bedecked inner-city stations famous from guidebook portraits of Moscow, which were begun in the 1930s and finished after the war. But its carriages are from another age: hard benches where spent springs exaggerate every jolt and bump and the thick, yellowing patterned wallpaper inside the wagons seem to hark back to an earlier reality, almost pre-Revolutionary in their crudity.

Babushki, those ubiquitous old women, their wizened features tied tightly inside rough woollen headscarves, shapeless creases of black coats wrapped around their formless bodies, worn felt *valenki* boots on their feet, crowd into the carriages, tugging huge and heavy bags and packages after them. Stray dogs and drunken men, the vodka vapours smelling strongly as the condensed clouds of their hoary breath hang in the air on a cold winter's day cram in too, fighting for space inside the old wooden wagons.

Riding the metro out to meet Tatiana was a journey into the past. The last time I had been beyond Fili Park station – a couple of stops out from Kievsky station, where the popular Gorbushka video market is a haven for bargain-hunting Muscovites unconcerned that most of the cheap CDs and videos are pirated copies knocked out illicitly in Bulgaria, China or closer to home – was in the spring of 1991, during my first stay in Moscow. Then I had been a guest of family friends, a former KGB officer and his younger wife, who lived in a similarly sparse and distant complex of concrete boxes to Tatiana, one stop closer to the centre, near the metro station Molodezhnaya.

Little of the landscape of run-down streets and untidy courtyards had remained in my memory – Moscow in the dying days of the Soviet Union remains for me at best a series of disjointed images of people, places and parties; of unexpected colours, incomprehensible customs and baffling bureaucracy.

In 1991 I had missed the last connection here at Kievsky station late one night, after lingering with a young woman too long as we walked across a Red Square romantically lit by the glare of the full moon. Coming up for air to the deserted apron of tarmac around the station's neo-classical white walls I stepped into the first cab I came across, realizing too late that two men were seated up front. My faltering Russian and proffered $5 note made me easy prey and a couple of hundred yards along the road the pair pulled over into a dark corner to beckon to their mates. Taking my chance, I had jumped out of the car and, despite the threats from the foul-smelling mouth of the swarthy driver, who followed me and grasped me by the lapels of my jacket, I managed to struggle free. I found my way to the brightly lit station entrance, having lost only the $5 and a little of my dignity.

Then as now, the Moscow *militsia* betrayed not the slightest interest in such street incidents, and I had had to find a more honest driver to make my way home.

As the metro wagon rumbled through the suburban stations, I wondered quite how I'd managed to explain in my pidgin Russian where I wanted to go, and how I'd even recognized the block of flats where I was staying in suburbs which still frequently look identical, putty-coloured, run-down and depressing.

Tatiana met me at the station, where a short straggle of market stalls selling fruit, frozen fish from cardboard boxes and various household items – cleaning products, underwear, useful knick-knacks – caught the passing trade.

The sense of stepping back in time intensified as we negotiated the dangerously slippery mountains of snow and ice lying between the grey concrete buildings and picked our way to her apartment house. Situated on the far side of the development, overlooking pristine white fields of snow, Moscow was a spectacular outline far in the distance. As we rounded the corner of yet another identical tower of glass and brick identified only by a set of fading six-foot tall numbers and slashes – *Dom* 12/4 (Block 12, building 4) – I saw a scene I hadn't witnessed in Moscow for years. A line of stolid, patient old women waited silently to reach the back of a lorry trailer mounted with a large, bright-yellow cylindrical tank. The women had the purposeful air of those who feel virtuous for having arisen at dawn and stood in line for hours to snatch up a bargain rarely seen on the streets.

Just such lines are for me an icon of the Soviet Union, when the inefficiencies and corruption of the command economy instilled in people the habit of joining the end of a queue regardless of what product was available – or even thought to be – at the front. President Boris Yeltsin's campaign strategists had leapt upon such images in the presidential election of 1996, when a strong showing from Communist leader Gennady Zyuganov in preliminary rounds of voting had prompted the publication of posters comparing the endless queues for sausage or cooking oil in Soviet times with the full shops of Yeltsin's era. You can find queues for cheap cooking oil and other products in marketplaces in provincial towns across Russia, where the free market is still a foreign theory found only in university textbooks and the cash economy is a fragile concept. But in Moscow – virtually a city state in Soviet times – where eight years of wild capitalism have transformed the economy and social practices, shaving copecks here and there from your shopping bill by queuing for hours for cut-price products has virtually disappeared. And the notion that something is scarce, in a city where everything has a price and anything – from university diplomas, exotic and endangered animals, to influence, sex and contract killings – can be bought, has become part of the folklore of the Soviet past. But here in the suburban fringes of a city which retains, even in its sophisticated centre, a village atmosphere where peasants in styles of clothing unchanged since the Bolshevik Revolution rub shoulders with urban young Russian yuppies, the Soviet Union appeared visibly resurrected.

'What are these women queuing for?' I asked Tatiana, whose short, unfashionably cut dark green woollen overcoat also seemed to belong to another age.

'Milk, they're waiting for milk.'

But milk isn't even remotely scarce in Russia today. Seven or eight years ago I remember packing cans of Marvel powdered milk to bring for friends, along with rubber shower attachments for their bathrooms, Marks & Spencer underwear and other rare and coveted items. But the economy, especially in Moscow, has been transformed since those chaotic early days of transition.

'Yes, you're right, milk isn't scarce and it's not even as if this milk, which is a couple of roubles cheaper a litre than that bought in shops, will run out. The tankers come down from a state farm a few miles away and if they sell all the milk they simply go back and bring another tankerful to the same spot,' Tatiana said. 'There's no reason at all for these women to get up at the crack of dawn and wait in line to fill their plastic bottles up with milk. They could come at their own convenience and buy as much as they wanted. But they're conditioned by years of hardship, shortage and poverty to believe that if you are to get something you have to make sacrifices. Besides, they can meet their neighbours here and enjoy a good grumble about how hard life is today and how much better it was in the past.'

Again I had the strange sensation that the years I had spent flying to and from Russia, the years I had lived here in this strange country, by turns exhausting and exhilarating, quixotic and bizarre, were being stripped away. I was back in the warm Moscow spring of 1991, when Yeltsin was wooing the voters to become president of the Russian component of the Soviet Union and the influence of Western fashions and ideas was still so new that the streets were peopled by women wearing summer frocks I'd last seen in London in the 1970s and a pair of my worn old Levi's could fetch 200 roubles in an illicit street deal at the giant open-air Izmailovsky flea market.

One day I had travelled by *elektrichka* out to the writers' village of Peredelkino, where Boris Pasternak and other icons of Soviet literary tradition had lived and died. It was a hot, drowsy sort of day when even the large country flies could hardly be bothered to stray from the shady undergrowth, and dirt-coloured dogs raised dusty trails as they trotted across the bone-dry mud roads that ran out at angles from the simple concrete platforms that served Peredelkino instead of a station.

A long crocodile of tired-looking locals stood in the harsh sunlight beyond the railway tracks waiting for service at the small windows of a concrete kiosk. Idly I inquired what they were waiting for and began shooting photographs as my Moscow guide, a young artist, explained that they wanted to buy *kvas*, a mildly alcoholic drink made from the fermented crusts of stale black bread. Bitter and fizzy, *kvas* remains a firm summer favourite in Russia; ice-cream is more often enjoyed from roadside stalls during the frozen winter months.

The appearance of a foreigner – especially one taking photographs among the tired and patient people – did not go down well with the denizens of Peredelkino. Harsh, unintelligible threats were made and a *militsia* officer appeared, demanding to know who I was and what I was doing. Hands grabbed for my camera and aggressive faces insisted I hand over the film. My guide tugged me away, explaining that the locals thought I was poking fun at Russian poverty and hardship by photographing the queue. Eight years later, Tatiana thought the *babushki* of Krylatskoye stood stoically in line out of nostalgia for the poor certainties of the past. Perhaps they had forgotten the shame of living in a society that spouted utopian slogans but, through neglect and indifference, heaped insults and injustices upon its people.

Tatiana's life as a poorly paid teacher was never going to be easy, even in Soviet times when she trained for a job she still loves. The new Russia has provided her and her husband with little in the way of material prosperity, at the same time as stripping away what social safety nets existed under Communism: unemployment benefits, subsidized holidays in government-owned Black Sea sanatoria, free medical care. And yet despite the objective statistics that would classify Tatiana as a loser in the market jungle of the new Russia, she is resolute that her life today is much better than it was when she was growing up and starting her family and career in Soviet times.

Tatiana gets by on less than the stark statistics of the average family living standards in Yeltsin's Russia. Russians spend nearly half their income on food – in America, the figure is less than 15 per cent. Housing accounts for just six per cent of spending. Health-care costs are surprisingly also greater for a Russian family, according to official statistics: American families spend less than 1 per cent of their incomes on hospital and other care costs, while Russians spend more than 15 per cent.

A casual visitor to Tatiana's apartment would not think of her as poor. There are televisions, radios, an electric sewing machine, a washing machine and the other accessories of modern domestic life. But Tatiana and her husband have spent more than twenty years carefully accumulating the small luxuries of life and on closer examination the family income provides for a standard of living barely above the breadline.

Tatiana has two jobs besides taking private classes as a *repititor* – cramming for students desperate to improve their chances of passing stiff university entrance exams. A graduate of the Lenin State Pedagogical Institute in Moscow, Tatiana knew that her life as a teacher would be no bed of roses when she graduated in the early 1980s. Teachers have always enjoyed high social status in Russia, but even in Soviet times only those research specialists in powerful defence or politically important nuclear, engineering or electronic industries and institutes earned good salaries. But in those days, when most people, including teachers, were paid an 'average salary', money was less important as there was little to spend it on beyond the basics of shelter, food, clothing and modest entertainment.

Her official job, at State Secondary School Number 91 in Arbat Street, a stylish old quarter of central Moscow known for its restaurants, bars and pedestrian shopping street, pays 400 roubles a month. A private school near the Moscow metro circle line's Taganka station pays 1,200 roubles a month, about a quarter of the $200 fees charged to the parents of children who attend the school. Tatiana, a small woman with a thick bob of short black hair which is beginning to grey, mutters, '*Dorogo. Uzhasno dorogo*' – 'Expensive. Terribly expensive' – under her breath as she recites the bald figures that dictate the financial constraints of her life.

She remains on the staff of School Number 91 because it is a specialized chemistry school under the supervision of the Russian Academy of Sciences, where advanced experimental chemistry is taught. Working at the private school, where she enjoys the perk of free places for her son and daughter, gives Tatiana a sometimes painfully acute insight into how the other half in today's Russia live.

Most of the parents of the fee-paying children at the school – not all the pupils, as the school converted from a state institution to private only a few years ago – could be considered 'new Russians' she says. Children of parents who own or run small businesses – travel agencies, commercial firms or those in some sort of higher government service, parliamentary deputies or members of the Federation Council, Russia's upper house – attend. 'The children of these sorts of people find it difficult to socialize with other children of their age,' Tatiana says, sipping tea at her kitchen table and gazing across the sunlit panorama of the Moscow skyline. 'They are very nervous and aggressive. They don't like to watch good cartoons, for example, with the other children.'

She finds it hard to define exactly why the children of new Russians exhibit such markedly different behavioural patterns from the others at the school – many of whom started at the school when it was still a free, state school and pay little or heavily discounted fees. 'Perhaps the children are deprived of love and attention by parents who are too busy earning money to spend time with them. Sitting together watching television never helps people to communicate.'

The conversation turns to the 'friendly, family atmosphere' that most of the teachers, parents and pupils feel at a school originally privatized as a means of providing a higher quality of education to the children of teachers. Tatiana's joy in her job is evident and comes across in the way her face softens and the tension in her relaxes as she talks about it. Just as in Soviet times Russian people found havens and respite from the heavy hand of the state in human relations, small intimate rituals, the everyday comforts of friends and trusted colleagues, so individuals today, tossed about by the vagaries of an economy with few rules in a society in transition, take succour from the small things in life. Tatiana doesn't dwell on the financially straitened circumstances of her life. Her husband Alexei, whose 2,000-rouble monthly salary as a computer specialist at a Moscow bank has been steadily eroded by inflation in the last few years, used to earn even less as an engineer at a research institute. But the indignity of doing a thankless job for a pauper's wage does grate. 'Sometimes I feel resentful about my lack of status and poor pay. There are certain days when it really hurts to think about it, especially when there is no money in the house and everyone is irritated. It's difficult to understand why you cannot provide for your own children.'

On days like this, Tatiana can feel her bile rise at the thought of the new Russians who ostentatiously flaunt their wealth, even if she – like many since the financial collapse of August 1998 – can also sometimes take a grim satisfaction from the losses some of these types suffered. 'It's difficult for me to understand the psychology of these new Russians. We tell lots of anecdotes about them,' she muses, referring to the rash of jokes about the brash new Russians that have sprung up in recent years to fill the vacuum left by the Soviet era's underground political humour. 'If we're telling these jokes about them, what sort of jokes do they tell themselves?' she wonders aloud. More seriously, she abhors the materialism of people who know the price of everything and the value of nothing.

'In Communist times people were not allowed to do anything or have anything. Right now there is the chance to earn heaps of money and people cannot conquer their urge and cannot realize what is most important in life and what is not. Very often people believe that the more they have, the better. There have always been such people in Russia, it's just that right now they are blooming and flourishing. At the same time, there are those people who believe everything is fine and money is not the most important thing in life.'

Tatiana is one of the few graduates from her institute who has stayed in teaching. Most of her old college friends fled the state sector years ago, as it became evident that the collapse of Communism meant the virtual collapse of the state too. Most moved into business or took office jobs with Russian or foreign firms. At reunions these friends tease her – 'Tatiana never left school' – but they respect her for doing a job which is essential in any society, especially one in such a state of flux as Russia. It's a shame that these old friends, who spend crazy sums of money on entertaining their pampered offspring, never think to put their hands in their pockets to support cash-strapped schools, Tatiana says. Perhaps it's a reflection of the shift from a society where the communal was trumpeted above the individual to one where selfish concerns and corruption have become leitmotifs for a new age, but the lack of any significant charitable movement in Russia and indifference to social concerns are overt characteristics of the new Russian psychology.

Tatiana has toyed with the idea of leaving teaching, but admits that notions of going to work for a company and earning a salary ten times as much boil down to little more than 'delusions' for her. 'I have thought about doing something else, but the thing is that I feel like this job is my place,' she explains with the air of one who long ago dismissed any arguments in favour of risking her fate in the vicissitudes of Russian commerce. 'During the summer holidays I miss school, the children, my colleagues. It's interesting for me to go to school and teach; it's always interesting to start up some fun projects with the kids. This is why I stay in this job.'

It's not an easy choice, but Tatiana insists she doesn't feel particularly deprived living on such a tight budget. Eight years after the Soviet Union was formally declared dead, when President Yeltsin and the heads of state of the Ukrainian and Belarusian republics, Leonid Kravchuk and Stanislav Shushkevich, met in an old hunting lodge in the Byelovezhsky Forest, near Brest close to the Polish border, Soviet-level public housing costs remain the rule rather than exception in Russia. Rent, heat, electricity and light for her three-room apartment cost just 350 roubles a month and Tatiana saves money on travel costs by buying a discounted metro pass for the equivalent of £1 a month. She should pay about six times as much but 'cheats the state' by buying a concession rate pass from people entitled to them – invalids, the unemployed, war veterans – who have no need of them. 'I'm trying to talk myself into thinking that the state cheats me by paying me so little. Still, I don't like to do this, but I have to,' she says, troubled by her admission.

The economic indignities heaped upon the Russian people by the failure of successive administrations and Kremlin cadres in the Yeltsin years, which many might fairly consider crimes of considerably greater magnitude than misuse of a discounted travel pass, don't figure in Tatiana's equation. Her simple faith in the essential benefits of Russia's transition from Communist state to supposedly free country remains undiminished by the grubby realities of greed, corruption and theft on a grand scale revealed during the country's first few years of post-Soviet freedom.

When her husband found his job as a computer technician at the bank several years ago, his salary was enough for the couple to immediately send their then twelve-year-old son, Ivan, to Oxford for a two-week English-language summer school. 'We promised the same trip to our girl, Olga, the next summer, but then found we couldn't afford it, and the way things are now she will never get to Oxford. Life had become much, much harder, even before the crisis,' Tatiana says referring to the rouble collapse of August 1998 and subsequent economic hardships. 'Inflation has eaten up my husband's salary and everything is much more expensive than before, but wages have remained the same.'

However, life is about so much more than merely money, she repeatedly insists. In August 1991, when, in a historically defining moment, Boris Yeltsin leapt up onto a tank outside the Russian parliamentary White House in the centre of Moscow to rally the crowds of pro-democracy demonstrators who had rushed to protect perestroika against the *coup d'état* by hardliners from the Politburo, Tatiana was there.

She felt the axis of her life, her country and her future shift at that moment. She and Alexei had lived through the years of Mikhail Gorbachev's glasnost; had believed in perestroika. This had been the oxygen that gave hope to a generation that grew up under the stifling stagnation and boredom of the Brezhnev years. You sense that no disappointment, short of a slide back into the grim grey grip of Communism in Russia, will taint Tatiana's approach to life with cynicism.

So, she's not sure if this year she'll be able to save the 2,500 roubles she managed to put aside last year for ten days of summer sunshine in Rostov-on-Don; she'll borrow if scrimping and saving falls short. The last time the family had a Black Sea holiday was four years ago; she has a friend married to a forester up in Karelia on the Gulf of Finland – where the tsars took their holidays and Yeltsin has continued the tradition – and knows she and the kids can stay there for free. So, she makes her own clothes and her teenaged daughter swears she'd far rather wear home-made than some cheap fashion garment found in the open-air markets. None of this can be weighed against what Russia stood to lose in August 1991.

'It happened that the day before the coup we were with some friends, listening to the songs of Alexander Galich, and one song has the words, "You may go out to the square. Do you dare go out to the square?" It's a song about revolutions, about the Decembrists, Prague. As soon as Alexei and I heard what was happening, we rushed to the White House, stopping by the school to take a bag full of gas masks from there. People at the White House were making speeches and saying gas masks might come in handy. I was there when Yeltsin got up on the tank. It was the first day and everybody was nervous and alarmed. Later more people came when the rumour started going out that General Lebed's assault troops from Ryazan would come and protect us, but the first day was scary. Nobody believed that those who had started the coup would allow people to make speeches or organize a public protest.'

Tatiana remembers the sea of 'good faces' in the crowd around her and the atmosphere of hope and support she felt as Russia's future lay in the balance during those heady days of August. Politicians made speech after speech: Yeltsin, Ruslan Khasbulatov – later disgraced in the October 1993 showdown between the president and parliament. 'Of course, I wouldn't give a copeck for their words today,' Tatiana says bluntly. 'But then I believed that the politicians were not simply in it for themselves, they were for the people too. I was stirred by Yeltsin's words, I wanted to believe in him and to trust him. It was especially nice because it looked as if he was not trying to become a person of importance himself, no. He sounded as if he was a person of great dignity, even towards Gorbachev. I realized that to protect and to save the reforms of perestoika, this was about ensuring that democracy was not killed in the cradle. I believed that at that time Yeltsin was really stirred and worried by this, that he was the man of the moment.'

Fearing for her safety, Alexei sent Tatiana home at the end of the first day of the coup, although he remained with the defenders of democracy behind the hastily built barricades of trolley buses and concrete paving slabs for a further two days. Tatiana sat by the picture window of her high-rise kitchen, looking out over the same panorama that greets her eye to this day, praying for her husband's safety. When radio station Echo Moskva reported that there was shooting around the White House, she feared for her husband, sharing the concerns of many throughout Russia and around they world. Alexei ensured that he found the opportunity to slip through the barricades to phone his wife and assure her of his safety. These were emotional days for Tatiana, who, despite the passage of years and death of hopes represented by the Yeltsin years, the corruption, the banditry, the disastrous war in Chechnya, still regards him as a hero.

'I simply think that it has been very hard in these short few years since those events to really do anything. I cannot even quite imagine how it was possible to come as far as we have. Maybe someone would be able to do a better job – but where is this person? All the people suggested as possible successors, none of them are as good as Yeltsin. All of them belong to the old guard, they have just changed their colours. Yeltsin has had a very difficult job, the most difficult in this country, but still we might say that everything now is more or less all right, compared with what we had. So, thank you, Yeltsin. You know, he is no Zyuganov, Lebed, Khasbulatov or Anpilov. It's scary to think of what would happen to all of us if these people were to come to power,' she said, referring to Communist and Nationalist faction leaders.

One image she recalls with particular anger was the indifference of most of her neighbours to what she understood as historic events. 'In the morning, before my husband called and told me that everything was fine, I went shopping. In the shop I was queuing for something and could see that for the majority of people nothing much had changed. I felt so angry at them for not caring. People were only worried whether there was sausage in stock.'

If the fact that sausage – at least in Moscow – is now always to be found in the shops and street markets is enough of an improvement for many people in today's Russia, Tatiana is not entirely disillusioned. She recognizes that as one of the many hopeful young people of perestroika her vision of a democratic, free Russia does not entirely correspond with the reality. But dreams when realized rarely do, she avers. She remembers the anger she felt as a teenager at how the masses acquiesced in a system that kept them in chains. Reading Alexander Solzhenitsyn's *The Gulag Archipelago* as a sixteen-year-old was the dawning of her political consciousness. 'It was unpleasant to realize that we were not allowed to speak out, to voice our thoughts. The reality of our life was frustrating and all our problems were connected with the political level. I so wanted change. It was difficult for me to imagine that people could always live under these lies.'

The chaotic political torrents of the post-Communist years might have driven out Tatiana's naïve faith in the power of politics in Russia to bring utopian change – she regards all politicians as liars and fact-twisters now. But life today is immeasurably better than in Soviet times, despite the financial hardships of her life. 'We always dream about something better than is realized. But you know, that queue we saw is something exotic today. We do not have to hoard food; it's a long time since we bought things by the sackful. It's possible to buy every book you want to read and even to earn some money and go someplace if you want to go there.' With something of a wistful note of nostalgia, she adds that in Soviet times if you saw someone reading a book by an unauthorized writer on the metro that could be enough to strike up a lasting friendship.

For a woman whose family has to struggle to make ends meet, it is perhaps not surprising that the elements in the new Russia Tatiana most dislikes are those dictated by money, consumption and the shifting currents of popular culture. She long ago stopped reading newspapers, something she and her friends consumed with alacrity in the days of perestroika. Most Russian newspapers today are full of crime, sex, scandals and gossip, or revolve around the lives of people concerned only with creating art or music in order to make money, she believes. 'I get really irritated when all you can see in the papers are stories about what huge amounts of money or property people have stolen and I'm sick of the new pseudo-culture of propaganda. Even if I don't want to know anything about the private life of the American president, I have to know because it's what everyone is talking about. When I watch television I skip channels to try avoid seeing or hearing anything about this.'

The new Russia has corrupted artists as well as politicians, she feels. Film director Nikita Mikhalkov, whose latest film, *The Barber of Siberia*, a $45 million Russo-French co-production, had just opened in Moscow when we talked, was an example of the disappointments of the new world of post-Soviet Russia. Russia's most expensive film ever, billed as an epic love story spanning continents and decades and described by its promoters as the '*Dr Zhivago* for the 1990s', was all over the media. Tatiana was not impressed with a man who had won an Oscar for best foreign film some years previously with his story of personal treachery and murderous purges in Stalin's Russia, *Burnt by the Sun*.

'Mikhalkov used to be one of our best directors,' she lamented. 'And now he is turning out films that look like *matrushka* dolls. It's so bad that he changed. He was a good guy and I believed that given some freedom he would have the chance to demonstrate genius. Instead in our new Russia he has sunk to this level.'

The abuse of freedom is perhaps the price Russians are paying for the years of repression, she feels. She hates the cheap and tawdry television shows and magazines aimed at the younger generation, teenagers who have little or no recollection of the past. While she remains confident that her two children are avoiding the worst excesses of popular culture – she approves of their friends and the sort of music they listen to – others are not immune. The sort of teen magazines that horrify parents in the West have become ubiquitous in Russia in the last couple of years. 'Children as young as ten or eleven are reading *Cool Girl* or *Cool* which are all about sex, the details and techniques,' she says, referring to two popular newsstand magazine for teenagers on sale at every metro and market in Moscow. 'Maybe these sorts of magazine are like some kind of illness. This sort of material was prohibited for so long, perhaps people need to eat as much of it as they can and then it will disappear.'

The turbulence of the new Russia – the collapse of the old order and fluidity or lack of rules under the new – has driven many of her friends into the embrace of religion. Tatiana, who follows her own spiritual and moral rules, has eschewed this path. For her parental duties, her friends and her mother have been the stabilizing factors of a life buffeted by economic winds unforeseen in her youth. The new Russia has dealt losing cards to most of its citizens, many of them the legacies of the corruption-riddled Communist system of old. Measures of national health have declined across the board. Alcoholism, drug abuse, sexually transmitted diseases, malnutrition and infectious diseases are rife. Tatiana knows she and her family are poor, but she doesn't feel like a loser.

'My mother warned me when I entered the Pedagogical Institute that I would be poor. But since my family has always been poor, that was not an argument that scared me. I believe a person is truly happy when they are doing what they want, then everything else will somehow work out. I may have little money, but whenever I see an old woman begging in the street I try to give her a few coins.

There may be some cheats and liars among these beggars, but what if there are? You have to help people.'

Vasily Filipovich does not look like a casualty of Communism. A tall man who retains a military bearing and the booming voice of a parade-ground martinet, if anything he is straight out of the mould of a Hero of the Soviet Union. The sixty-eight year old retired Soviet army colonel and his wife, Raisa Alexeyovna, a surgeon who spent her working life treating patients in military and cosmonaut hospitals in Russia and Ukraine, bristle with confidence and assertiveness.

The parents of Andrei Pedorenko (see Chapter 2, 'Winners'), the couple live in a huge four-room flat in a modern high-rise apartment block just off Prospekt Mira, in Moscow's northern suburbs. The flat is well furnished and wood-panelled throughout – thanks to Vasily Filipovich's handiwork. Few pensioners in today's Russia enjoy such creature comforts as they do. Colour television sets, a mock open fireplace and glass-fronted cabinets displaying the best china reveal a high standard of living. Vasily Filipovich and Raisa Alexeyovna are products of the élite of Soviet society and their neighbours are drawn from a similar milieu – retired Communist apparatchiks, military men and administrators. The very position of their apartment block – on a shady boulevard a stone's throw from one of Moscow's main thoroughfares, in a district developed in the 1950s for families of the nomenklatura – tells people all they need to know.

But to talk to Vasily and his wife about their ideas and beliefs is to be left in no doubt that the transition of Russia from the Soviet path to the patchwork affair of capitalism, cronyism and nascent democracy of today has left them high and dry.

Vasily Filipovich describes himself as an 'ideological

Communist' who owes everything to the Soviet Union. Born just two months after Boris Yeltsin in 1931, Vasily's life followed much the same path as many of those former loyal Communist Party members who so swiftly took up the mantle of democracy following the putsch of 1991. He and his wife met in the first class at school in 1939 and married in 1956, when they were both in their mid-twenties. Theirs has been a happy union, Vasily says, with the cheerful encouragement of his wife, because 'we understood each other from the first moment and share the same views'.

Those views, shaped by their careers within core structures of Soviet society, remain firmly Communist, and the couple recently co-authored a book arguing that the only viable political system for the twenty-first century is an evolved form of socialism – 'self-organizing socialism' – radically different from that practised in the Soviet Union of old.[1] Theirs is not the revisionist ideology of the embittered old Stalinists who swell the ranks of KPRF (Communist Party of the Russian Federation) demonstrations on the anniversary of the October Revolution, chanting a soothing mantra of ancient slogans and demanding a return to the perceived security of the past. Vasily and Raisa are a lot brighter than that. But their impassioned argument that Soviet Communism failed because it lacked stability and eroded the support and goodwill of the people through forcing the pace of change too quickly seems just as out of place a decade after the Cold War regimes across Europe began tumbling. True socialism, they argue, can emerge only when the political structures employ both the energy of the productive sector of society and the wisdom of the non-productive but experienced older generation. Any political society based on two points – such as Western parliamentary democracy, revolving around opposing parties, or the Soviet model emphasizing just party and the workers – is bound to fail. 'A stool with only two legs will always fall over,' as Vasily puts it. 'The most stable system is one that stands on three points – like religion, with God the Father, God the Son and God the Holy Ghost.'

The October Revolution in Russia came fifty years too early, Vasily and Raisa think. Like a ship setting out to sail its maiden voyage without properly working engines, the Bolshevik Revolution relied upon the enthusiasm of the workers to set about building a modern economic engine, while the ship was propelled by the first wave of revolutionary fervour.

Vasily, eyes closed to aid concentration and one finger held aloft in the air, explains: 'We supposed the engine would be built while the ship was afloat. But no one thought about the construction of the ship, what was needed under the waterline, or above it. The ideas about productive relations advanced by Marx and Engels remained below the waterline. Non-productive relations, where children and pensioners fit into the scheme of things, was left hanging in the air. Pensioners ended up with no rights, no place in society. The ship remained afloat for more than seventy years only because of the enthusiasm of ordinary people and the authority of the Communist Party. But enthusiasm cannot remain strong for ever, it cannot be a permanent engine, and when Gorbachev destroyed the party's authority the ship of socialism had to sink.'

Unlike many members of the generation born in the 1930s who grew to maturity during the upheavals of the war years and Stalin's last years, they aren't clinging to a notion of political security fixed at some point in the past. Vasily, who justifiably argues that he 'owes all to Soviet power', readily volunteers that the slogans he uttered so faithfully in the past look like little more than fascism from today's perspective. But that does not mean that the Soviet period has nothing of value to offer Russia's future.

His father was killed at the front outside Moscow in 1942. Aged forty-four at the time, he was among the last call-up of men over forty desperately needed to plug the gaps of regiments bled dry by the Nazi onslaught. In 1947 his mother died, leaving him to find his own way in life in the chaos of post-war Russia. The couple left school in 1949 and Raisa entered the Leningrad Medical Institute, while Vasily, despite being four inches too short and desperately thin, managed to secure a place in a Kiev military college. The discipline of military life appealed to him and he joined the Communist Party in 1952, the same year he graduated with a 'Red Diploma' and gold medal, awarded to the best students who scored top marks in all courses. 'I was especially good in the field of Marxist-Leninism,' Vasily recalls with marked pride. He went into teaching in military schools before later specializing in complex engineering systems and radar. Raisa joined him in Kiev and they started a family. In the early 1960s promotion brought the family to Moscow, where Vasily put his considerable energy into both work and organizing a cooperative to build garages for residents of the apartment block.

'Everything was very clear. I never doubted [Communism] and all the people I knew never doubted. Everything was clear for them – the theory of Marxist-Leninism, they found very interesting, and they knew who was the enemy!' says Vasily with a smile, pointing in my direction. 'Capitalism was the enemy! We were building socialism and we were sure we were building this. We believed all the slogans. We never doubted ourselves or thought this was all some kind of an obsession, although of course if we think about these slogans now we find them ridiculous.'

Life may not have been very easy during the first decades after the war, but it was interesting and people felt good, the couple recall. The unity of the party system and ideological slogans and campaigns provided the energy to work towards a brighter future. Only later, when the internal contradictions of the command economy began to break down – during the long years of Brezhnev's stagnation period – did the dream begin to fade.

Vasily retired from the army in 1978 and went to work at an electro-technical scientific institute – a smooth transition along the well-oiled track of a Soviet career. But cracks were beginning to appear in the façade of Soviet society and Vasily relates his experience of brief suspension from party membership in the mid 1980s and his trial under the Party Control Commission as part of this process.

Since the mid-1970s, Vasily had been chair of the local garage building cooperative. It was his job to ensure that the necessary land was found, licences procured and garages built for those who paid into the fund. There had never been any great problems with managing an organization that was nothing more than a neighbourhood microcosm of all collective property agreements common throughout the Soviet Union. Then in 1987, a couple of years after Mikhail Gorbachev's perestroika reforms began, 'a division in life appeared between the left, where all had been clear, and the right, when nothing was clear any more,' Vasily says. Abel Aganbegyan, the scientific secretary of the Russian Academy of Sciences, briefed by Gorbachev to advance new economic models for the Soviet Union, proposed the adoption of a soft form of a market economy, a system of 'self-financing' enterprises, as Vasily puts it. 'His proposal was like that of someone suggesting that a man who can't swim drop into the water to test whether he sinks or not. Aganbegyan told us that if we did not know what to do, we should try, and see what happened.'

Vasily's response to what seemed like a direct attack on the tenets of Communism was to set to work on developing a counter-argument to disprove Aganbegyan. 'The new director of my institute asked me to elaborate an alternative mechanism to the principle of self-financing. We were able to prove that the situation was nothing like that described by Aganbegyan, that he had not really thought about things at all and that his concepts were incorrect,' he says.

A decade later, in 1999, Aganbegyan's energetic approach to the free market was once again under the microscope as he was investigated on suspicion of abusing his position as rector of the Moscow Academy of Economics to transfer buildings belonging to the institute to a private Higher School of International Business he owned.

If Aganbegyan's philosophy did not take root in Gorbachev's Russia, it set off a questioning of many accepted norms of Soviet society. Vasily, who for years had been using his spare time to ensure that everyone who wanted garages eventually got one, had been denounced for abusing his position and securing land to build his own private dacha – a plot, in fact, to which he was entitled as a military officer. In 1985 he was dismissed from the Communist Party pending a trial. The two-year investigation and trial into the allegations coincided with Gorbachev's early attempts at introducing market mechanisms into the economy and Aganbegyan's sacrilegious suggestions.

'I was busy building garages. There were two queues for these garages. During the building process everyone was friendly, but when half those waiting received their garages the arguments broke out. One person thought his garage was not big enough, his neighbour's was bigger . . . Allegations flew hither and thither. Our board of directors was made up of élite types – generals, administrative officials. People felt offended.'

The petty clash of egos convinced Vasily that his experience of years of running the cooperative was correct, he says with a knowing grin. 'Every person is just a complete shit. If you do something good for a person, often a little later they don't remember a thing about it and can do you harm.'

The allegations were groundless, the charges, under Communist Party rules, were eventually dropped and Vasily resumed his membership. But the affair and the schisms he saw opening up around him as Gorbachev continued wrestling with the reformers and conservatives within the party left a bad taste. Vasily may still have had his party card, but he chose not to rejoin the Communist Party of the Russian Federation when the post-putsch ban on the party was lifted by the Constitutional Court in late 1992.

Vasily and Raisa's energies during the early years of transition from Soviet power to today's Russia were occupied with research for and the writing of their book. They brush aside the events of August 1991 and remain convinced that the current political complexion of Russia is but a temporary phenomenon on the path to a true socialism, one which recognizes the acute demands of the world's environmental problems and draws upon the experience of the older generation, which laid the foundations for the creation of socialism in Russia.

But their frustrations at the path Russia is taking today have been given outlet in more than writing. In October 1993, quite by accident, the couple found themselves swept up in the thick of the dramatic and bloody clash between Boris Yeltsin and rebellious elements in his administration and the parliament.

Tensions between Yeltsin, his vice-president, Alexander Rutskoi, a gruff airforce major general and Hero of the Soviet Union for his service in Afghanistan, and the Soviet-era parliament, the Congress of People's Deputies and the Supreme Soviet had been growing since the introduction of economic shock therapy under acting prime minister Yegor Gaidar the year before.

Repeated clashes with the Supreme Soviet, the representative body of the much larger Congress of People's Deputies, through late 1992 and the first half of 1993 both forced the question of the constitutional basis for the new post-Soviet Russia and highlighted the precarious relationship between a powerful president and a truculent parliament. Russia was still very much feeling its way blindly through the rapids and switching currents of the new political conditions. The Communist Party of the Soviet Union may have disappeared as a functioning entity, its property and privileges abolished, but memories of its power remained fresh. Yeltsin's clear contempt for a parliament which just four years before afforded him the platform to make a political comeback, after Gorbachev had forced him out of the Politburo, allowed bitterness to fester and anti-Yeltsin alliances to grow. Yeltsin had not been in parliament for a year before that October and his refusal to work with what he dismissed as 'soviets' gave radicals the opportunity to seize control of key levers within the parliament. A stubborn clash over the budget, where parliamentary deputies dismissed a deficit-cutting government measure to propose one which critics said would fuel hyper-inflation, ended in stalemate. On 21 September Yeltsin, in characteristically bellicose mood, dissolved parliament, a move which was promptly declared illegal by the Constitutional Court. The scene was set for a historic clash of wills. Deputies proposed Rutskoi as acting president and the parliamentary headquarters, the Russian Federation White House, on the banks of the Moscow River, was put under siege.

Interior ministry troops were mobilized to surround the tall, marble-faced building with razor wire, and Moscow's mayor, Yuri Luzhkov, a Yeltsin loyalist, cut electricity and phone lines to the White House. As Muscovites went about their daily business, barely concerned with the political drama unfolding in the city centre, hardliners barricaded within the building took control. They included embittered Communist and anti-Semite General Albert Makashov and Viktor Anpilov, the leader of extreme-left Working Russia. In August 1991 tens of thousands of ordinary Muscovites had crowded into the streets and parks around the White House to defend democracy and rally to Boris Yeltsin's cause. In September 1993 it was the disaffected and warped who joined forces in a strange union of die-hard Stalinists, neo-fascists and monarchists.

Vasily and Raisa were not among those who dashed to show their colours, despite their disgust at Boris Yeltsin and his notions of the new Russia, although on a couple of occasions in the final days of September they dropped by the scene of the stand-off out of curiosity.

'We're very busy people and we were not planning to save the White House,' Vasily says with characteristic humour. 'It was clear that this was an illegal attempt to overthrow a legally elected legislature and the government's action was banditry and nothing else. But by this time I was the director general of a watch-making enterprise and I didn't have a chance to take to the rails together with [Gennady] Zyuganov [leader of the Communist Party of the Russian Federation] and [Viktor] Anpilov. We were not interested in this at all – our mentality differed completely from that of the mob.'

But on the morning of 3 October their path and that of the mob crossed and the couple found themselves involved in the armed clashes which afforded Yeltsin the pretext to order the tank bombardment of the White House the next day.

Vasily had arranged to meet a business partner outside the metro station at October Square, near Gorky Park. The square, a small hilltop area overlooking the Moscow River and dominated by a massive statue of Lenin, had also been chosen as the rallying point for members of Working Russia, staging a demonstration in protest at a government ultimatum the day before that the White House must be evacuated within forty-eight hours. Working Russia's members had a reputation for violence: five months earlier a police officer had been killed when thugs among their May Day demonstration attacked the police cordon.

The Pedorenkos found themselves surrounded by crowds of angry demonstrators waving placards. 'Yeltsin – the enemy of the people!' read one, they remember. Portraits of Stalin jostled with icons of Nicholas II, the last tsar. Among this confusion, Vasily and Raissa lost each other. Looking for a way out, Vasily eventually found himself outside the police cordon and in front of the mob as it began to make its way towards the White House – and a line of OMON (special police SWAT squads) ranged behind aluminium shields on Krimsky Bridge over the Moscow River.

Sitting in the cool, wood-panelled living room of their apartment, recollecting the events of that day, Vasily's deep bass voice grows louder as the excitement and emotion of the moment come back. He turns to the table to sketch a map of the scene on a piece of paper for emphasis. 'Members of the OMON were running up the stone steps onto the bridge to reinforce their comrades as the demonstrators moved forward towards the line. At the front [of the marchers] there were three people, deputies of the

Supreme Soviet. Behind them a Soviet army colonel, Pedorenko, Vasily Filipovich,' he says with a grin as Raisa remarks, 'Yes, as always in the thick of it.'

It's clear that October 1993 has left a lasting impression on Vasily and his wife, and distaste for the Yeltsin administration. Vasily continues: 'I started to give orders to this column, with all these young people at the front. Since I'm a military man, I managed to give orders to the right flank and the left flank so they could move at the same tempo. Once they got organized, we started approaching this aluminium wall of OMON shields.'

A request by the Supreme Soviet deputies to the police commander to let the marchers pass was refused. They turned back. But the demonstrators were determined. Ordering the front line to link arms, Vasily and the 'huge snake of people' advanced the remaining thirty yards towards the police.

'So, there was this Soviet army colonel and a mass of people . . . and, singing the patriotic song about the Russian warship *Varyag*, a song that makes the hairs on your neck stand on end, we marched towards the police.'

The unarmed demonstrators met the police and a brief skirmish ensued. Vasily recalls feeling as if he were in an old black-and-white film; there was an unreal quality about approaching the police lines. His sense of the drama of the incident is borne out by the events of the day and subsequent official explanations. The OMON lines melted away after the briefest of skirmishes with the Working Russia demonstrators and the interior ministry troops which had been enforcing the blockade of the White House disappeared as the mob approached, leaving cars and trucks with the ignition keys still in them. The ease with which rebellious White House parliamentarians, led by the vice-president, Alexander Rutskoi, were later able to storm the nearby Council for Mutual Economic Assistance

(CEMA) building and then make their way in an armed convoy of trucks and stolen armoured personnel carriers (APCs) to the Ostankino television centre suggests that a cleverly executed trap was sprung. If the precise reasons for the police withdrawal on 3 October remain unclear, the bloody events of that day were certainly the reason Yeltsin gave for ordering the tank fusillade against the White House the next.

Vasily knew nothing of this, but even as he met the line of OMON shields head on, it seemed strange to him that they fell back so quickly. He grappled with the OMON officer, who was raising his truncheon for a second blow, and managed to grab his arm. 'At this moment I thought – time to get out of here. But suddenly the line went down,' he says, as Raisa adds, 'As if it were a provocation.' The demonstrators surged ahead and ran on as the police retreated.

Hundreds of people were to die over the next forty-eight hours. The official death toll – almost certainly an underestimate – was 147.

As events unfolded, both Vasily and Raisa sensed an element of stage-management. The 'enraged mob' surged forward, attacking OMON officers as they ran. Raisa, somewhere in the crowd far behind Vasily, had a clearer view of what was happening. 'The crowd was mainly made up of young people. There were women there too. Next to me was a teacher and other people from the intelligentsia. Not hooligans. But when the OMON retreated, out of nowhere in the crowd there were people of very strange appearance, they were provoking us, screaming 'beat them!' We women were trying to protect these young policemen – boys of nineteen who had been ordered to stay there. As soon as the OMON retreated these people appeared like devils, throwing something. It was well-organized provocation by the government,' Raisa asserts.

Sketching rapidly on a loose sheet of writing paper,

Vasily charts the progress of the mob of demonstrators as they moved towards Smolensky Square, where the day before a drunken crowd of 1,000 had erected barricades near the Foreign Ministry building, under the eyes of police who made no moves to stop them.

Here, in Smolensky Square, the crowd seized abandoned vehicles and swarmed onto coaches full of OMON officers. Vasily, who had picked up a long rubber truncheon and metal shield, argued with excited demonstrators who wanted to attack the trapped police. In the chaos the first injuries occurred as people were crushed between vehicles trying to manoeuvre through the crowds. It was two years after the fall of Communism and frustrations with spiralling inflation and rapidly falling living standards were being vented in the fury of the moment.

Ineffectual police attacks using tear gas and water cannons further angered the crowd and the column of people, several thousand strong, pushed on towards the White House, picking up discarded police equipment, paving slabs and metal pipes from a construction site as they went. Coming towards the river embankment where the White House is situated, Vasily saw dozens of abandoned police vehicles and small, disorganized groups of police. He talked with a section officer, urging restraint. The officer's response again suggests a design to the police reaction that day. 'I said to him, "Keep Quiet," and he agreed his men would do nothing against the crowd.'

By the time the crowd reached the White House the cast of the day was already set. Shots were ringing out around the wide road intersection where Kalininsky Bridge from Kutuzovsky Prospekt crosses the Moscow River. The government later claimed that the firing was coming from the White House, but the lack of police casualties and eyewitness reports at the time suggest the it was from official forces.

Vasily took shelter behind a granite wall at the CEMA building, which housed the mayor's office. 'I could hear automatic rifle fire coming from this building. Kneeling by this wall, I again found myself in an absolutely unreal situation. Somewhere in front of me I could see a man lying, not moving at all.'

The shooting went on for about ten minutes. Raisa, who was still separated from her husband, was also in the area and recalls the horror of realizing that people were dying around her. 'There was a young man of perhaps nineteen nearby. He had a gunshot wound to the head and was lying in a pool of blood. It was a terrible scene.'

The firing stopped and Vasily made his way across the road to the White House, where the vice-President, Alexander Rutskoi, parliamentary speaker Ruslan Khasbulatov and prominent nationalist Sergei Baburin were waving victoriously to their supporters from a balcony. The siege of the White House had been lifted and its defenders believed they had won. Bloodied by his early clash with the police, Vasily found time to have his wound dressed and witnessed the storming of the mayor's office in the CEMA building by Rutskoi's men, who crashed through the plate-glass façade with a seized APC. Sensing victory the nationalist forces began to call for an assault on the Ostankino television centre in the north of the city. Sergei Baburin famously announced, 'Let's go to Ostankino and capture the narcotic needle.'

Looking around him, Vasily saw sections of the crowd attacking foreign-made cars parked near the mayor's office, 'sheer vandalism' by provocateurs, as he puts it, and again decided it was time he left.

'Now that I think back to the events of 3 October, I can't help thinking that everything was very well directed. I witnessed many people within this crowd provoking others, acting illegally and trying to make the crowd into an uncontrolled mob. After Smolensky Square the crowd thinned out – probably these provocateurs left and went to get paid.'

Whether Vasily and Raisa's views on the extent to which provocation played a part in the violence of that day are coloured by their political attitudes or not, the blood-letting at Ostankino and the degree to which official sources played up the clash there later that evening remain a dark stain on the Yeltsin era.

Tired and anxious for his wife's safety, Vasily decided the best thing to do was to go home. He hitched a lift in the convoy heading for Ostankino, which lies a mile or so away from his apartment. 'The convoy set off for Ostankino. Moscow looked absolutely empty, only here and there people peering out at the street from their balconies. Driving up Prospekt Mira, we passed some armoured vehicles and people cried out to them to join us. When we saw the officer stick his finger up at us, we understood he did not share our patriotism. We were relieved when these troops took a different turning from us and headed out of the city.'

Despite the conflicting feelings Vasily and his wife have about being mixed up in the violence that day, the sense of power and gratification the revolt gave is evident in their account. Vasily remembers one man sitting near him in the back of the canvas-covered lorry they were riding in, remarking that he had neglected his son's birthday celebration that day, but wouldn't have missed the lifting of the White House siege for anything. The excitement of the events also had Vasily in their grip. He didn't get off at Prospekt Mira, but continued to the television centre, where later that evening scores of civilians and a number of journalists and cameramen among the crowd of 4,000 nationalists would die in a hail of fire from within Ostankino.

At Ostankino Vasily saw a small crowd of Cossacks standing around General Albert Makashov on the steps of the television centre. Makashov was demanding entrance to the building. In a fateful encounter Vasily introduced himself and, meeting with a rude response, decided that it was indeed time to go home. 'This man was wearing a general's uniform. I introduced myself as a Soviet army colonel in reserve. He said, "And I'm a general, so what?" The man is an idiot. I felt so angry I was ready to spit in his face, but being an intelligent man I didn't. I could see that if this fool was in charge it was hopeless and left for home.'

Vasily's decision probably saved his life. Interior ministry forces and OMON special police units had arrived at Ostankino an hour before the nationalists and taken up positions within. When a shoulder-fired grenade was launched into Ostankino's front entrance by someone from within the Makashov forces shortly after 7 p.m., the government forces opened fire. Dozens of people among the largely unarmed crowd died and more were killed when interior ministry reinforcements arrived soon after. Makashov's armed men, about 100 in total, drew back after some ten minutes, but Yeltsin's forces continued firing throughout the night, from within the television complex and from armoured vehicles driving around the nearby streets.

The curious and the foolhardy, drawn by the sound of shooting and the sight of tracer bullets cutting through the cold autumnal night, flocked to Ostankino. Many were killed by troops apparently under orders to shoot at any gathering of people.

Safely home and reunited, Vasily and his wife slumped in shock at what they had witnessed. 'We could not believe that such terrible things were happening here. The young people we saw killed . . . nothing in politics is worth this.

No one has been able to explain to me the point of these deaths,' Raisa says.

The slaughter was not over. Of the four young men – sons and grandsons of their neighbours – who left the apartment block that night to go to Ostankino, only one came back. The tank assault Yeltsin ordered the next morning on the White House, witnessed the world over thanks to CNN and other international news channels, left an enduring sense of injustice and anger among many Russians. It was a 'spectator coup', where Muscovites who went to watch the fireworks, eating ice creams as the tanks blazed way, confirmed Yeltsin's position, but it also poisoned the sense of hope and euphoria many had for the new Russia.

For Vasily and Raisa, Boris Yeltsin lost any legitimacy he might have had during those turbulent days in early October 1993. 'I was ashamed of our government – but they weren't ashamed of themselves,' exclaims Raisa. 'Yeltsin is worse than [Chilean General] Pinochet.'

The couple argue that Yeltsin's actions were those of a 'criminal attempting to escape punishment for breaking the [Soviet] Union'. Their assertion that Yeltsin has remained in power through 'the inertia of the Russian people' has some validity, but at the end of the decade which witnessed the collapse of Communism, their continued faith in ideological solutions to Russia's social and political ills seems increasingly anachronistic.

For Vasily and Raisa the Russia Yeltsin has created is anathema. Their son Andrei may be doing well in the free market economy that has emerged, but they remain convinced that nothing good will come of it. Paraphrasing the final lines of Nikolai Gogol's *Dead Souls*, Vasily remarks that time will tell what lessons Russia today has for the world: 'Russia is like a troika that is rushing ahead. All the countries look back and give way to it. Only

Russia can show to the world how to move away from the precipice, when all societies and governments are ready to drop into it.'

5

The Sexual Revolution

Sex and power, greed and individualism are at the centre of the personal revolution Tanya, a young single mother living in Moscow, has experienced since the collapse of the Soviet Union. From devoted wife and mother to a businesswoman surviving in a man's world and enjoying sexual and personal freedoms undreamed of in her youth, she is living a life for which nothing in her conservative Communist upbringing could have prepared her.

A linguist and trained teacher, Tanya was a twenty-six-year-old housewife, the mother of a three-year-old son, when Boris Yeltsin's bold clash with the architect of perestroika, Mikhail Gorbachev, sparked the end of the Soviet empire in the summer of 1991.

A native of St Petersburg, which she still refers to as Leningrad, as it then was, Tanya had lived in Moscow for just four years after moving to a flat in the capital to be with her young husband Sergei, a captain in the Soviet army's military intelligence corps. Her life revolved around home and husband. Her job at a state building-materials research centre was undemanding and her social life centred on providing the best for visiting family and friends the couple's limited income allowed. Life might have been a little limited, but it was stable, secure and safe.

Sitting in the kitchen of the same two-bedroom flat on the twelfth floor of an already crumbling modern high-rise apartment block on Moscow's northern fringes, Tanya, a small, dark-haired woman with a ready smile and bright, intelligent eyes, gazes across the panorama of box-like residential blocks and the far-off peaks of city-centre Stalinist skyscrapers, and looks back at a time which is already a different age, as remote from today's Moscow as the court of Tsar Nicholas II.

'I was sure nothing would happen to me. I could be sure what my salary would be for each year of my life to my death. Of course I would not earn a lot of money, but I would always have enough to have a good life. I would never be given the opportunity to try to earn more money; what opportunity was there?'

She pauses to pull a loose-fitting silk dressing gown more closely about her, in a gesture which combines a slight shrug of resignation with modesty as she reflects on how different her life is from the one anticipated by a Soviet upbringing. 'Today all my life is constant opportunity. Every day I have to make decisions. I have a lot of freedom, but it frightens me. Sometimes I don't know what to do with my freedom. I'm even frightened to have too much money, as too much money in today's Russia simply brings too many problems.'

She pauses, sadness hovering about her small, apple-shaped face as she contemplates the shifting challenges of life in modern Russia, before continuing: 'In my life before that moment in August 1991 when everything changed, we never said that our happiness depended on the sum of money we had; our happiness depended on everything. But today I can tell you that I may be happy if I have money. If I do not have money, I can tell you that I am not happy. I don't feel shame to say that money may bring me happiness. We all understand that this is not the only way to be happy, but of course without money a person cannot be happy.'

Tanya's moral revolution is not limited to her changed attitude towards money – a common shift among the majority of Russian people in the years of transition since all the old certainties were swept away. Her whole moral compass has been spun around by the influence of forces present but hardly acknowledged in Soviet times: greed, sex, power and individualism. The years since 1991 have been a roller-coaster for millions of ordinary Russians. Tanya, now thirty-four, is no exception.

In August 1991 she had been married five years, had a small son and an officer husband in his mid-twenties. Today every day is a challenge as she struggles to reinvent herself as an independent businesswoman whose newly rich 'new Russia' husband has left her for a younger woman, leaving her to bring up Nikolai, now eleven, alone.

Her business cards describe her as the deputy managing director of the Moscow office of a foreign company which sells expensive German-made clocks in Russia. But even though she earns $600 a month, and receives a further $300 from her estranged husband in child maintenance, Tanya's days run on constant anxiety and fear for the future.

A proposed sexual favour between two old friends offered her an opening into business – an opportunity which came her way, like so much in today's Russia, by chance and via a peculiar avenue. Tanya, who has always considered herself a very sexual woman and talks openly about her sexual feelings, relates the bizarre story as if it were a commonplace occurrence. 'The lover of one of my oldest friends had always been very fond of me. He knew that there could be nothing between us because I couldn't go behind my friend's back, but knowing Sergei had left me and that life was difficult, he wanted to do something to help me, so he offered me to his friend, who runs this clock business, as someone who might be useful in the office and pleasurable in bed. I wasn't attracted sexually to the man, to whom I was introduced, but was desperate to prove that I could be of use to his business. I was asked to help in the organization of a festival in Moscow, something he also had interests in. My salary at this time [summer 1996] was paid half out of his pocket and half from my friend's lover. On the first day my new boss, whose wife and family were then living in Almaty [Kazakhstan], suggested that I come back to his place for dinner. He said he wanted me as a woman, but that it was my choice. I didn't want to put him off completely, so I merely said that I didn't want to go to bed with him right now, leaving open the possibility of some future liaison. I didn't want to have sex with him, but also I didn't want to lose the possibility of proving myself in business.'

From this dubious start Tanya rapidly proved her worth as a businesswoman, winning the man's confidence in her ability to translate his ideas into polished business deals. When his wife, an accountant in her forties, joined him in Moscow, she was convinced Tanya was having an affair with her husband. Understanding that even the notion of this could jeopardize her position in the company, Tanya began a very public, albeit fictional, affair with another senior manager, a former actor from the Moscow Art Theatre.

Sex, like money, has become one of the dominating themes of Tanya's life in the new Russia. Soviet propaganda liked to pretend that there was 'no sex in the Soviet Union', a lie which only partially obscured the truth. Tanya remembers that the ramshackle management atmosphere at the technical institute where she worked in the early 1990s was due less to poor leadership than to sexual intrigues. The head of the institute made it his business to seduce every new, young and attractive female employee, discarding his last lover each time to begin a fresh conquest. 'He had every pretty woman in bed there except me,' she recalls with an ironic grin. 'Embittered ex-lovers did their best to disrupt the smooth running of the institute. I remember one woman was convinced that I had usurped her and she was always spitting venom at me.' Sex, greed, violence, power games: all were features of life in Soviet times, when real power and authority were denied the vast majority.

'Times change, but people do not. I think that sex is one of the essences of a person. Of course our parents knew nothing of erotic films or pornographic magazines, but I'm more than sure that they did something in bed and today is no worse. But sex in those days was hidden and limited by walls and doors. Everything now is much more open. If I want to be sexually active, I can show it, but it must not be vulgar – it's normal for a young pretty woman to be sexually active.'

The explosion of sex in Russia in the first half of the 1990s cannot be attributed simply to a stripping away of decades of suppression: sex games, extramarital affairs and sexual intrigues were discrete but ubiquitous features of Soviet society. In a system where most people knew and understood the futility and emptiness of the slogans that echoed throughout the nation from the Kremlin downwards, insincerity and boredom were dominant trends. In a closed system where money had no real meaning and position was sought less to wield power for positive purposes than to win perks and influence, the majority of Soviet citizens knew the rules of the game: we pretend to work and you – the state, the Communist Party, the institute director, state farm boss – pretend to pay us. Playing the game to win was pointless for the vast majority not involved in Communist Party political games. So sex became the diversion, the main way of assuaging boredom.

Dissident writer Yuli Daniel's short stories, published in the West in the 1960s under his pen name of Nicolai Arzhak, caused a Soviet sensation in 1966 when he and fellow writer Andrei Sinyavski were brought to trial, charged with writing 'anti-Soviet propaganda', an allegation strongly denied. Found guilty of 'disseminating slander dressed up as literature', they were sentenced to five and seven years' hard labour.

Daniel's short story 'This is Moscow Speaking', a dark satire of the Soviet's state casual attitude to the lives of its citizens, threw an uncomfortably harsh light on subjects the Kremlin preferred to remain unexamined. Centring on a Politburo announcement that Sunday, 10 August 1960 was to be declared 'Public Murder Day', giving Soviet citizens over the age of sixteen the right to 'exterminate any other citizen' with the exception of children, members of the police and armed forces, transport workers on duty and 'murders committed in the course of robbery or rape', the story explored subjects that went to the core of the Soviet state.

Daniel defended 'This is Moscow Speaking' and two other overtly political short stories as literary interpretations of the denunciation in 1956 by the Communist Party's Twentieth Congress of Stalin, and the cult of personality and deviations from socialism during his rule. 'Atonement' examined the psychological turmoil of a man falsely accused of denouncing a colleague. 'Hand' was a complex depiction of a Stalinist secret police executioner, portrayed with some sympathy as a fellow victim of totalitarianism.

Daniel was also charged in connection with another story, one which he seems to have regretted and sought to distance himself from. 'The Man from MINAP' was a whimsical tale of a handsome young student, a member of the Young Communist League, who possesses an extraordinary ability: to determine the sex of the children he fathers, by intensely visualizing the features of Karl Marx for a boy or socialist heroine Klara Zetkin for a girl.

His talent is discovered in the course of a summer love affair, and the man from MINAP soon finds himself in demand by those eager to satisfy their desire for a boy or a girl. When he eventually gets caught in bed with a woman by her outraged husband, the man from MINAP finds himself at the centre of an institute show trial – until, that is, a party organizer hits upon the use to which his abilities can be put for Soviet purposes.

Translator Max Hayward's introduction to *'This is Moscow Speaking' and Other Stories*,[2] quotes Daniel as saying at his Moscow trial, 'I don't like this story: it is poorly written, crude and in bad taste.' Hayward observed:

> But this is surely too self-deprecating. His idea was to defy the prudish conventions of socialist realism, to poke a little harmless fun at the holy figure of Karl Marx himself, and also, more seriously, to satirize the scientific charlatanism which flourished under Stalin. Whatever one may think of its literary qualities, however, it is absurd to view it – as the court did – as anything but an honest attempt to break taboos that nowhere else would be regarded as such.

Despite Daniel's misgivings, he was reflecting an undeniable fact of Soviet life – especially among the urban intelligentsia – that the Marxist-Leninist dream had turned into a farce.

More than thirty years later, the legacy in today's Russia is a society where sexual morals and the relationships between men and women are profoundly different from those generally found in the West. The rapid development of a sex industry and the prevalence of prostitution on city streets, fed by teenaged girls fleeing rural poverty, are only the most visible signs of a society suffused with a raw sexuality. In a nation where young women in their twenties and thirties significantly outnumber young men, sexual attractiveness is at premium, putting enormous pressures on women to conform to the frequently chauvinistic notions of Russian men.

Tanya may feel freer to exercise the power of her sexuality, revealed through such casual remarks as, 'In the past, before I became independent, I was the servant in the house and always wanted to be the boss in bed; today, when I have quite a number of men under me at work, in bed I want to be the slave, I want to be dominated.' But she remains imprisoned by sex and attitudes to women. Despite working in a senior position in a highly pressured business atmosphere where she is able to daily demonstrate her value and abilities within the business world, Tanya lives in fear that she will lose her position to a younger, sexier, more attractive woman. 'I'm afraid of being kicked out of my job. Our economy is so unstable it may not matter how hard I work. But also every day I fear that I am not young enough, that the English I use is not good enough, and that every year there are more and more younger girls with longer legs and prettier faces who are graduating from college with much higher levels of English. I know that my boss values me for my experience, but I still worry that one day he will find a young girl with long legs and throw me away.'

The fear in Tanya's dark eyes is evident, reflecting her continuing struggle to unite the two conflicting aspects of her personality: that part of her which she grew up with and which was dominant when she married – a quiet, shy, mouse-like person, 'a grey little thing,' as she calls it; and that part which was always latent, hinted at in her references to her sexually dominant nature, a drive to succeed and use her natural wit, energy and vivacity in a business environment.

The character of life in Russia today, the way her own life has developed and matured in the boiling fulcrum of Russian society since 1991, reflects the burst of unformed, raw, even savage human energy that was suppressed or sublimated during the long decades of authoritarian rule. Musing on the way her life has moved on and that of her estranged husband, Sergei, Tanya attributes their choices to seek a new way forward in business to genetic inheritance. 'We both had something in our blood that pushed us towards trade and business. Sergei worked in military intelligence, not in the field with soldiers, but in an office with computers. He used to dress each morning in his beautifully pressed uniform and leave for work carrying his small attaché case. But in his blood he had the genes of a merchant. His great-grandfather had been a merchant – just like mine – and when the old regime collapsed he saw the chance to realize his deeper needs. My dream was to work at an international level, trading between companies. Even when I was working at state institutes in the old days, through using my English language skills I found ways to be involved in such projects.'

Sergei's early business ventures were characterized by risk. He obtained a licence to purchase mammoth tusk ivory from geological survey teams in Siberia, where test drilling and digging in the permafrost frequently brought to light ancient bones. Long trips into the wilds of eastern Siberia were undertaken with armed guards and Sergei would return with tens of thousands of dollars' worth of ivory tusks. But this enterprise coincided with a worldwide ban on trading in ivory and he failed to find the export markets he was convinced would make him rich.

Turning back to his roots in the rural Yaroslavl region, where he spent summers with his grandmother as a child, he moved on to butter and milk product packaging. With Tanya's support, the couple scraped together their savings and set up a packaging and trading business in 1993. The business prospered and Sergei soon realized his dream to get rich quick, one he held in common with many 'new Russians'.

But doing business in Russia's unregulated market was not without its risks, Tanya recalls, as she starts to discuss some of the more alarming turns her life has taken in recent years. 'All businesses in the new Russia run on credit and you have to be careful from whom you borrow money and need to invest in the appropriate level of protection. No business can operate here without its own *krysha*,' she says, a common euphemism for the Mafia. 'Sergei claims that his *krysha* are former police and military men, who are generally considered among the best, most effective and strongest *krysha*, but a lot of things suggest to me that Sergei never has had very strong *krysha*.'

One incident will remain with Tanya for ever: the night she lost the child she was carrying, the child which would have been a brother or sister to Nikolai had her pregnancy run to full term. Sergei owed a large sum of money to a group of men from the organized crime squad of a regional city. Quite what the relationship between regional CID officers and money lending was, Tanya cannot say, but in today's Russia the distinction between arms of state power and organized crime, money laundering and what Russians collectively dub 'dirty business' is often blurred.

'One night I was at home alone in the flat. Sergei was in the city, busy with some business or other. Before he left he told me that he was in trouble with some bad men and that I should not answer the door to anyone. I was frightened and waited at home, hoping nothing would happen. That night a group of Ukrainians came to the flat. I believe the regional organized crime squad sent them. They had guns and demanded that I let them in and give them the money Sergei owed. I was terrified and just waited inside the flat, quivering with fear. I didn't know what would happen if they broke into the flat. Eventually they left, shouting threats, and I was alone again. After this I lost my child.'

She says it bluntly, in a matter-of-fact way which seems to suggest a callous, uncaring attitude to a dreadful occurrence. But the way Tanya relates this experience, like so much she reveals of a life turned upside-down, suggests that her way of coping with the challenges and pressures is to distance herself from their emotional impact; to protect herself by disempowering their explosive potential by retelling them as simple stories.

If the loss of her child wasn't enough to destroy the couple's marriage, other insistent pressures in the new Russia were. Early on, Tanya was offered a job as head of international relations with a recently established business organization representing casinos and gaming outlets across Russia and the CIS – the Commonwealth of Independent States – a successor body to the Soviet Union, loosely linking former Soviet republics. Her job would have involved meeting prospective clients and businesses interested in making connections with casinos in Russia. The nature of the business meant she would have been working late at night.

'This was an opportunity that I could never have dreamt of before: I could not believe I had the chance to work in this sphere. I'm more than sure that if I had been able to take advantage of it, today I would be a very rich woman. But when I came home and asked my husband, he said no.'

Sergei forced Tanya to bring their son, Nikolai, back to Moscow from St Petersburg, where her mother, as was common practice in Russia where both partners in a marriage work, was bringing him up. 'Sergei insisted on this, even though I suggested we could afford a nanny if I took this job. He pretended he was worried about Nikolai, but in truth it was because he understood that this presented a serious danger to him: that I would be happier and more successful than he was in business.'

But the connection with the casino didn't end there. The couple began using profits from the butter business to play on the gaming tables. They were successful and won a lot of money – so much so that, after taking more than $20,000 one night at their favourite casino, they were asked to leave and forbidden to play there again.

Sergei began gambling every night, regarding it as a way of earning money, rather than an occasional diversion. 'He started going to the casino as if it was his business,' Tanya recalls, sitting at the table in a small, cramped kitchen – like so many in Moscow's modern flats – where only a few years ago the couple would count out piles of green dollar bills they had won after a night at the gaming tables. 'But this was the beginning of the end,' Tanya says. 'It was in the casino that he met this blonde he is with now and he started going to the casino to earn money, and I knew that nothing would be right after this moment. The casino became his illness. One night we had spent a nice evening together and I asked him not to go. We had had a nice meal, nice sex. But no, he said he must go. I prayed to God that night that he would lose everything. And he did, more than $16,000.'

After this point her husband entered a 'new stage of illness', Tanya says. He desperately wanted to win back the money he had lost. 'After this he could not stop. I shall never forget how once he told me that he witnessed a man who lost his Mercedes at the gaming table. The man went away, then returned determined to win it back, and ended up losing his apartment. Sergei told me he would never forget the look in this man's eyes when he had lost everything. But I think Sergei forgot.'

Sergei left home for a peroxide blonde a lot less bright – and less challenging – than Tanya. His leaving was not unusual. One of the less noted effects of the economic and social turmoil of the new Russia is the impact on marriages. Sitting in her car early one evening in the middle of a heavy traffic jam on Moscow's central Prospekt Mira, Tanya glances around at the male drivers nearby, waves her hand wearily and declares that she would put good money on the fact that all these new Russian men have left their wives and families to take up with younger women with longer legs, firmer breasts and smaller brains since they began enjoying their swiftly acquired new riches.

Sergei's addiction to his recent wealth has brought out the weakest and most venal side in his character, Tanya claims. Attempts to maintain a semblance of family life for the sake of their son have led to an uncomfortable double life in recent years: the couple spend time together with Nikolai as if nothing was amiss, before Sergei returns to his mistress, gambling and the ducking and diving of *bizniz*.

A desperation to prove himself important, coupled with an inner conviction of his own weakness, seems to bring out the worst in him, Tanya alleges, as she launches into a nightmarish anecdote about the miserable side-effects of Sergei's failure to make it big in Moscow.

'You know, Sergei's just a small fish in this city,' Tanya says, leaning forward conspiratorially. 'But back in the village where his granny brought him up, he's the big shot. He has a new, three-storey dacha there and struts around this village like he owns it. Last summer he wanted to take me and Nikolai there to stay with his grandmother. But Nikolai was already in Leningrad, so, perhaps to spite me, Sergei took his blonde with him. One night he was drinking with some business associates – local lads – and there was an argument. Sergei and his Moscow mates wanted to prove a point, so they took one of these men in the boot of their car to the river bank, tied him to the back of the car and dragged him through the dirt streets of the village. Next time they would drag him from his wife's bed and through the streets to the main square if he didn't know who the boss was, he was told.'

Whether the story, which Tanya was shocked to hear from her husband's own mouth, is true or just a case of warped posturing by a man enmeshed in the less savoury side of life in new Russia hardly matters. The moral compass of the couple's lives had been irrevocably altered since 1991.

Sergei, a slim wiry man with thinning blond hair and piercing blue eyes, once admitted in a rare candid moment that life in the new Russia wasn't as wonderful as its desperate proponents like to pretend. It was the summer of 1993 and as we left his apartment one evening and walked past two old men playing chess in the peculiar light of a northern summer, he lamented that these days business left him no time for such simple pleasures. 'You know, I used to be happy to spend an evening playing chess and drinking a little vodka with my friends. We would talk of philosophy and love – yes, women and sex too, but our subjects were gentle. Today all my friends want to know is whether they are keeping up with me in the number of TVs, videos and other gadgets they can afford with their dollars.'

Three years later, on the next occasion we met, Sergei's separate life was already a fact. With his blonde mistress we went to buy a cassette player at VDNKH, the old park of Soviet economic achievement in north Moscow, a vast formal area dotted with neo-classical buildings, porticoes, columns, massive social-realist statues, gilded fountains and acres of well-tended lawns. Faded slogans bearing witness to the clumsy posturing of Soviet propaganda still hung from the sides of buildings, trumpeting the triumphs of nuclear power workers or advances in technology. Beneath, the pavilions were now subdivided into a warren of small shops and trade stands. When I went to buy the cassette player, Sergei pulled a wad of 100,000 rouble notes (then worth around $15) from his pocket to pay for it – an offer swiftly declined. He protested that he had plenty of money, but had missed the point; I'd not gone to VDNKH with him for charity.

Tanya's experiences in the new Russia seem to have brought out a strength of character, combined with mental agility, that enabled her to meet the challenges of change without succumbing to the temptations of greed and vanity. She too sails close to the wind, like so many making their way in today's Russia, but while she may tack this way or that, she hasn't allowed herself to be blown completely off moral course.

She is a realist and she understands that the only factor she can really control in her life is her own response to what each day brings. Her wits and her drive have to serve her now, where in the past the rigid precepts of the Soviet system provided answers to virtually all aspects of life, public and private.

'I've changed a lot and my character has developed. Tomorrow my company could lose all its money, not because we're bad at business, but just because of the situation in Russia. I'm the only breadwinner now in my family; I can rely only on myself. The regime at work has changed me. I used to be very shy and it was very difficult for me to make business phone calls and be rebuffed with a no. Now I've toughened up and this is no longer a problem, but when I get home in the evening I'm very tired and just want to eat and sleep.'

The days when Tanya worked hard to be the perfect mother and housewife are gone. She rarely cooks the special dishes, the time-consuming *pel'meni* (Russian dim sum) or *pirozhki* (cabbage, mushroom or meat-filled pies) or prepares the exotic salads of her early married life. These days she struggles home on the crowded metro, often sipping from a can of gin and tonic, drops into the new twenty-four hour Western-style supermarket that has been built at the base of her high-rise apartment block, where scruffy grass verges and rusty bus shelters once greeted the eye, unlocks the twin steel security doors in the vestibule to the apartment and drops exhausted into a chair.

'Nikolai is having to grow up very fast,' Tanya reflects. 'He's always worried that his mum is so tired and wants to help and look after me. I'm usually too tired to cook, so I just warm up some convenience food from the supermarket and am in bed not long after Nikolai.'

Tanya knows that the cares of today's Russia present mixed blessings, but is clear that her life, however hazardous and haphazard it sometimes appears, is a vast improvement on what the old system had mapped out for her.

Her upbringing in a conservative, military family in Leningrad, where her parents, mindful of future opportunities, nudged her away from a scientific education and towards languages, could not have prepared her for situations which today are almost commonplace, but would then have been considered scandalous. Tanya talks about her knowledge of and acquaintance with members of the Mafia with the ease of one who has simply had to accept this as part of the reality of her new life. 'Russia's *krysha* appeared from the underground of Soviet society. In Soviet times these Mafia groups were hidden. Now they are an official reality of Russia,' she says.

The Mafia touches virtually every part of Russian society. Wherever money can be made and influence exerted, the Mafia is to be found – in business, government, public institutions and the church. 'I myself know the literal godfather of an ecclesiastical Mafia,' Tanya says. 'It's a fact that our church has become very popular among people in Russia today, new Russians especially, because business is always a risk and everyone feels fear. A man may be very respectable, but inside him there is a simple and primitive soul. He'll go to church to get some kind of support – and that support may often be more than spiritual.

'This particular priest I know considers his service to be just a job. He has his own life and needs a lot of people with money or influence with, for example, the Federal Bureau of Security [a successor body to the KGB]. He is the head of a church that was badly damaged during Soviet times, when it was used by the government as a warehouse. His ambition is to be a member of the highest council of priests in the Orthodox Church, but for this he needs to prove to the Partriach of the church that he is a man of action who can do a lot of things – like restoring his church, which was reduced to little more than four walls by the neglect of Soviet times. For this he needs a lot of money, to show how powerful he is – how he can make something out of nothing. So, he has "friends" and tries to make money,' Tanya says, glancing out across the Moscow skyline over the remains of what were once villages, swamped in the last twenty years by the march of cubist apartment blocks thrown up swiftly and cheaply by army conscript labour.

The organization of the cleric's Mafiosi is little different from that of any other *krysha*, Tanya says. The priest has contacts through his Church circles in towns and cities the length and breadth of Russia and the former Soviet republics. Protection and shady business deals are the key features of the group's activities.

The extent to which the Russian Orthodox Church has abused government tax exemptions on humanitarian aid, designed to provide indirect subsidies for the repair and restoration of churches destroyed or damaged during Soviet times, has already been widely documented in the Russian press. A scandal broke in 1996, when allegations surfaced that the Church had used the tax breaks to import hundreds of millions of packets of duty-free cigarettes into Russia, effectively handing over its special tax-free status to private businesses in return for a cut of the profits.

Tanya's first-hand contact with this *krysha* offers a rare glimpse into the minutiae of organized crime, as ubiquitous in today's Russia as membership of the Young Pioneers, the Komsomol or the Communist Party once was in the Soviet Union.

The priest's group, like so many other Mafia groups, runs three different types of vehicles, reflecting the differing needs of various Mafia missions. Simple Ladas, still the most common car on Russian roads, are used for most urban journeys. Jeeps are useful for trips into the countryside, where roads are still largely unpaved and tend to turn into muddy quagmires at the first touch of rain. Sleek Mercedes 600s are reserved for more formal and ostentatious activities.

Position within a Mafia structure is reflected through personal jewellery. Members of *krysha* literally wear chains of office, Tanya says, adding in an amused digression that little has changed in this aspect from the clerics of tsarist times. 'This priest wears a heavy gold chain and crucifix worth at least $5,000. A *krysha* member's position is reflected in these chains. In this the priest is no different from any other in the Mafia. His position is shown through the weight of the gold chain, the precious stones in it and its cross.'

The priest has a gun, but tends not to carry it, Tanya says. The services offered by his *krysha* differ little from those offered by any other Mafia gang. When a business associate of Tanya's boss had trouble with Ukrainian clients who had refused to pay for a delivery of raw materials, the priest offered to collect the debt. In this case the deal was never agreed; threats made against the lives of the man's wife and children were taken sufficiently seriously for him nervously to decline the priest's solution.

Tanya sees a change in the way the Russian Mafia has developed. 'In the past the majority of Mafia groups were gangs of strong young men who needed money. To do this they operated as informal debt collection agencies, making their money from the cut they received from persuading someone to pay their debts. Now there's a new tendency. Mafia groups are formed from the police or members of the military who fought in Chechnya. They're older, more experienced and more clever. I know one guy who was a member of a Moscow city police subdivision who was the official bodyguard for an American film star when he came to the city. He fought in Chechnya and is on a military pension at the age of forty-two. What can a man of forty-two living on a Russian military pension do?'

The trend of businesses paying their own *krysha* for protection is also evolving. Many of the new generation of Mafia groups are setting up their own businesses, legitimate or otherwise, and then providing their own security.

'These guys combine business and defence of themselves. They put their money into profitable places – shares, for example, where they know they will get a good return. They have handgun permits and are organized in similar ways to the other Mafia. The idea behind this new type of Mafia business is that it's just too complicated to try to cheat them and expect to go without punishment.'

Tanya steers clear of this side of things in her business life: simply saying that although she knows the company of which she is deputy managing director has a *krysha*, she has never seen them. 'I know we have a "roof", and I know that it is not strong enough. If it were, we would have had less bother with our creditors and more success with our debtors.'

However, Tanya has not totally jettisoned the moral values she grew up with. She's painfully aware of the influence of the modern Russia and its new freedoms on, for example, the development of her son, Nikolai. But she seems to accept that the sudden new freedoms thrust upon Russian society since 1991 allow her to exercise considerable choice and pragmatism in their interpretation.

So, for example, if she or her firm was in trouble with a creditor company's Mafia and there was the opportunity to solve the problem through sexual favours, Tanya sees nothing wrong in using sex to her own advantage, although she does acknowledge that fear plays a part in this response. 'I know what it means to be frightened. I've been through a lot of frightening things that I thought would never happen to me, of course. But I think that if it is necessary, I have something to offer . . . although this is also why I am afraid that I am not so young, so pretty or so slim, because any situation can appear in this country. To survive in this country you have to be young, healthy, strong and, for a woman, pretty enough, because morality is not too strict today and this can be a very severe country. If I had to [use sex to my advantage], I would never refuse, provided what was on offer wasn't very perverted. If it's not harmful, why not do it, if someone expects payment in a form other than money?'

For all Tanya's apparent strength and control in the face of the unpredictable life she is forced to live – a life where she feels 'as if I'm the one with balls between my legs' – the collapse of moral and social boundaries in today's Russia takes its toll. Involvement in an unsuccessful attempt to set up a medical referral business in Moscow, offering private medical treatment in the West for wealthy Russians fearful of submitting to their own country's decrepit state system, gave Tanya an uncomfortable insight into the medical consequences of contemporary pressures. Young men in their late twenties were referred for heart attacks and strokes, while other clients sought help for sexual impotency.

'Our businessmen are overloaded. The result? Impotence! They put all their forces into work, leaving nothing for sex. I'm not afraid to say that I believe the majority of men in their mid-thirties in Russia are impotent. They are always frightened; always thinking of their business; any minute their mobile phone might ring, they can get a shock; they can never relax. I remember when Sergei and I were still together, he was reading the paper one morning and suddenly went white with fear. One of the men with whom he had been drinking the night before had been shot dead on his way home, barely an hour after they had been together. That's why all today's businessmen know that today they are alive, but God knows what will happen next to them.'

Tanya worries about her eleven-year-old son and his daily exposure, through the media and commonplace conversations, to the harsh and licentious world of Russia today. Erotic movies and sexually suggestive advertisements are aired on prime-time television in the early evenings. Teenage girls seem to vie with each other to wear the shortest, tightest, most revealing clothes during Moscow's long, hot and dusty summer months. Prostitutes barely out of secondary school hang about street corners in the city's central, and expensive, neighbourhoods. Newsstands at metro stations overflow with cheap sensationalist rags, draped with front-page photographs of naked women and violent crime.

She shrugs. A single mother. A businesswoman. A 'frightened little grey thing'. A woman who feels as if she has 'something between my legs'. Her roles are constantly shifting and every day she must make choices, trying to relate them to some kind of frequently shifting moral code. Tanya knows all she can do for now is take each day as it comes.

'All the barriers and walls that we lived with in Soviet times have been broken down and we've been given an enormous amount of information, of rights and freedom. But we do not know what we want to do with this freedom, or how to use it. This is just a bomb that has exploded in our lives: we simply don't know what to do with everything that has been given us.'

Thirty-year-old Muscovite Nina has lived through the same explosive years as her friend Tanya, but seems to have shielded herself almost totally from their fallout. Her personality, less extrovert and gregarious than Tanya's, offers some clues to the steadiness of her moral compass during these years of shifting magnetic forces. Hers is a simpler universe, sketched in plainer outlines with fewer of the complexities which both excite and beset Tanya.

Nina, an interpreter and translator, was born with almost crippling short-sightedness, a factor which may help to explain her totally different reaction to the emerging new Russia. An only child whose technical college teacher parents divorced when she was still very young, she grew up in a small three-roomed flat in a post-war apartment block just off Leninsky Prospekt in the city's Oktyabr'ski district, one of Moscow's central residential areas.

To suggest that her life was somehow narrower or more restricted than that of many other young women growing up in the dying years of the Soviet Union may not be entirely fair, but the circumstances of her upbringing, with her mother and an aged great-aunt in a home crowded with bric-à-brac, ephemera, family portraits, heavy old furniture, including a baby grand piano incongruously wedged in a corner, combined with severe short-sightedness only marginally improved with the aid of bottle-thick glasses, gives some insight into Nina's determined, unflappable character.

Unmarried at thirty-two and the effective bread-winner in her small female nuclear family, Nina maintains that her life today differs little from that which she believes she would have lived had Communism survived. 'My life today is more or less the same as it was in 1991: it's private language students, translations, work, shopping, friends. Of course it's different in detail from how it might have been had the Soviet Union still existed, but it's difficult to say whether it's better or worse.'

Today Nina no longer wears glasses and dresses more fashionably than she did in the past. Her acute short-sight has been corrected through a series of operations performed by the Russian specialist Svyatoslav Fyodorov, famed for his 'conveyor belt' operating technique. She holds one regular job, a seasonal position as interpreter to a promotional firm connected with a Moscow ice-hockey club, but the bulk of her income, which averages around

$400 or $500 a month – considered a decent living wage in Moscow – comes from her private work: language students keen to improve their English skills before taking university entrance exams, or younger children striving to push ahead. Translating Western paperbacks into Russian – romantic pulp fiction for popular consumption – or more serious documents also keeps her busy.

She went freelance in 1993, after spending three years as a translator and subtitler for a small private film company. Through her work with the ice-hockey club, she has twice been on competition tours in America, an opportunity which may not have been afforded her in Soviet times. She helped write the subtitles for a biographical film about Boris Yeltsin's life, *Yeltsin: Vicissitudes of Fate*, which premiered at the Rossiya Cinema on Moscow's Pushkin Square in May 1991, shortly before the former regional party boss from Sverdlovsk (now Ekaterinburg) was elected Russia's first president and only three months before the August coup attempt pressed the Soviet Union's self-destruct button. However, Nina views these events as distant, far-off sounds when she considers the plot of her own life.

At the age of eight she became an 'Oktyabryonok', a member of the Communist Party's most junior youth wing. She graduated to the red neckscarves and blue caps of the Young Pioneers, learning Marxist-Leninist ideology at summer camps and through books, lectures and songs. At fourteen she moved on to the Komsomol, the Young Communist League, where she would have remained until the age of twenty-eight, when she would have been offered the choice to apply for full Communist Party membership.

A slender, serious and studious woman, Nina dismisses any notion that these years of preparation for a life meant to be lived by Communist ideals really had any effect on her character, attitudes or world-view. 'You have to remember that none of this was sincere. I was never really bothered about a career or money, and never intended joining the Communist Party. That would have been much too serious. At college I was a Komsomol *prozhektor* [searchlight], an ideological critic. It was my job to keep other members in line. It was fun. I could write poems and make cartoons to stick up on the college Komsomol notice-boards. I would criticize such things as smoking in the toilets, the dirty and untidy conditions of some parts of the college, litter – harmless things like this. But you have to remember that none of this was taken really seriously, half an hour later you would be laughing and joking with the same people you had just criticized,' Nina says.

The power of ideology and the influence of Communist Party organs on young people were waning by the time Nina graduated in 1990; Komsomol was 'dying a quiet death'. She attributes her cynicism and insouciance in the face of Russia's changes since 1991 to the conflicting influences of her formative years as a teenager growing up during the 1980s. 'Anyone who grew up in Russia in the twenty years before the Soviet Union collapsed can't really claim to be surprised by how the country has turned out now,' she asserts. 'I was fourteen when Brezhnev died. Here was someone who had been in power my entire lifetime and of course I wept and mourned with the rest of the nation. But then there is a new guy [Yuri Andropov, Brezhnev's successor] who dies fourteen months later, who is buried to the strains of the same music with the same pomp and ceremony. And then there is another one [Konstantin Chernenko], who dies six months after that, and it's exactly the same deal and the whole country is wondering who will be the head of the funeral committee, because that man will be the next leader of the Soviet Union. And then this guy [Mikhail Gorbachev] starts all this talk of perestroika and the next thing you know it's the summer of 1991 and there are tanks on the streets. That's not exactly surprising, is it?'

Given these interpretations of the formative external events in her life, Nina's cynicism is hardly surprising. Casting her mind back to August 1991 when rows of tanks stood at the bottom of her street, engines running, ready to drive into the centre of Moscow, a journey of just a few miles, she asserts that of the thousands of Muscovites who flooded to the hastily erected barricades around the White House, hardly more than a handful were really serious. 'Show me one who was running there to defend democracy! Show me! I want to see this monster! Mostly people went there because their friends were going, or they thought they would be in the spotlight of the world's mass media,' she exclaims, in an uncharacteristic outburst of anger.

Nina saw through the system she grew up in and used it to put herself in a position where she had some choice in her life. The graduates of her college, the Moscow State Pedagogical Institute for Foreign Languages, named after Maurice Therez, were considered the Soviet Union's best linguists. Nina knew that the top students were habitually recruited by the KGB under a system known as *raspredeleniye* – distribution – where graduates were directed to spend three or four years in a particular job before being allowed a choice of career. Obligatory obedience to the directives of *raspredeleniye* had been abolished in 1985, after Gorbachev came to power, but in 1990 Nina and her classmates still felt its heavy influence and the KGB had the money and clout to offer students very attractive inducements: secure, well-paid employment, perks in the shape of allowances for further education or accommodation and other benefits.

'I was called in for chats with KGB recruiters on several occasions and was eventually offered a very good job in a

Above: Andrei Pedorenko at School Number 279, where history and tradition provide a thread of continuity in a country in transition.

Left: Vasily Filipovich and Raisa Alexeyovna, Andrei's parents. A former Soviet army colonel, Vasily's faith in socialism remains undimmed by Communism's collapse.

Left: Stability in the midst of chaos. At School Number 279, Inna Kore and Regina Mamlina remain positive despite poverty-level wages.

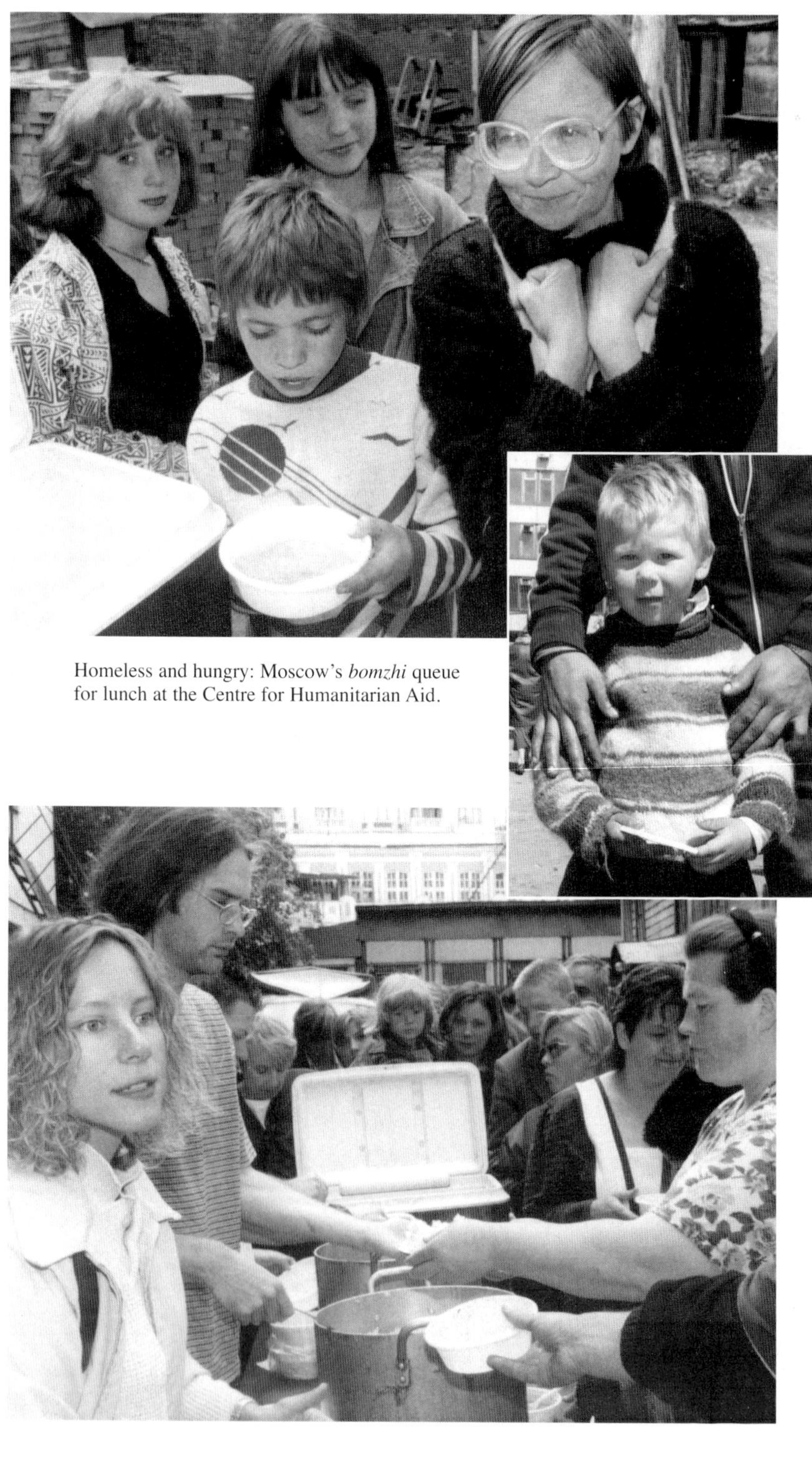

Homeless and hungry: Moscow's *bomzhi* queue for lunch at the Centre for Humanitarian Aid.

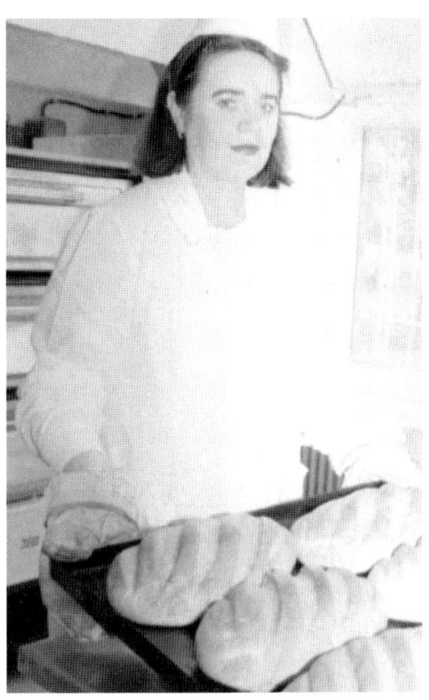

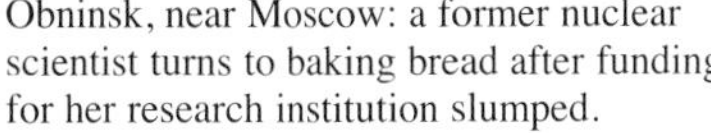

Obninsk, near Moscow: a former nuclear scientist turns to baking bread after funding for her research institution slumped.

For the lucky few, today's Russia remains a land of wealth and opportunity. Shopping for winter fur, Moscow, December 1998.

Muscovites reading anti-Yeltsin posters opposite the State Duma during the unsuccessful impeachment hearings against President Yeltsin, May 1999.

Above: For most people, hunting for a bargain in wholesale or open-air markets remains an essential part of the daily routine.

Above: This metro advert purports to offer young women the chance to fulfil their dreams: 'Want to be a film star? Non-professional actresses, 18 and upwards, required.'

Left: Refugees from the Caucasus are a common sight in Russia's street markets.

Above: Professor Yulia Tourchaninova with her daughter Alice. Personality, confidence and humour have remained her shields in times of adversity.

Right: Leaving Russia: Vladimir Kariakin, a former rocket troops colonel, is now running a small hotel in Prague.

Biologist Alexei Stepanov: life in America failed to impress and, for better or worse, he returned to his motherland.

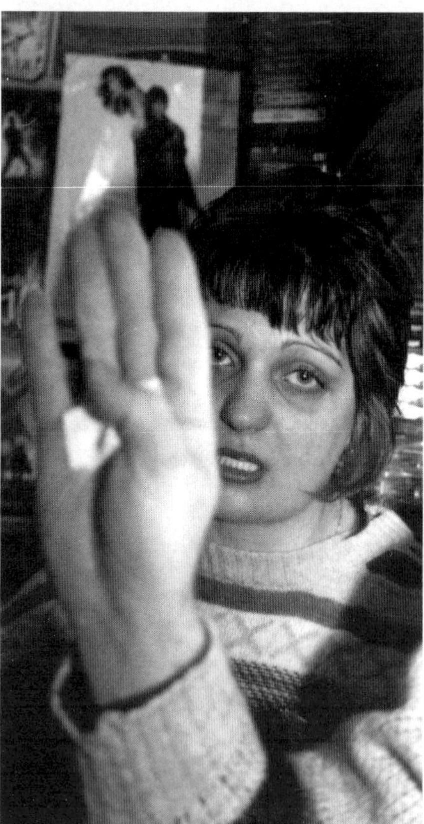

Raids on illicit video kiosks keep the pressure up on Russia's video pirates. Armed police seize thousands of contraband videos during a typical raid, leaving tearful and frightened vendors in their wake.

Left: Monarchists and Nationalists, as frequent a sight on Moscow's streets as red-clad Communist demonstrators.

Below: Moscow State University students making their own entertainment on a sunny afternoon.

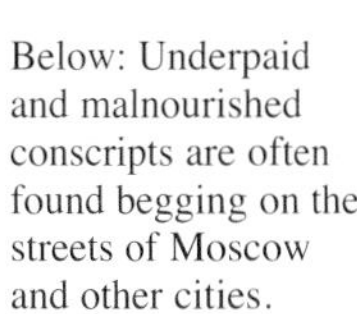

Below: Underpaid and malnourished conscripts are often found begging on the streets of Moscow and other cities.

Entertainment of a more risqué nature: the Hungry Duck night-club, Moscow, where young women perform impromptu strips on 'Ladies' Nights'. (BEN ARIS)

KGB high school, where KGB operatives were taught foreign languages. I knew that I would never pass the medical because of my poor eyesight, but I did not want to say no,' she recalls, adding with a knowing but humorous look, 'Never say no to the KGB.' She went through the whole charade, obediently responding to requests to provide her mother's and grandmother's passports; giving details of the birthplace of her great-grandparents and information about her father.

'Of course, I failed the KGB medical. But after this everyone at the institute knew that I was "reliable", that I had been quite right to co-operate with the KGB, that I was an active member of the Komsomol and I had done my duty. After this I was left alone and allowed to have a free choice in what I did after graduation,' Nina says, adding that of those of her friends who did take the KGB rouble, most, she thinks, are still working for its post-Soviet successor organization, the Federal Bureau of Security.

It's through this shrewd manipulation of the system that Nina believes she would have been granted the freedom to follow her own working choices in her life, Communist system or not. She began taking in private students as soon as she left college and remarks that tutoring students in summer crammers for university entrance exams has long been a ubiquitous, if barely approved of, sideline among Russian university staff and postgraduates. She may have had to take some small, approved job in order to legitimize her working life, to gain the necessary official stamps in her internal passport, but with the easing of the old rigid economic controls under Gorbachev's Soviet state, the sort of flexible self-employment Nina enjoys today would, she believes, have appeared anyway.

Her life is little changed from the one she had mapped

out for herself: busy autumns, winters and springs, with a slower pace in the summer, allowing long, languid weekends to be spent out of town at friends' dachas in the rural areas around Moscow; the colder months of the year given over to outings to the theatre and more intimate social events for friends and families. But the lives of other young Russians around her have changed dramatically, she agrees.

In her youth the Soviet Union's key personal concern seemed to be to present a fiction of perfection. The country looked relatively beautiful, lip service was paid to the inner concerns of its people, but in reality, by this time, no one really gave a damn what people were thinking about inside their heads, provided they didn't act on it in public. In today's Russia, 'People can do what they want; see what they want; wear what they want.'

As far as Nina is concerned, that's great. But she despairs that the nation has lost all concept of ideology; that young people in today's Russia have no organizing principal in their lives beyond making money. 'Look at my eleven- and twelve-year-old students – they have no ideology at all. There should be some core ideas for people to unite their attitudes around. Russia is going through a very interesting period right now, trying to gain what other countries had 100 years ago. We have the chance not only to create leaders but also to accumulate some of the worse aspects of Western development. It would be very sad if in the next five or six years people failed to find some kind of idea, whether it is the reunification of Russia, the restitution of the Soviet Union or just some cultural concepts. Call it what you want, people need something to organize around, not just wages, prices, the cost of living. Kids should be given something to dream about, not just fat wallets or luxury cars. There should be some centre to life.'

It is when Nina addresses these issues affecting the new Russia that it becomes clear, that for all her denials about the effect of her ideological upbringing and the insincerity of life in the Komsomol, of society under Communism, that something rubbed off. Her moral compass may never have pointed with any integrity towards Communism's precepts, but her own, often contradictory, attitudes towards the new Russia suggest a yearning for some unshakeable foundations in life.

During the presidential elections of 1996, when Russians faced a clear choice between the unstable, often chaotic new world of incumbent Boris Yeltsin and the security of the revisionist policies offered by the Russian Communist Party, personified by the soothing, avuncular image of its new leader, Gennady Zyuganov, Nina, like the vast majority of liberal, urban intelligentsia, hoped and prayed that Yeltsin would win a second term; that Russia would not have suffered a false dawn and be reconsigned to the heavy greyness of the Soviet past.

The very day the result of Yeltsin's narrow victory became known, securing for Russia a freer if unpredictable future, sealing the lid on the past, Nina became obsessed with doubts. What if Yeltsin died in office? What chaos awaited Russia from a premature end to the only man capable of holding together the vast and painful reforms the country was enduring? Maybe Russia would have been better off under Zyuganov – he was younger and fitter and could, presumably, be relied upon not to die in office. For a woman who had, just days before, been complaining about the infantile beliefs of her vehemently Communist-supporting great-aunt, the volte-face was astounding. And yet, when challenged, she merely shrugged her shoulders and said, 'I'm Russian, what do you expect? We barely understand ourselves, so how can foreigners ever hope to understand us?'

The ease with which Nina can hold contradictory attitudes underlies her sense of living from a consistent moral focus. The world around her may have shifted and continues to change with disorienting rapidity, but her personal universe remains steady, if somewhat fatalistic. 'I wasn't shocked, and remain unmoved, by the changes in 1991 and since then. It may be that I don't think about these things. Of course, during times such as the period of intense inflation [1992–3], it was strange to see the prices changing between morning and evening, doubling or tripling. But that was only for a short time. Of course it was unpleasant at the time, but it's all over and I would say life is slowly getting better. Of course people want things to be all right all at once. Of course it's sad to see what's going on in the countryside, where older people are dying and the youngsters are leaving to become prostitutes or thieves. Of course it's unpleasant, but what can we do?'

Nina may think that her own life continues largely untouched by the currents of the new Russia: she rarely watches television and the surface world of fashion and consumerism, which occupies the minds of so many in the new Russia, holds no interest for her. She supports her mother and her great-aunt, whose salary and pension combined bring into the household less than $200 a month, and spends her savings on a good summer holiday, favouring Egypt and Spain, two increasingly popular holiday destinations for Russians.

For those whose lives are entirely caught up in Russia's wild free market economy, the 'new Russians', she has charitable words rarely encountered among the wider public. 'Unfortunately, the general opinion of new Russians is that they are idiots, but they are not, as I have seen myself in Spain. The parents might wear heavy gold chains, but they have kids who speak fluent English. It's good to see the parents giving their children an education, something they themselves missed.' The popular image of loud, brash, ostentatious, rich and vulgar new Russians has more than a grain of truth, she concedes. But the chance that the second generation of newly moneyed Russians, like succeeding generations of new money anywhere in the world, is likely to be more sensitive and intelligent gives Nina hope for the country's future. 'At the same time as representing an ugly face of the new Russia, these people actually are doing quite a lot for the country. Many of them might have started out as simple shuttle-traders and now they have companies of their own. After all, they are the ones who provide clothing and food for the vast majority of normal people who do their shopping in the street markets. These people are intelligent and smart. What else does a country need?'

Other aspects of life in the new Russia also impinge upon Nina. Working at the hockey club means the occasional brush with the Mafia. Like every other commercially lucrative sphere of life, sport is heavily entangled with organized crime. Mafia turf wars over the income to be made from a protection racket within the ice-hockey club's arena, where numerous small business and concession stalls operate, have already led to one group of 'monkeys', as Nina calls them, being ousted – with more than a few deaths and casualties – and another taking their place. Her job keeps her one step removed from most of these intrigues – she works for a company involved in organizing sponsorship and promotional deals for the club – but when the boss of the old Mafia made a comeback recently and offered her a job within the club, she began thinking very carefully about leaving her own full-time job altogether. 'For the time being I'm playing it by ear,' she says carefully. 'This guy has a 100 per cent criminal past and is swanning around the club every night with a new girl on his arm. As long as he is just there and does not smile at me, that's fine by me. But if he starts pestering me to work with him again, I'll simply leave.'

Life may not be easy, or particularly pleasant, for most people in today's Russia, but the country is moving forward, she feels. 'For the majority of people outside the capitals [Moscow and St Petersburg], life is not great. They are earning several times less than urban Russians and don't feel nearly as secure. Maybe in the long run, in fifty years' time, we shall say that this period was necessary, if tough. For those who live in the capitals, life is complicated. Now even children can earn good money, it's very easy for them to stop thinking about education. We have choices and we are not always responsible about which choices we make. I feel confident about my life and future, but I know that for people of my mother's and great-aunt's generation, life is very, very difficult. My mother finds it very difficult to adjust to the fact that things are changing. She lived the largest part of her life in the Soviet Union, and to see things clearly today is virtually impossible for her.'

6

Harbours in the Storm

The stoicism and patience with which the Russian people have endured the rude and alarming changes forced on them since the collapse of the Soviet Union is one of the most remarkable aspects of the stormy transition witnessed since August 1991. As republics on the periphery of the Soviet Union descended into conflict and inter-ethnic violence after the rush to independence, the relative calm that has characterized Russia has confounded the doomsayers of the early 1990s. As Baku, Tbilisi, Yerevan and other cities in the Caucasus erupted into outbreaks of bloodshed in the first months of the new post-Communist era, Moscow remained quiet. The civil war in Moldova in 1992 saw Russian troops under the leadership of General Alexander Lebed mobilized to prevent the break-up of a republic with a large ethnic Russian population. Citizens of Moscow, St Petersburg and the other large urban centres cast their eye over the newspaper headlines and got on with the struggle to survive in an economy where hyper-inflation was already raging. In Central Asia in Kazakhstan, the second largest former Soviet republic after Russia, where 40 per cent of the population is Russian, fears of an ethnic backlash were high in 1992. But the iron grip of the country's ruling oligarch,

President Nursultan Nazarbayev, prevented unrest and Moscow didn't have to cope with a mass of Russian refugees. Civil war in Tadjikistan and Islamic unrest in Uzbekistan raised the spectre of the contagion of religious conflict throughout the 1990s. Although the Tadjik civil war was formally concluded with an UN-brokered cease-fire in 1998, the capital, Dushanbe, remained subject to outbreaks of violence between tribal warlords and an unofficial curfew continues to clear city streets by early evening. The messy and costly war in Chechnya barely caused a ripple of upset in Moscow, a couple of terrorist bombs on the metro and a city-centre bus aside.[1]

Moscow's streets remain practically as safe as they were under the watchful eye of Soviet times. Mafia crimes apart, the absence of street crime makes it one of the more pleasant capitals in Europe. Old-established rules of public etiquette on the metro, buses, trams and trolley-buses mean, for example, that young single women feel free to travel home alone late at night, confident their journeys will remain problem-free.

Russians have seen their savings disappear through inflation. They have witnessed the wealth created in Soviet times stolen from under their noses in rigged privatization schemes. They have been the victims of fraudulent investment schemes, like the MMM pyramid savings scheme, which collapsed to a clamour of pensioners demanding the return of their life savings in 1994. They have suffered the indignities that followed from the loss of the social safety net which gave them a measure of security in the past and have seen already meagre standards of living decline throughout most of the country. Two-thirds of the population feel 'lost and abandoned', according to the official surveys, and half the population live below the poverty line. Wages in the public sector are low and payment is erratic. Teachers, doctors and academics have long become used to receiving their salaries months in arrears. Most Russians earn little more than $50 a month – in Moscow perhaps double that – from their official employment. And yet they remain stubbornly resistant to calls to take to the streets and force a change for the better. A resolute awareness among all except the blindest old Stalinists of the horrors a return to the past would bring, is a continual reminder of the benefits of living in a free society. The chaotic economy and at times anarchistic political atmosphere are unpleasant and cause hardship, but life is immeasurably better without the clammy grey hand of the party on your shoulder.

Russians have survived, endured and overcome the privations thrust upon them through the economically stormy years of transition from the Soviet period in typically Russian fashion. Friends, family and the workplace all figure prominently in the tools ordinary people rely on to enable them to put one foot in front of the other.

Inna Kore and Regina Mamlina have taught at the same Moscow inner-city school for more than fifty years. Both pensioners, they continue to work part-time not so much for the income – less than $15 a month each – as but for the emotional and psychological support afforded by familiar surroundings and long-established friendships. As pensioners and state employees, statistically they are among the poorest of Russians, the chief victims of Yeltsin's new Russia. But joining the ranks of the poor pensioners and placard-waving trade unionists and Communist rabble-rousers who spill out on to the streets of Moscow at every old Communist holiday to demand Yeltsin's resignation and vent their anger at the theft of their retirement dreams doesn't interest them. Not having to lie to their schoolchildren and the freedom to discuss ideas and philosophies override any worries about the difficulties of getting by on a tiny pension of 400 roubles a month.

School Number 279, '*imeni Tvardovskovo*' – named after the poet Alexander Tvardovsky, as both women chime in when asked – has long been considered by those who have worked there as a special place. A strong literary and artistic tradition gave it a certain cachet for the more intellectual and a reputation for tolerance and democracy was already well established in the darkest days of Stalin. In the post-war years the principal, Lydia Nikolaievna Yegorova, a redoubtable woman from an ecclesiastical family who had been educated before the revolution, strove to create a secure, protected space within the school for children and staff.

That Inna and Regina, who have taught generations of children, including the school's current head teacher and deputy, regard the school as a special place, one which has been a haven throughout the Soviet and post-Soviet periods, is not unusual. The role of the workplace in Russia as a key agent of social stability is perhaps more important than in many other societies. In a country which emerged from feudalism only fifty years before it was plunged into war and revolution, the sense of social identity afforded by the collective was a key factor in the cohesion of Russian life. Denied, officially at least, the comforts of religion during much of the Soviet period and with many of the functions of the family taken over by the Communist Party and the state, the workplace became the focus for meaning and support in most people's lives.

Accommodation, leisure activities, childcare, summer camps for the young and holidays for the workers, evening classes, clubs and societies, all were organized through the workplace. The end of Communism and the collapse of vast swathes of the old, inefficient industrial plants across Russia have dealt a heavy blow to this network of social care and support. The notion of the workplace as an anchor in lives subject to the switching winds of politics and economics remains a strong feature of the Russian psychology.

For many Russians today, not just those like Inna and Regina who are officially retired, the official workplace is an essential source of legitimacy. An officially issued 'work-book', like the British P45, is as important a document to a Russian citizen as the registration papers allowing residency in a particular town or city. Their salaries may amount to little more than a pittance and they may spend much of each day away from the office or workbench, attending to their own private business, but the fact of their employment – membership of the collective – gives people a source of stability and support without which life would be immeasurably harsher. Inna and Regina's school is situated in a relatively well-off residential district around Prospekt Mira in central Moscow, near VDNKH. The school has a particularly strong sense of history and democratic traditions. But most schools, state companies and industrial concerns in Moscow and throughout the country, have adapted and carried over traditions developed in Soviet times to today.

In the winter of 1998, on assignment for the *Times Higher Education Supplement*, I travelled to Tula, the industrial capital of an administrative region just beyond Moscow. Tula is noted for its arms factories and the fact that the governor, Vasily Starodubtsev, was a member of the hardline Communist coup committee of August 1991. Interviewing teachers at a run-down state general school about the threat of looming food shortages that were then being talked up in the press and among Western aid agencies, the power of collective identity and solidarity afforded by the workplace in Russia was clear. The head, Larisa Klimenko, a tall, elegant woman in her fifties, became animated when discussing the subsistence standard of living forced on her and the school's seventy members of staff. Salaries ranging from 300 to 600 roubles a month ($20 to $40) had more than halved in real value since the August banking crisis and the regional education authority persistently paid teachers three months in arrears.

'People are living off their garden plots, those allotments where we used to grow flowers. Spring and summer evenings and weekends are spent working the soil to ensure we have enough potatoes, cucumbers, onions, beetroots, carrots, tomatoes and fruit to get through the Russian winter,' she said. 'Of course, if we had enough money to live on we wouldn't bother doing so much hard work. We would relax more, be able to dress better and could pursue other interests outside work.'

Her all-female staff related how they were finding ways to beat the chronic crisis of poverty-level wages. Giving private lessons in maths, physics, foreign languages and other popular subjects could bring in up to 100 roubles a week from children with better-off parents, but tightening the purse strings remained the best tool for survival, they said. Marina Mikhailova, thirty-five, a senior history teacher with ten years' classroom experience, reckoned she had spent 100 roubles in the previous few days on shopping for essentials. Married with a fifteen-year-old son, her family's income totalled less than $80 a month. 'For the last six years all teachers have been growing their own food to avoid spending money at the market. I don't worry about the future. We've all learned to take one step at a time. We have to remain optimistic for the children we teach – it's not their fault that today's Russia is so complicated.'

Maths teacher Tanya Matrokhina, thirty, agreed. She was worried that the diet she could afford to provide for her eight-year-old daughter was poor and tried to save enough money to buy vitamins to make up for it. Eschewing talk of the immediate future, she said, 'I'm not afraid. My parents and grandparents lived through much worse than this. The next year or two will, of course, be very difficult, but in the long-term Russia's future will be good.'

The formal interviews over, I stayed and chatted with the women about the things in life that really mattered to them: going to the theatre, devising ways to make themselves fashionable and expensive-looking clothes and organizing extracurricular events at the school. Mrs Klimenko bemoaned the fact that too many spring and summer evenings were taken up with visits to tend her vegetable plot at the dacha, when she would rather be at the ballet or theatre. But overall there was a Dunkirk spirit: whatever slings and arrows the chaos of Russia's transition could throw at them, they would endure, survive and even thrive in the face of adversity.

At the school a key agent of cohesion is the Poisk – Search society. Like many schools, colleges, factories and offices throughout Russia, the old Soviet emphasis laid on the communal sacrifice of the 1941–5 Great Patriotic War remains a visible presence today. The foyers or landings of few organizations or workplace departments are free of wartime battlefront maps, contemporary photographs of Red Army soldiers and the stolid, medal-ribboned images of former students and employees who fought in the war. The war and its huge sacrifice in human life and property – as many as 25 million Soviet citizens died during the period – retain a meaning and force that go beyond mere propaganda. When the nation remembers its war dead on Dyen Pobedy – Victory Day – each 9 May, frontline veterans go into schools to tell their stories. Children and young people who probably never even met the grandparents or great-uncles who fought in the war spend hard-earned roubles on red roses to lay at the memorials and eternal flames found in every Russian town and city.

Over the last thirty years students and teachers from

School Number 279 have traced the graves and last-known resting places of scores of its former pupils who fought and died on all the fronts of the war against fascism – Stalingrad, Leningrad, Novgorod, Smolensk, Pskov, Minsk, the Baltics. Parents and staff lead summer expeditions to educate each new generation in the true horrors of war. The Poisk society, set up by Inna and Regina in 1968, did not always find official favour in an era when Politburo propaganda wished to emphasize the heroic collective nature of the conflict over any individual sacrifice. The school frequently found official archives and army sources unwilling or uncooperative when seeking information to help in the search. But Inna and Regina persevered, not only because each had grown up in the war years and lost brothers at the front, but also because they felt the importance of allowing young people to truly understand what the war meant for Russian people, beyond the political hyperbole of the Kremlin. 'So, through Poisk it was not just with the help of words, but with action to help the children feel themselves part of a big family and explain to them how horrible any war can be. I believe this was very important and definitely affected the formation of the personalities of our children and probably continues to do so to this day,' Inna says, adding that it brings to life the words inscribed on the blockade memorial in Leningrad: 'Nothing and no one is forgotten.' She continues, 'The war was something all people took part in and it was their victory. Many are unknown; many people died and were not even buried properly. This is why we remember these people, not the recognized war heroes.'

The work of Poisk continues to this day under the direction of teachers who had themselves been pupils and members of the society at school in the 1970s. A large map of European Russia, Ukraine and Belarus, showing where the school's wartime pupils died so soon after they had graduated to join the army, is displayed on the wall of a reception area of the school. In the corner of a stairwell a stone memorial, the names of the dead picked out in gold leaf, reveals the gradual work of Poisk in finding and honouring the sacrifice. A small museum recounts through photographs and personal histories how so many seventeen- and eighteen-year-old boys and girls went virtually straight from school to the front in the summer and autumn of 1941, barely trained, to die before the onslaught of the Wehrmacht. Battlefield finds – rusting bullet-scarred helmets, defused mortar bombs, jagged fragments of exploded grenades, cartridge cases and ammunition tins – bring something of the dreadful reality of the time home.

The activities of Poisk reflect the ethos of a school which has, through successive decades, maintained an atmosphere in which inquiry, mutual support and trust have flourished, to give its community a space safe from the turmoil of the outer world. As an indication of the power the war continues to contribute to a sense of social cohesion, the last ten years have seen a mushrooming of similar groups. Finding the battlefield corpses of millions of Red Army soldiers denied a proper burial through neglect, wartime chaos or official attempts to limit knowledge of the true cost in blood of the conflict has become something of a national obsession.

The school supported all the social policies of the Soviet world before 1991, with active Young Pioneer and Komsomol units organized by staff and students, but its reputation established its role as a safe haven for those not entirely in tune with the regime. The part the school played in providing a refuge for Jewish staff in the 'anti-Cosmopolitan' repression of the post-war years, when the infamous show trial of a group of leading Jewish doctors was only the most visible of a series of Stalin-inspired anti-Semitic measures, is remembered to this day. Inna and

Regina, who are both Jewish, still appreciate the shield it put between them and the repression of the late 1940s and early 1950s, when they were junior teachers just beginning their careers.

Inna, a tall, slim woman, her beauty undimmed by age, recalls how the purging of Jewish intellectuals during the period perversely benefited her. Sitting in a chilly, empty classroom on a winter's day, she says, 'The best teachers from the universities were made to leave during this period of repression and they started working in very small institutes, such as the city teacher training institute, from which I graduated in 1947. This meant I had something of an élite education.'

Directed to teach at School Number 279 under the Soviet system of *raspredeleniye* – official employment directives – Inna discovered that the pre-revolutionary codes of moral conduct demonstrated by the head, Lydia Nikolaievna Yegorova, meant it attracted those subjected to Communist Party hysteria. 'Lydia Nikolaievna came from a priest's family. You can imagine that the traditions and rules of her family and her behaviour were those of pre-revolutionary times. When these so-called "cosmopolitans" were repressed, she took a lot of teachers who were made to leave many other schools because of their origin. All the people working here are still, to this day, very grateful to this lady and perhaps this is why we continued working in this school. The times were not very friendly – there were endless horrible articles in the press against the "cosmopolitans". In many other schools teachers and kids were made to vote against some of the teachers. Perhaps this is why I, and Regina when she came, felt particularly comfortable in this school.'

The development in the school of a literary drama society, based largely around an appreciation of the work of the poet Alexander Tvardovsky, gave focus and purpose to the school community. Tvardovsky, who during the 1960s was the editor of the progressive intellectual journal *Novy Mir* – (*New World*), is considered to have heralded many of the later democratic changes in Russian society through the journal's articles and poetry.

The work of the Poisk group and day-to-day absorption of busy workloads for Inna, a literature teacher, and Regina, a chemist, allowed the years to go by largely unaffected by external political events. Within the school a new world was created, one in which people treated each other with respect as human beings, and trust and a degree of openness were the rule rather than the exception.

The women recall few unpleasant occasions, but acknowledge that the weight of having to teach the 'lies' of officially sanctioned courses, particularly for Inna as a literature specialist, remained a burden throughout the Soviet era. 'It's no longer our duty to lie to the pupils. We're allowed to say what we think, and this makes up for a lot of the material difficulties we have to endure today. Everything is pardonable. We may forget about everything because of this atmosphere of freedom,' Inna says.

The school's ethos continued to give stability and shelter through the break-up of the Soviet Union and the chaotic emergence of the new Russia, the women say. 'We subscribed to Tvardovsky's journal, *Novy Mir*. We believe that all the changes that have been happening in people's minds were prepared by this journal, and we cultivated these attitudes in the children. We wanted to keep up the memory about the war and educate honest citizens of the country, citizens who would hate everything that was false. That was our task. We're pleased to see when we meet our former pupils that they are all democratically minded people.'

On the whole the school community supported the changes heralded after August 1991 enthusiastically, although economically events took a turn for the worst. The keener, older members of the school's Komsomol chapter clashed with some members of staff who weren't sure whether they should rush to embrace the changes lest the old order be reasserted.

'It was a very difficult time. Everyone had to digest all these changes and comprehend what was going to happen from then on. It was very difficult to work with the pupils because in their minds there was total chaos,' Regina, a small dark-haired woman with a gentle smile, recalls, before Inna takes up the theme. 'After everything that happened, strange as it might seem, they could not agree to the positive approach of the teachers. They couldn't understand why we were so positively minded to the changes. Maybe it came from families or parents, but the kids were mistrustful of what was taking place and of the teachers' efforts to have a new look at literature. Of course they felt a certain degree of freedom here in school, the regulations relaxed and allowed us to change the teaching programme and introduce new topics prohibited before. The kids were not willing to accept this at first. Books that were critical of the Soviet system were something they were initially very reluctant to accept. The human mind is very conservative – it's very difficult to get rid of dogmas. It was a very difficult time. There were real battles with the kids.'

The transition from the stability of the social and political world of the Soviet Union to the uncharted territory of the new Russia was something the students at the school found much harder than the staff, the women recall. A lifetime's experience of having to keep their thoughts to themselves or the most trusted of friends was a heavy weight to bear. The collapse of the old order brought relief and a sense of freedom to many of those who had grown up under such a burden. The children took longer to adjust, unhappy with seeing familiar texts and themes discarded overnight. Eight years later a new generation with barely any recollection of life under a different political regime is much more receptive to debate and argument, Inna says, drawing on an example of classroom discussions over the message to be found in the works of Fyodor Dostoyevsky.

'Today the youngsters can see why Dostoyevsky's books were not allowed for so long, because the writer was against bloodshed in any revolution, as if he foresaw what was in store for Russia. But a few years ago the children were inclined to say, "No, this is not right. Revolution is something very different. Revolution takes place for the good of the people and bloodshed should be allowed for the greater good." This was something that several generations of Soviet children were fed on.'

Less than a decade after the old order disappeared the new generation, at least in their school, has lost its lust for blood. Today's youngsters are far more likely to argue that no slogan or ideology is worth shedding blood for than was true in the past. 'Today, in my classroom, I feel as if I'm talking to people who believe in the same things I do,' Inna remarks, although she adds darkly that too many teachers remain stuck in the old cast and continue to propagate Communist ideas to this day.

If the day-to-day political switchbacks of Russia's parliamentary and Kremlin antics continue to maintain a sense of uncertainty and the fluctuating economic fortunes of the country make planning a futile exercise, the small island of stability offered by the school provides a welcome respite. Both Inna and Regina should have retired years ago, but the comfort they find within the school community helps them 'forget about all the horrible things' happening outside its doors. The examples of students who return each year for the traditionally well-attended school reunions give the women faith in the future.

'We see that people are now beginning to learn to cope with their problems themselves. At a recent reunion I talked with graduates of the last ten to fifteen years. After the financial crisis of last year [August 1998], whoever was asked how life was with them, everyone was saying, "Great!" Probably not everyone's situation is brilliant, but these people have been taught to look at life from a different angle. There is no despair; there is no indifference. This is a very positive change in mentality.'

The women have not been spared the vicissitudes of life since 1991. They remember the sense of unease and fear they felt that August when one morning at their country dacha they found they couldn't tune in to Echo Moscow, a popular liberal news station. 'Echo Moscow was silent. The next station was silent and so on until we found just one station playing classical music. We realized something terrible had happened and, gathering up our clothes, we ran to the railway station,' Inna says.

The fevered talk on the *elektrichka*, rumours of tanks on the streets, stumbling back home to find only Tchaikovsky's 'Swan Lake' playing on the two channels, all seemed a nightmare. Regina went to the barricades around the White House, taking food and drink for the defenders of democracy, while Inna remained at home, 'sitting, trembling'. All the long years of hoping that one day they would be free of living two lives – the external face of conformity and the inner dreams of being free of Communism's straitjacket, came into sharp focus.

In October 1993 the women, who share an apartment overlooking Prospekt Mira, saw the trucks and buses rushing towards Ostankino television centre trailing red banners proclaiming, 'Kill! Beat! Reveal Yeltsin's Lies!' Once again they felt horror and dread at the prospect that the new Russia would slip back into a version of the old. The 'mob of hooligans' who were rushing to the deadly clash at Ostankino brought to the surface all their fears.

'We felt horror. We were not afraid for ourselves, but for the fate of what had already been fought for. We were afraid for democracy. We didn't fear a return to the dreadful system of Stalin's gulags, but feared that the glasnost and freedom our students had been enjoying would be torn away from them.' Ironically, a close friend of theirs, a woman who had worked in the apparatus of the Central Committee of the Communist Party during Soviet times at Old Square, near the Kremlin, calmed their fears. 'This friend, who was always something of a white crow within that crowd at Old Square, simply said, "They will not pass. These people are fools, the most inferior we have in the country. Don't be afraid of them." '

As the 1990s draw to a close, life in Russia remains like 'living on a volcano' and Inna and Regina remain anxious about the future for the young people they teach. Political instability continues to provide ripe conditions for extremist rabble-rousing. Neo-fascists hold rallies of black-shirted young toughs beneath flags adorned with swastika-like devices; Communist factions and Vladimir Zhirinovsky's misnamed Liberal Democratic Party target the young. But life remains hopeful and promising despite all.

'Of course everything has turned out a little differently from how people envisioned the new era and one has to hope that our democracy will stabilize and the democrats unite, but now, provided we don't slip back, the prospects are hopeful,' Regina says.

The financial crisis of August 1998, when the rouble crashed fourfold against the dollar and a wave of banking and financial institutions went to the wall, was a cruel blow to many. The women's standard of living was not particularly high, but with their pensions worth $80 before the crisis they could afford to live reasonably. The economic crisis hit them hard, but their way is not that of those who are 'constantly screaming and chanting'. Their part-time positions at the school give them a continuing role in community life and teaching private lessons – an essential feature of the Russian education system, where young people traditionally cram for university entrance exams – affords opportunities to earn upwards of $150 a month.

Asked what, if anything, they lament about the collapse of Communism and the rise of the new Russia, the women pause and think. The decline of organized sports and cultural activities for young people are all they come up with. They cannot say they suffered unduly during Soviet times, neither was ever called before the KGB, although both had occasionally uncomfortable run-ins with the local party committee. But the summer camps, team sports and inexpensive cultural activities sponsored by Soviet Communism were part of the social contract. 'We were not dissidents, we only did what we could to fight against the pressures within the system. But not everything was bad. The lack of nationally organized youth activities these days is a problem. We try to set up what we can in school and the politicians sometimes talk about creating something with the help of retired military men, but the absence of organized groups for young people remains a problem,' Inna concludes.

After a lifetime lived within the close grip of Communism there are minor regrets. For Inna and Regina the freedom they have enjoyed since August 1991 is priceless. 'No stability, no economic security is worth going back to what we had before. Nothing material could compensate for what we have in Russia today,' they say.

In the summer of 1968 Yulia Tourchaninova was a sixteen-year-old Moscow Komsomol leader in charge of a group of younger Pioneers at a special camp at Artek, near Yalta in the Crimea. There were thousands of young Communists from all over the world at the international summer event, where young people from Eastern Bloc countries and Western socialist organizations could meet, share experiences and participate in ideologically and physically healthy activities. The summer camp president was traditionally chosen from a country other than the Soviet Union and so it was that a boy from Nice, in the French contingent, drawn from that country's strong Communist youth movement, was appointed leader. Yulia, considered a rising young talent within the Komsomol, was made vice-president. It was a high-profile position, putting her in more regular daily contact with the adult members of the Komsomol and Communist Party organizing the camp than with her young charges. Then something happened which forced Yulia to make a choice that changed the way she saw and thought about the Soviet world.

'Czechoslovakia was invaded. All the groups from the larger, more important socialist countries had their own separate dormitories. The next day, after news of the invasion had reached us, there was a kind of vacuum around the Czech house. All these young Pioneers with their international ideas were forbidden to approach the Czechs and Slovaks. But those from the capitalist countries just rushed there with presents and toys. Leaders of the capitalist contingents even addressed their embassies, pleading for permission to take the Czechoslovak children home with them.'

Yulia couldn't stand by. She too went to the Czechoslovaks, the only Russian – the only Eastern Bloc – youngster to do so. The experience was to mark her for life and leave her with an enduring inner strength that enabled her to follow her own strongly individualistic path under Communism and since its collapse.

'It goes all through my life. In crisis situations I don't think, I just act,' says Yulia, now a professor of pedagogics (education), mother to a young daughter and freelance translator of educational, historic and scientific books.

Her actions at the Pioneer camp drew no sanction from the authorities; after all she had only followed the strict letter of the law on international friendship towards and support of a group of fellow Communists. But she did face persistent questioning and attempts to persuade her not to display her solidarity. Drawing deeply on one of the pungent Bulgarian cigarettes she habitually smokes, Yulia says the incident did not cause her to question the whole basis of the Soviet world's ideology, but did force her to distance herself from the party, its activities and ideas.

'I became very practical and pragmatic. I felt that this experience proved that one could use the whole Communist construction against Soviet society, doing exactly what was written there in the rules of the party, Komsomol or whatever. That was my position from that moment until I finally quit the Komsomol in 1974 at the age of twenty-two.'

If Inna and Regina found their shelter in School Number 279, Yulia – who would later teach at the same school for a number of years – found hers within. A petite, feisty woman with a sharp wit and energetic nature, Yulia was determined to follow her own inner direction, regardless of what the prevailing slogans or trends dictated. During a career in teaching and educational psychology, she has always trodden an iconoclastic path, switching jobs whenever a particular field became too restrictive. Today at forty-seven, she is the mother of a new daughter, twenty-six years younger than her first, and is making a living as a freelance translator alongside her husband, physicist and psychologist Ernst Goussinsky. She is on maternity leave from her position as director of the Russian national in-service teacher training institute and enjoying a break from a demanding lifestyle despite the paltry $10 a month maternity pay and child benefit she receives. Translating books such as Chicago University history professor Richard Hellie's monumental *Slavery in Russia*, writing articles on education for Internet newspapers and undertaking private commissions enable her and Ernst to work from home, a spacious three-room apartment in the Izmailovo district of north-east Moscow. Caring for baby Alice, born two days after the birth of Yulia's first granddaughter in an adjoining hospital room, has introduced a different tempo to her life after years of being a career woman.

Yulia's attitude to life could perhaps be taken as a model by anyone in any society. A healthy psychological strategy, she defines it as remaining true to her own principles, while being flexible and willing to take risks and act upon opportunities. If the conventional picture of life in the Soviet Union suggested a rigidity of social structures where career progression depended largely on a good party record, Yulia is the exception to that rule.

Dissuaded from joining the theatre by her actor father, who warned that only the very best can ever hope to be happy in that world, she intended to enter Moscow State University's chemistry faculty, fired with enthusiasm by one particular teacher. On the day she was due to sit her entrance exams, her father died and she failed to take the test. Despite her grief, she later found a place on a teacher training course combing physics and languages. She married and divorced young and gave birth to her first daughter, Olga, before she had graduated. She had no idea what she wanted to do with her life, but, finding that she enjoyed teaching practice during her studies, decided to go into teaching. Her experiences during these years left her with another conviction that has served her well. 'The message I gave myself from this time is that I must be open to chances, looking around ready to spot my path,' she remarks, as we talk in the cluttered kitchen of her ground-floor flat, occasionally interrupted by the sound of Alice's crying from the next room, where Ernst is combining work and baby-sitting.

This philosophy made her open to the changes happening in Soviet society, despite a natural cynicism about politics. In what Yulia describes as one of her personal triumphs, over twenty years she consistently pushed the case of a freer society with her mother. 'Mum was a judge and a member of the Communist Party. She was one of those people who had a once and forever frightened conscience – people who could not imagine how they could let themselves open their eyes and see things as they are. So it took me twenty years to explain something, by which time she was perfectly ready and absolutely positive about what was happening,' she says, kissing the tips of her fingers in a joyful gesture. 'I can appreciate it because I saw many people of her age in an awful condition psychologically when everything started to break down. They saw how everything their lives had been about was announced to be wrong, unfair, dishonest – it was horrible for them – but Mum was OK, which was my greatest pleasure.'

Perestroika and glasnost did not give Yulia any great sense of confidence in the future. Observing the changes in Eastern Europe, she remembers feeling that the Kremlin would never allow such freedom in the Soviet Union, that 'generations would pass until the shelves of our shops would be full . . . but, well I like to be mistaken in this way!'

August 1991 came, therefore, as a complete surprise, but Yulia immediately knew what she had to do. Hearing about the seizure of power by the Kremlin emergency committee and seeing television pictures of small numbers of demonstrators rallying to Boris Yeltsin's side at the White House, she began phoning around friends. 'As I went to dial the phone it rang and the very friend I was intending to call was there, suggesting exactly what I was going to say – let's take food and go down to the White House.' And so it was that Yulia, her daughter, Ernst and friends, plus suitcases bulging with food went to join the crowds of Muscovites determined not to allow the grey men of the Politburo reverse the revolution Gorbachev had sparked.

'Walking down to the White House from Barrikadnaya metro station, there were crowds of people and an atmosphere of common joy. People from all over were flooding there and we saw lots of familiar faces – actors, writers, journalists. The funniest thing about it was that everybody was carrying food – we must all have seen the same television pictures. When we got to the White House someone had set out these huge restaurants canteens, marked 'eggs', 'cheese', 'bread' and we just deposited what we had there.'

The carnival atmosphere of the first day became more tense the next, when Yulia, a number of her students from the teacher training institute and Ernst stayed all night at the barricades in the drizzle, expecting gas or tank assaults at any moment. Yulia, whose flat was being redecorated at the time, had taken plastic dust covers with them to keep the rain off and she and Ernst slept as best they could during that fearful night. As is common with great historic events, small personal incidents are what persist in the memory of participants. 'The family joke ever since that night has been that Ernst spent his first night with me under the sheets waiting for the tanks to come. Being a gentleman, two years later he had to marry me!' says Yulia, laughing.

Once again during the events of August 1991 Yulia had done what she felt was right, had taken action without thinking, knowing only that this was right for her. Soon the rapid release of energy created by the swift collapse of the old order was translated into one of her most exciting projects: a retraining programme for teachers that directly challenged the psychology of years of Soviet practice.

In January 1991, after a varied career that included teaching secondary school physics, a spell as a researcher at the Academy of Pedagogical Sciences of the USSR and lecturing at a top teacher training institute, Yulia moved to RIPKO, the national professional training body for teachers. The institute had long been a dumping ground for former education ministers, local authority chiefs and other officials and had a reputation for being one of the last strongholds of rigid orthodox ideology. Despite her feelings about perestroika, the mood of the country had changed and the purges that Boris Yeltsin, onetime head of the party organization in Moscow, had overseen within political structures eventually reached RIPKO. Reforming the organization was impossible, so the entire staff was forced to resign and Yulia, along with many of her colleagues from education, took over. She was rapidly promoted to head of the department of pedagogics and psychology and set about reinventing teacher training.

Untainted by ideology – she'd moved into teacher training in 1985, after key Marxist-Leninist elements of the curriculum had been removed – she understood that if people were to follow politics, changes of a more profound nature than the name of the country and the language of reform had to be introduced. Equipped with a $300,000 grant from the George Soros Foundation and a further $200,000 worth of textbooks and visiting professors from European and American universities, she set up a nationwide two-year retraining programme for 500 teacher trainers that owed more to Big Sur than the Soviet Union.

Using the language and tactics of Californian personal growth workshops, Yulia, Ernst and a team of bright and committed young postgraduates invited 500 teachers, students and professors from dozens of regions of Russia to come to Moscow for a series of residential weekends. The seminars, where all expenses were covered from the moment the participants arrived in the capital, would mark the beginning of profound change in the lives of many of the teachers.

'I felt very much that you can tell whatever truth to a person if you really manage to make him believe that you are not against him personally. More than that, that you love him and care about him, that you don't have any hidden motive. This was the problem we faced. I had to create a fully astonishing psychological situation of the kind none of them was used to,' Yulia says.

For people used to the conformity of years of Soviet-style management and professional courses, the likes of which still dominated their profession, Yulia's deceptively simple invitation to a sanatorium-based retraining seminar was indeed 'fully astonishing'.

Designed to be the very opposite of what the participants might have expected, the seminars deliberately mixed people of different experience, seniority and rank. The programme was packed with workshops and discussion groups, attendance at which was entirely voluntary. Yulia and her team dressed casually and deliberately avoided using the stuffy conventional forms of address where a person's name and patronymic were always coupled with the formal *vy* rather than more personal *ty*.

Thus it was that revered heads of university-level institutions arrived at the seminar, held in the town of Dzerzhinsk, near Moscow, dressed in suit and tie, only to be greeted by Yulia in old jeans, a baggy sweater, crew-cut hair and a pungent cigarette hanging from her mouth.

'There were many shocks at this seminar. This full shock they received on the first day after their arrival had very many aspects, not least the fact that the whole thing was free of charge,' Yulia recalls. 'These people, Sovki – Soviet citizens as we always called them – had never found themselves in a situation fully paid for by someone without making an effort to get it. Here other people had chosen them, quite by chance. They could not find any personal merit why this crazy American [Soros] should give money to this crazy woman who is doing what she likes. They felt very strange because someone was making them happy without them asking for it.'

Many participants, unaccustomed to receiving something for nothing and rather suspicious, arrived with 'large sums of money'. Most were dressed formally – Yulia laughs at the memory of the tight skirts and high heels many of the women wore, recalling that after a few days a deputation came to ask for half a day off to go into Moscow to buy more casual clothing.

Participants had to share rooms and senior, long-serving professors were deliberately housed with young students to increase the sense of total disorientation from everything they had expected. The rigid status-obsessed Soviet system was and remains a strong feature of official life in Russia, and treating people who expected special favour in so casual a manner was designed to shock.

'The team who ran the seminar had an order to be informal to the furthest extent. Workshops and meetings took place in halls where many people sat on the floor, and discussions and parties were carried on long into the night,' Yulia says.

The approach drew some complaints initially and tempers became frayed once or twice, but mostly people soon took to the freedoms offered by the seminar with enthusiasm and vigour. Yulia remains convinced that it was the abundant 'love and appreciation' that made the difference, and months later, when following up the professional changes the seminars and subsequent workshops had made, participants kept on coming back to a key feature. 'Many of these people felt they had never before just been allowed to be themselves and to be accepted as such, and this gave them the ability to go on and make changes in their lives,' she says.

Professional promotion opened up to many participants; career changes and even personal moves resulted from the seismic shifts people experienced during the seminars. Many 'old, boring and absolutely rigid' marriages came to an end when people felt free to be themselves. Other changes were less immediately apparent. Yulia had deliberately invited an elderly professor who was regarded as one of Russia's leading authorities on the history of education. He appeared very tense, closed and official when she first met him and he remained distant, though attentive, throughout the seminar. Later Yulia had a surprising letter from him, telling her how his students had reacted to him on his return to his university. Several young women had come up to him and asked him what had happened to him at the seminar – he looked different, more relaxed and open. The man was astonished. In all his years in teaching, no one had commented on how he looked. There were internal changes too: he rewrote his courses, removing years of stolid and hackneyed ideas.

Yulia's teacher retraining seminars may have directly affected only 500 people, but the cascade effect allowed the message to spread much further. Later, travelling across Russia to give lectures and address meetings, she and Ernst concluded that 'the whole of Soviet Union could have done with one of these courses', such was the yearning for change in people's lives.

Yulia's path may have been more erratic than that of Inna and Regina, but like them she too found a way to survive the changing times. Living from conviction and acting with certainty – even when the odds seemed stacked against her – have enabled her to achieve much that she wanted, party dictates and economic crises notwithstanding.

Despite, or perhaps because of, her political cynicism, Yulia has not been disappointed by the new Russia. Mikhail Gorbachev's perestroika contained little to impress her, and although she was one of those who defended democracy at the White House in 1991 – because she knew there was no future for her under Communism – she was never a great fan of Boris Yeltsin. 'I never expected anything, from Gorbachev, Yeltsin or anyone else. I didn't believe either of them and did not expect anything from them. I can't say that I wanted something specific. The only thing I wanted can be stated in negative terms. I did not want the Communist Party on my head and after my family, my work, my going abroad, what I eat and what I wear. I just don't want anyone, except those I choose myself, on my back.'

Convinced that the Communists, and more generally politicians, 'never did and still don't control anything', Yulia has devoted her life to setting and meeting her own targets. A witness to the way 'things go their own way', she is confident that Russian society will eventually settle down and stabilize, and she works towards the future without the burden of anxiety so many carry in Russia today.

'I'm not disappointed with Yeltsin because I was never charmed by him. I'm not disappointed with Gorbachev because I was never deceived by him. You know, we have a saying in Russia, "they have their own wedding and we have ours". They are playing their own games, but the more they are playing their games the more chance that life has to find its own way. This I'm sure about, because when they stop playing and start ruling that would be a real mess.'

7

Mafia

Moscow, April 1999. Three men in their late twenties and early thirties are eating dinner on a warm spring evening at the Aeroflot Hotel on Leningradsky Prospekt. The hotel is neither cheap nor expensive, an anonymous sort of place frequented by commercial travellers and Russian businessmen of a certain class and type. Few Westerners ever find their way to its steel-framed doors and dusty foyer. Another man enters the bar, approaches their table and draws a pistol. Aiming at thirty-one-year-old Andrei Kuznetsov's head, the man fires. His aim is poor and Kuznetsov suffers a flesh wound where the bullet grazes his neck. His colleagues, Igor Pospelov, also thirty-one, and Alexander Likhachev, twenty-eight, prefer not to wait for the police and instead drive Kuznetsov to Sklifosovsky casualty hospital, a few miles away, near Komsomolskaya metro station on Moscow's Garden Ring Road. Hospitals are safer than hotels, especially when the police may not arrive very speedily.

Pospelov and Likhachev make sure their partner is attended to and finally emerge from the hospital's main entrance just after 1.30 in the morning. They don't notice the red Moskvich parked nearby with its engine idling. Moskvich cars are the Ford Fiestas of Russia, so ubiquitous they are practically invisible. Perhaps Pospelov and Likhachev are tired, senses dulled by the shock of the shooting; no one will ever know why they are so fatally relaxed. The men sitting in the Moskvich are armed with pistols just like the one used against Kuznetsov earlier. They fire rapidly and accurately. Both men are hit in the neck and chest and, despite the best efforts of doctors at the hospital, die shortly afterwards. The killers drive away at speed from the hospital on Grokholsky Pereulok. Armed police officers standing guard at the nearby Portugese Embassy fail to stop them.

The shooting and killings make a few paragraphs in the next day's newspapers in the city, where police speculate that the attack was typical of a criminal *razborka* – a dispute between gangs. The wounded man and dead men were involved in shuttle-trading, shipping goods from China and the Far East to sell in Russia. It's a lucrative, Mafia-dominated business and there is much competition and jostling for market positions. The attacks were most likely linked to this, police say.

Moscow, June 1998. The forty-three year old owner of the bar and sauna in a city suburb knew the man in dark glasses who came in one evening. Customers told police later that the two had chatted for an hour or so over several beers before the man, whose glasses hid an ugly blue bruise on his cheek, pulled an army-issue Makarov 9mm pistol and shot the proprietor at point-blank range in the chest. The killer may have had a female accomplice with him, witnesses were not too sure, but the man and a slender blonde both ran out of the bar seconds after the killing. Popular newspapers showed photographs of the portly victim lying on his back, his sweater pulled up to his chin, revealing a large, round belly and messy wound in his chest. Pressed for possible motives, police investigators were quoted as saying that the businessman had been shot at before, a year earlier, when a bullet clipped his neck as he was coming out of the entrance to his apartment block. The man had registered at a local hospital but immediately checked out again and disappeared for a month or so. Again, a business dispute was the likely reason for the killing.

Moscow, November 1996. Paul Tatum, a forty-one-year-old American entrepreneur, has been involved in months of wrangling with his Russian business partners in a struggle for control of the Radisson-Slavyanskaya Hotel, adjacent to the city's central Kievsky railway station. Tatum hasn't kept the dispute to himself; locked inside his office in the hotel, surrounded by bodyguards, for weeks he has kept up a high-profile press campaign via fax. Advertisements calling for Russia to uphold the rights of foreign investors are published in leading Moscow newspapers. A special defence fund to promote free enterprise and investor rights in Russia is launched. An arbitration court case is launched in Stockholm. One dank, dark night, Tatum leaves the hotel with two bodyguards and walks the couple of hundred yards to the entrance to the Kievsky metro station. As he descends the concrete stairs from the street to the underpass, a man who has been loitering behind a parapet leans over the stairwell and fires several bursts from a Kalashnikov assault rifle. Tatum dies instantly, despite the body armour he is wearing under his jacket. He is hit by eleven of the twelve shots fired from the 5.45mm AK-74, with five entering his body at the neck, above the bullet-proof jacket. Further proof of the skill of the assassin is witnessed by the fact that neither of Tatum's two bodyguards are hurt. The assassin escapes, leaving his automatic rifle behind him. No one is caught for the killing and soon after the neon sign reading 'Radisson' atop the hotel is removed, leaving only the word 'Slavyanskaya'.

Mafia killings have become so commonplace in Yeltsin's Russia they hardly merit a page lead in the popular newspapers unless the victim is high-profile or the modus operandi particularly gruesome. Violence as a way of solving disputes and removing problems is no stranger to Russian society, but the unprecedented explosion in private, as opposed to political, crime in the years since the collapse of the Soviet Union has left few in the new Russia untouched.

Large Western multinationals which have taken the risk to invest in Russia frequently claim they are above dealings with the Mafia, but ask any company how many security guards it employs, and the answer is likely to be twice as many as it really needs. No office building or shopping centre in Moscow, and most Russian cities, is without its complement of paramilitary-attired young men, or broad-shouldered be-suited guys with fists like hams. The companies that supply security are usually part of a Mafia group's portfolio of business interests and the fees and numbers of men a firm takes are usually not open to negotiation. Joint ventures between Western firms and Russian partners often operate on the understanding – tacit or explicit – that it is the domestic partner's job to get their hands dirty. Deals with crooks are hidden in cross-payments, allowing firms to get around such obstacles as the American Foreign Corrupt Practices Act, which forbids payment of bribes abroad.

Ordinary Russians brush shoulders with the Mafia all the time. Members of the Mafia, after all, are ordinary Russians themselves. The businessman who is owed money rarely turns to the courts – the police and judiciary are widely viewed as corrupt, inefficient and self-serving. He'll turn to his *krysha* and have pressure applied that way. The chances are that he is already paying somewhere between 10 and 20 per cent of his profits to a *krysha*, whether he likes it or not.

The streets of Moscow and St Petersburg are full of young men in sharp suits and smart cars, coming and going from restaurants and gyms at all times of the day. They may have legitimate jobs that give them access to such a high standard of living, but again the chances are they are part of an organization that at its core is criminal.

The emergence of the Mafia, of organized crime, in Russia in the post-Soviet period is a complex story with roots going far back into both Soviet and tsarist Russian history. Underpaying state officials, particularly tax collectors, as a means of encouraging them to use their powers to find means of support for themselves while hitting defined revenue targets, the tsarist system of 'tax farming' saved the exchequer money by tacitly supporting corruption. In Soviet times the heavy cost of running and policing Stalin's gulag – Glavnoe Upravleniye Lagerei, Main Administration for Prison Camps – was lightened by the use of professional criminals, the so-called '*vory v zakone*' – thieves in code – to police the political prisoners. The close relations between state and criminals left a legacy that spread throughout Soviet society and officialdom, as the opportunities provided by post-war economic plans, so cosily engineered within the corridors of power, opened up a new realm of lucrative alliances between apparatchiks and criminals. The Uzbek Cotton Affair of 1988 – the embezzlement of billions of roubles to pay for fantasy cotton production – involved not only the leading senior officials of the Uzbek Communist Party but also top protectors in Moscow, including General Secretary Leonid Brezhnev's son-in-law, Yuri Churbanov. Politburo leaders launched anti-corruption drives from time to time, the most notorious of which was Gorbachev's ill-fated anti-alcohol campaign of the mid-1980s, which served only to boost illicit vodka production and launch the criminal careers of thousands of alcohol king-pins. Petty thieving, bribe-taking, corruption and pilfering from the workplace in the Soviet period were so endemic as to be all but acceptable.

The loosening of social and political sanctions against wrongdoing which began to accelerate in the finals weeks and months of Gorbachev's rule swept through Russia with the collapse of the Soviet Union and the release of the restraints of old. Party apparatchiks and members of the nomenklatura seized the opportunities afforded them by access to funds, connections and power to begin building private wealth and business organizations. Police, military men and members of the security services saw openings to use their specialist knowledge and skills for private gain. Academics, local government officials and managers of state factories all seized the moment and set up businesses from their workplaces. Old friends and protectors within the party or official structures helped with security and keeping red tape to a minimum. Although the Soviet-era constitution and criminal code remained on the statute books, in the new Russia the only real rule was to get away with what you could. In an environment where a new system of laws and criminal code are only slowly and fitfully being introduced, the rule of law remains little more than a vague notion.

By 1998 it was estimated that as much as 40 per cent of the Russian economy fell under the influence of organized crime and Russian officials – using rather loose definitions – claimed there were as many as 5,000 Mafia groupings in the country. The true figure is probably closer to 350 genuine organized criminal groups, including the top dozen or so major gangs.

The Russian Mafia tends to make the headlines only when killings are carried out, but the extent to which organized crime has become an integral part of the business and political culture of the new Russia has moved one iconoclastic politician to urge the state to strike a deal with the Mafia to raise revenue through collecting not taxes but tribute – with a profitable cut for supplying the service.

Irina Khakamada, a half-Japanese businesswoman and economist who leads the Common Cause faction in the State Duma, defines the contemporary Russian economy as 'neo-feudal' and argues that since the state is no longer able to fulfil its proper functions, it should recognize the extent to which criminal groups have privatized many business and security functions once reserved to government.

She believes Russia needs to replace taxation, both direct and indirect, with a 'quasi-tax, a fixed payment, like the tribute of feudal times'. Taxes would be levied in two key ways under her plan: an individual poll tax set at a low and affordable level, such as the equivalent of $1, would give the government a fixed budget source. Businessmen would pay a tribute tax, collected not by the underpaid and corrupt tax police but by private companies, which would be required to assess their region and make an advance payment before collecting the full amount, minus their share. Those firms that made the best bid in an open tender, guaranteeing the largest advance payment and fairest and verifiable system of collection, would win the business.

'You can't have officials living on the $200 a month they officially get in Moscow today – that's an open admission of corruption. We need to separate capital from the state,' Khakamada says. 'Our problem is not a lack of investment but a lack of transparency. Businesses have to become transparent, and then we can move towards modern market relations.'[1]

The idea may not be as absurd as it sounds. Dr Mark Galeotti, an expert on the Russian Mafia and director of Keele University's Organized Russian and Eurasian Crime Research Unit, observes:

> The *mafiya* are both cause and effect of the central state's lack of authority. Its inability to control terror and organized crime is undermining Moscow's moral and practical authority . . . The *mafiya* is at once a loose collection of criminal entrepreneurs, a dominant force behind the new Russian capitalism and a natural response to the failure of the state to carry out various basic social functions. As a result, tax evasion has become widespread, not just because the authorities cannot adequately police the revenue, but because businesses feel evasion is their right given that they are having to pay separately for services the state should provide.[2]

Ordinary Russians both fear and admire the Mafia. When the Swiss authorities dropped their criminal case against an alleged Mafia godfather, Sergei Mikhailov, also known as Mikhas, the head of the powerful Moscow Solntsevo Mafia group, in December 1998 for lack of evidence in an organized crime trial, most Russians saw the returning mobster as a hero. Fear of crime, on the other hand, is what prompts middle-aged university professors in Moscow, for example, to carry gas pistols or young men to enrol in martial arts classes. Trusting the police to provide for secure streets and public places has never figured strongly in the attitudes of most Russians, particularly today when underpaid and unmotivated officers often moonlight as private security guards or act as a *krysha* themselves.

Andrei, a twenty-nine-year-old security specialist with a privately-funded agency in Moscow, has combined military, police and security work with a brief spell as a bodyguard for a Moscow Mafia gang boss in the years since he left the army and fled ethnic violence in Azerbaijan. The extent to which the Russian Mafia relies upon recruiting ex-security service personnel is reflected in the way Andrei, a Russian by birth, slipped from police service into *krysha* service. A short, stocky, olive-skinned man with crew-cut black hair and brown eyes, he enlisted in an élite parachute regiment in Baku when he was called up in 1988. Soviet troops had yet to be withdrawn from Afghanistan and the riots between Armenian and Azeris that were to mar decades of peaceful coexistence in Baku that year were still some months in the future. He joined the *desantno-shturmovaya brigada*, aerial shock troops trained in the mountains of the region in preparation for service in Afghanistan, but was never sent there.

'My military service coincided with that period we called *perestroika-perestrelki*, Andrei says, using a punning phrase referring to the last years of the Soviet Union, when Gorbachev's policy of rebuilding Communism degenerated into nationalistic squabbles and ethnic violence in the republics. It was a time when it was impossible to avoid direct involvement in the policing of ethnic clashes that were eventually to lead to the outbreak of a rash of small civil wars in the region. Andrei saw service in the incipient violence in Nagorno-Karabakh, and the riots of Azerbaijan and in the chaos following the massive earthquake in Spitak in December 1988, when humanitarian aid deliveries from the West sparked anarchy and fighting between troops and thousands of homeless victims. In 1990 he returned to Baku, just as inter-community violence there was reaching a peak. Tensions between the regional KGB and Soviet security forces during this time, when local security services demonstrated reluctance to police the ethnic clashes with sufficient vigour, led to the establishment of locally recruited units to replace Russians taking orders directly from Moscow. Andrei found himself called up into an interior ministry unit, where his duties included working in the personal protection detail for the Azeri leader, Ayaz Mutalibov, then chairman of the republic's Communist Party and later the first president following independence in 1991.

'It was a time when I learned a lot. Although I didn't like having to serve in the forces again after my time in the army, I realized we were working with older, very experienced people and they taught us a lot that would be of great value later on,' Andrei recalls, referring to his KGB officers. 'We provided the whole spectrum of services to Mutalibov. We had to protect him at home, outside in the city when he was walking or being driven somewhere, and in his meetings with other politicians. He had of course his own Soviet guards, it was a time when local forces were not greatly trusted, but we were under orders to carry out our duties too.' Despite the confusion and overlapping spheres of command that existed in Azerbaijan, as in other republics in the twilight days of the Soviet Union, Andrei's service protecting a head of state provided a solid basis for his later work in the Mafia.

Like the majority of young men who have found their lives leading towards the Mafia in post-Soviet Russia, Andrei claims he didn't plan a criminal career. Eventually released from military service, he enrolled at university in Baku to study geology, graduating in June 1992. He completed his studies against the background of an increasingly fractured society, as Azerbaijan struggled to find national equilibrium in the early months following the break-up of the Soviet Union.

'Looking back, it's clear that Soviet times weren't so bad. When I was in the army I knew that the state would take care of its citizens to the best of its ability. But with the break-up came a rise in national tensions and our position as Russians in Baku became increasingly difficult.'

Andrei's experience in the army and interior ministry forces made him an attractive target for Azeri forces seeking to recruit men for the war in Nagorno-Karabakh. 'They wanted men who could act as trainers and offered us a car, a flat and good money. But I knew this would mean serving at the front and didn't want to do it. I was young and stupid and said, "we choose the colour of our flag just once."' It was a dangerous comment to make in the heated atmosphere of war-torn Azerbaijan and that night a military truck packed with armed men in combat gear stopped outside Andrei's flat in Baku. He didn't wait to find out what fate they had in mind; instead he clambered over a balcony and made for the safety of a relative's flat. He realized he had no future in Azerbaijan and, after making plans with some friends, drove to the border with Dagestan and fled, using false documents – 'In Azerbaijan if you have money you can buy anything,' he remarks. 'We crossed the border in broad daylight with stonily set faces. We waited for the mid-afternoon when the sun was at its warmest and the border guards were most sleepy – you know how much these Muslims like to relax. Then we walked across,' Andrei says with a smile.

His Azeri wife also found an ingenious escape route. A stewardess on the national airline, she had been prevented from trying to skip plane on two earlier occasion, but finally managed to escape with the help of similarly forged documents. By January 1993 the couple were in Moscow and trying to create a new life together, with the help of relatives in the nearby city of Tver. The only work experience he had was in the security forces, so he went directly to the local police and found a job with the special forces, the regional SWAT squad. His experience of active service and internal conflict in Azerbaijan appealed to police far from such upheaval, but within three months he was dismissed after a personal conflict with his superiors.

'They wrote in my dismissal papers that it was possible that I was an Azeri spy and that I should not be employed by any branch of the interior forces. But I was a young guy, a good shot, I spoke English and was trained in hand-to-hand combat. I returned to Moscow and started talks with a special crime squad there, but when they saw my papers they turned me away.'

It was at this point that the gamekeeper turned poacher. 'I was in Moscow, I had a wife and a child on the way, I had to find some way of earning money.' Old school friends, sportsmen Andrei had trained with, advised him to offer his skills and experience to one of the city's Mafia gangs. Andrei's move from police officer to new member of the Koptevskaya-Dolgoprudnaya criminal gang was simple and without compunction. His past as a personal guard to the Azeri leader ensured his swift appointment as bodyguard to one of the gang's senior leaders, enabling him to bypass the usual system of having to bring something to the gang when you join: some local rackets you already control, a large amount of money for the gang's *kassa* – war-chest – the offer to undertake a shooting or beating to prove yourself.

Andrei worked for the group for six months before easing himself out to a job in a private security firm with the blessing, he says, of senior men. But his experience reveals the degree to which Mafia groups in modern Russia have re-created the security of the old Soviet social system in the way service and loyalty are rewarded with protection.

Andrei's Mafia group had evolved out of the old-fashioned *vory v zakone*, with a distinct hierarchical structure and the discipline lacking in some of the new groupings, dismissed as *banditi* – bandits – by long-established professional criminals. New recruits to the group were known as *byki* – bulls – a term that has become synonymous in today's Russia with any well-built, broad-shouldered young man assumed to be involved in illicit activities. These *byki* were the foot soldiers of a group numbering well over 100, which was divided into different sections under the command of a man known as the brigadier. *Byki* carried out the strong-arm functions of the group, threatening recalcitrant businessmen who were late in paying their protection money, beating up members of another gang who had crossed them, running errands for their bosses.

Bound by their common criminality and peer pressure, once a member of a gang the only way out for most *byki* was through injury and retirement, imprisonment or death in the line of duty. Those men who showed particular talent or aptitude could rise up through the hierarchy of the group, which in some ways resembled the disciplined military and sporting organizations from which most members were drawn.

Loyalty to the group was fostered not only through pressure and the threat of violent punishment for those who broke its rules, but also by ensuring that members and their families were well looked after. In a country where all vestiges of the Soviet social security net have disappeared, the provision of pensions and support for widows and orphans among Mafia groups is a significant attraction for men with few other ways of earning a living wage.

Andrei's particular experiences, especially his active service in the army and stint as a bodyguard to the Azeri Communist Party boss, ensured that he bypassed the *byk* stage. Childhood sporting friends and other men who, like him, had served in élite parachute regiments vouched for him and he entered the group as the bodyguard to a brigadier, a man in charge of a section of up to thirty junior Mafiosi.

For Andrei the fact that he was working as a bodyguard was an important distinction: 'I was not dealing with businessmen, like the *byki*. I had a particular goal in front of me: to protect my boss and make sure that he was not shot. I had to be aware at all times that some situation, perhaps a car crash or some other incident, was not an opportunity for an assassination attempt. The only moral qualms I had about doing the job was that I had to carry an unregistered gun. Other than that, as far as I was concerned it was just the same as protecting the Azeri leader, only at a different level.'

He doesn't regret his period with the group, reflecting that it was a lifeline for his family at the time and noting, with professional pride, that his boss is still alive, living in Spain and 'feeling fine'. The same cannot be said of many of Andrei's colleagues from the group. Sipping at a cold bottle of Baltika beer in his office on a warm, sunny afternoon, Andrei's face clouds over at the memory of the cost of Mafia association to many gang members. 'The group is still there, but the guys I was with – some have been shot, some are in prison, others have fled from the police and gone overseas. A few have managed to transform their lives and are doing something else, like me, and some are living on their pensions – Mafia pensions, rather good.'

The scope of the Koptevskaya-Dolgoprudnaya group's activities and business interests is not something Andrei is willing to discuss, skating over questions on its detailed functions by explaining that an unwritten rule of such gangs is, 'If it's not your business don't ask. If you need to know, you'll be told.'

Studies of the Russian Mafia list six key areas of activity: racketeering and extortion, vice, the sale and hire of guns and paid assassins, smuggling, economic crime and counterfeiting, and illicit or semi-legal businesses. Gangs such as Andrei's – an old, established grouping with roots running far back into the Soviet criminal past – would have run a mixture of such ventures, from providing services of value and effectiveness in a chaotic economy, such as helping to arrange bank financing for business, to more straightforward protection rackets.

Andrei's next comment reflects the skill and sophistication of the operations run by such gangs, as much as his own attempt to downplay his involvement. 'I was not really deep into the gang. I was not privy to everything about it. I had a very definite aim and I kept my sights on that.'

As a bodyguard to a brigadier Andrei was expected to dress smartly, keep in shape and be discreet. His first task as a group member was to draw a thick wad of dollars from the *kassa* (cashier) and go out shopping for Italian tailored suits, shirts, ties and leather shoes. Dressing the part is as important to the Russian Mafia as playing the game to win.

A typical working day began in the gym and swimming pool before the day's business agenda was discussed over lunch. Lists of problems to be solved, money to be paid or collected, and businessmen to be visited were agreed and a schedule of meetings to which his boss and he were to go was drawn up. Afternoons might be a flurry of meetings at markets, shops, kiosks or in restaurants, or another round of body-building exercises in a well-equipped gym. Evenings were spent in expensive restaurants and at nightclubs, where more business was conducted as Andrei kept an ever watchful eye. It was the mid-1990s and although many of the most violent wars for control between different Mafia gangs in Moscow had already been fought and won, there was always some aspiring gang of *banditi* trying to muscle in on the Koptevskaya-Dolgoprudnaya's territory.

Such clashes would often result in violence and gang members were involved in shoot-outs and assassinations, but generally the unwritten rule of the *vory v zakone* groups was to resolve such differences without the use of firearms where possible. Andrei remains proud of a professionalism that meant during the six months he served as bodyguard to the brigadier, he never once had occasion to use the pistol he always carried. 'The job of a bodyguard is to do everything to avoid a shoot-out. You should do anything else instead. When there is shooting, it's a mistake, especially when you're in charge of such a person as I was. You don't want to attract attention to him.'

One memorable time he drew the pistol to threaten a gang of baseball bat-wielding thugs who had been sent to beat up a businessman whom his boss was pressuring for protection money at a meeting in a Moscow café. 'As we were talking a gang of about twenty muscular young guys came in carrying baseball bats and they started threatening the businessman. Like us, they also wanted money, but this wasn't something I could allow to continue. I asked which of these football hooligans was the boss, the senior man, and as I did I took hold of a heavy telephone that was sitting on the table. This guy stepped forward and I hit him very hard in the face with the phone, breaking it in the process. He went down and I drew my pistol from the back of the waistband of my trousers. I knew if they were a serious gang they would be carrying weapons too. I was ready to use it but didn't have to – with their top man down and me pointing a gun at them they backed off. Fast.'

For a job that required total commitment and not inconsiderable risks, Andrei didn't exactly earn a fortune. He could expect to take home between $200 and $250 a week, depending on exactly how heavy a schedule he worked. But with all his daily expenses and clothing needs taken care of, it represented a lot more than most honest toilers in the new Russia could expect.

Andrei expresses no regrets about his time spent in the Mafia group. Although his career up to that point had been within the security services, his anger over his abrupt dismissal from the police in Tver was such that he took considerable pleasure in switching sides and using the knowledge he had gained in official service against the state. 'Despite the reputation of the Mafia and the fact of illegal activities the group engaged in, I know that the men I worked with in the Koptevskaya-Dolgoprudnaya group were honest and courageous. Whatever happened they would take care of me and my family.' It was more than could be said of the army, police or the Russian government, then or now.

Andrei left the group when he was offered a well-paid job using his knowledge and skills to offer protection to businesspeople through a personal security agency. The fact that his brother had considerable influence in the Mafia group eased his path out. As a professional bodyguard, his exit was simpler than that of a mere *byk* and he left on good terms with his former boss and colleagues.

The extent to which branches of the state security services overlap and feed the ranks of organized crime is revealed by such high-profile scandals as the autumn 1998 allegations by members of a Moscow KGB unit that senior officers had ordered them to draw up plans for the assassination of Boris Berezovsky, the billionaire financier and former chairman of the Kremlin security council. The allegations, made on national television by officers disguised in ski masks, created a country-wide sensation.

When raids by the tax police, such as those carried out in December 1998 against Sergei Lisovsky, a wealthy young television advertising mogul and former leading light of the Moscow Komsomol, involve masked police, the severe beating of security guards and strip-searching of female office staff, the line between legal and illegal security forces becomes a fine one.

Oleg Gladnitsev, senior investigator with the Russian Anti-Piracy Organization, a Hollywood-funded joint venture with the Russian government which combats video piracy and copyright abuse, says the extent to which police and the Mafia are linked and share common interests is an open secret in security circles. Video piracy, which accounts for more than 80 per cent of all home videos sold in Russia, is a huge and lucrative sector of the business portfolio of many Mafia groups. With virtually no rental market for videos in Russia, selling pirates copies of Hollywood blockbusters such as *Titanic*, *Men in Black* or *Armageddon* for prices as low as 50 roubles ($2), is big business.

When RAPO investigators go on raids against copying laboratories or wholesale video markets like Moscow's Gorbushka Rynok, they go with *militsia* or OMON units armed with Kalashnikov assault rifles. 'We always keep the date, place and timing of our raids secret because we've learned that if we tell the local police in advance, the chances are that no evidence of illicit videos, copying equipment or fake video sleeves will be found when we go on the raid – the pirates will have been tipped off.'

In one raid on a video production plant outside Moscow the RAPO team's OMON support squad got into a fight with armed guards at the factory. It was only after some heavy exchanges of gunfire that the OMON officers realized they were being shot at by uniformed *militsia* officers moonlighting as security at the plant.

The problem, according to Oleg, a thirty-five-year-old former Soviet Army special ranger and OMON officer, is not only that poorly paid and motivated policemen see moonlighting for the Mafia as a lucrative source of a second income, but that for many ex-servicemen who have seen fighting in Chechnya or other conflict zones, civvy street offers few career opportunities. 'These are people who are well prepared for killing, fighting, for armed conflicts. These are people who have already overstepped this line of pity or mercy – people who have already committed murder, for whom it is not a problem to do it again. Men are under pressure to provide for families and to retain their self-respect through doing a job. With the help of friends and friends of friends, they do all they can to find work. This is where the so-called "kind people" turn up. First of all they offer some trifle – for example, take a bag with money and carry it from one place to another. Or perhaps use force to get some money out of someone. Gradually the noose gets tighter and tighter until there is no way out.'

The wave of gangland murders that has swept through Russia in the Yeltsin years bears all the hallmarks of the work of highly trained specialists, Oleg says. 'Between 1991 and 1993 in Moscow there was virtually a war going on. Every day some people were shot and there were explosions reported everywhere. I'm sure these were the work of high-quality, well-trained specialists. It's not everyone who knows exactly where to place a grenade in the most vulnerable place of a vehicle and thus fulfil the order. Dozens of these orders were fulfilled. Take, for example, the killing of Otari Kvantrishvili [a leader of Moscow's Georgian Mafia murdered in April 1994]. That was the work of a specialist. He was shot by a sniper from a roof of a building as he came out of the *banya* [sauna]. Definitely the work of a specialist.'

Without well-trained snipers or experts in explosives, many of the Mafia assassinations simply would not be possible. Military *spetsnaz* – special forces – from Moscow's 16th Brigade in particular, have been linked by the press to key roles in some of the professional killings carried out during the most violent Mafia turf wars in the capital in the first half of the 1990s. In a country where the vast numbers of military and security forces built up and supported during the Soviet era find themselves increasingly impoverished and surplus to requirements, the natural way out is into crime.

The precise role of former security forces specialists in key Mafia killings during the Yeltsin years is difficult to prove, if only because most murders remain unsolved. Estimates of the extent of Mafia killings in Russia have been put at as high as 70 per cent of all premeditated murders. Certainly the skill with which leading business, social and political figures have been eliminated makes for a grim *Who's Who* of modern Russia. Key figures killed by Mafia assassins include *Novoe Vremya* publisher Sergei Dubov in February 1994; investigative journalist Dmitri Kholodov of *Moskovsky Komsomolets*, who died when a booby-trapped briefcase he believed to contain documents on corruption in the armed forces exploded as he opened it in his Moscow office in October 1994; Vladislav Listyev, a state television executive who had frozen advertising while he studied dubious accounting procedures, shot down at the entrance to his flat in January 1995; Ivan Kivelidi, president of Rosbiznesbank, who died in August 1995; and Mikhail Manevich, deputy governor of St Petersburg, assassinated in August 1997.

When radical democratic State Duma deputy Galina Starovoytova was killed in St Petersburg in November

1998 by a killer using an American-made Agran-2000 submachine gun left at the scene, police concluded it could only be the work of 'those with strong inter-regional links' – well-connected Mafia. The automatic rifle, used by US special units, had become a favourite of Moscow Mafia gangs in the preceding months and the public outrage at Starovoytova's killing spilled over into mass demonstrations of mourning and anger throughout Russia. At her funeral in St Petersburg, more than 20,000 mourners queued for hours in sub-zero temperatures to file past her coffin. Mourners included the great and the good of Russia's liberal democratic movement of the 1990s: former prime ministers Yegor Gaidar and Sergei Kiriyenko, privatization guru Anatoly Chubais, and Nizhny Novgorod's former governor and ex-deputy Russian prime minister Boris Nemtsov.

But murders that sparked waves of public outrage, such as Starovoytova's and those of Listyev and Kholodov, young popular icons in the media eye, are the exception rather than the rule. The controversy that raged after Kholodov's murder finally brought enough pressure to bear on the police to see some results. In February 1998, after years of campaigning from the editor of *Moskovsky Komsomolets*, two senior army officers, Major Vladimir Morozov and retired Colonel Pavel Popovskikh, reportedly a former head of paratroops intelligence, were arrested. This marked the first progress in a police investigation which had been criticized for sloth over the previous three years. Prosecutor General Yuri Skuratov also suggested that the former Defence Minister Pavel Grachev, who was head of airborne troops in the early 1990s and had earlier been questioned in connection with the case, should be brought back for further inquiries. At the time of writing, five years after the Kholodov murder, investigators in Moscow had finally drawn up charges against a number of serving and former army officers in a case demonstrating the extent to which Mafia tactics have infected state forces. Listyev's murder is occasionally referred to by politicians claiming knowledge of high-level collusion in the killings, but for the most part Mafia victims are rapidly forgotten by all other than family and friends.

Fortunately for most people, these extreme forms of Mafia activity impinge upon their lives only through newspaper headlines and television or radio reports. But the tentacles of the Mafia *sprut* – octopus, as organized crime is familiarly known – are far-reaching and will touch the lives of all Russians in some shape or form.

A conversation with any Muscovite involved in business or commerce will reveal at least a passing knowledge and experience of the Mafia. Many people don't like to talk frankly about the extent to which Mafia activities poison daily affairs and euphemisms abound when a conversation turns to the topic. Office managers in, for example, a sports wear firm might refer to the fact that a new group of 'monkeys' has taken over control of the sports stadium where they are based. A boss may have to 'take a holiday' because the 'pressures of work' have become too much. An understanding of the Russian business environment soon allows one to decode such statements.

Others are less squeamish. A driver for one of Moscow's large telephone taxi services had no qualms in detailing for me the way the Mafia affects his business. Cash-rich businesses like a taxi service are an obvious target for extortion by the Mafia, but the driver's perception of the protection money his firm paid each month cast them more in the light of a service combining police, office of fair trading and taxation functions.

'Our firm has about 600 drivers on its books – some with their own cars, others driving the firm's Volgas [the sturdy, if old-fashioned, Russian-made saloon],' Oleg said as he picked his way through Moscow's fume-choked traffic jams on the way to the airport one afternoon. 'Until the crisis [financial and banking collapse of August 1998] the firm was paying about $6,000 a month to our *krysha*. I don't know how much we're paying now, probably a little less, but for a firm of this size it's a normal payment.'

The taxi firm's *krysha* was to take care of any problems that might come up: other Mafia groups trying to muscle in, police harassment of drivers, licensing issues. When a particularly nasty or difficult problem needed to be resolved, the *krysha* might resort to a *razborka* – a battle with another Mafia group.

The notion that paying a criminal group a large sum of money each month simply to ensure the firm could continue to operate didn't strike Oleg as unusual. A fit, muscular man of thirty-four, he had been driving a cab in Moscow for fourteen years and valued the comparatively good income it gave him – 16,000 roubles a month ($600). If paying the Mafia enabled him to continue making good money, he was happy with that. 'It's all very normal. We pay the *krysha* money; they look after us. That's how things work in Russia.'

Oleg neither admired nor abhorred the Mafia; he simply accepted it. Even where Mafia activities had an obviously negative impact on him – for example, in the rising petrol prices during the summer of 1999, caused, it was said, by a major *razborka* between rival oil and gas Mafia groups in St Petersburg – he simply noted it with a shrug of the shoulders. This acceptance of the role and position of the Mafia within Russian society is widespread, particularly among businesspeople.

Valentin, a slim, prematurely balding man in his mid-thirties, has a lifestyle the envy of many Russians. A successful self-made man in the meat processing and packaging business, he drives a latest-model foreign car and owns apartments in Moscow and a large, newly built dacha on a plot of land near Tver in Moscow's 'Golden Ring' region of historic cities. A career army officer in Soviet times, he negotiated his way out of military service within a year of the putsch of 1991. Early efforts in trading gemstones brought rich rewards. It was a dangerous business – he relied on good information and official contacts – but with returns of around $20 for every dollar invested, gemstomes soon gave Valentin an income he could only have dreamed of in Soviet times. Within a year he had made more than $100,000 and he and his wife went on a spending spree, emptying the *antresoli* cupboard above the kitchen door and spending the money on televisions, cars, cameras, clothes, holidays and property. 'I was thirty years old and had never known such wealth. But when my partner in the gemstone business died of cancer, business became difficult and I started looking around for something else.'

Valentin went back to his roots in a rural district outside Moscow and saw the chance to set up a more steady business, bringing high-class meat products to a wider market through modern factory processing and packaging methods. The business appealed to his sense of patriotism. Domestically produced food products were considered inferior to expensive foreign imports, but Valentin knew just how good locally cured and cooked meats were and determined to compete with the imports.

In any other European country a range of support services, from financial and legal to governmental, would have been available to help him set up the business and create employment. But in Russia, Valentin says, the government and Mafia combine to put obstacles in the way of any wealth-creating enterprise as a means of creaming something off for themselves.

The early days of the new Russia – the first half of the

1990s – were a chaotic and wild time. Soviet-era rules had disappeared and the Mafia was busy carving out areas of influence. Small kiosk owners, traders and others who were visibly turning over sums of cash, however large, were targeted by the more organized old criminal gangs, but other, less visible business people were left alone. Valentin certainly knew that he needed to pay his way in his early money-making days, when frequent trips to the Siberian 'wild east' necessitated paying off officials along the way. But direct contact with Mafia structures was rare.

This changed when he moved into the more stable meat processing business in the mid 1990s, a time when, he says, 'a symbiosis of power and money appeared in Russia'. 'Doing business in Russia has never been easy, but what happened after the first few years of freedom was that an oligarchy of extremely wealthy businessmen appeared. At the same time bureaucratic power became stronger and more powerful again, and it seems to me that the Mafia groups and the bureaucracy came to some kind of agreement on how they operated within the same area,' Valentin explains. 'Today, if you want to do business, you cannot do this without the say-so of the authorities or government. You have to negotiate both with officials and with the 'others' [Mafia]. It's like some game you have to go through. In any business you have to deal with some form of taxes. In Russia whatever type of business you have there are "crows" waiting to attack you. The result is that the financial and legal system doesn't support you. If you follow the laws you can't do business. You have to break the laws and the Mafia exploits this.'

While some, like the cab driver Oleg, see the Mafia as little more than an expensive privatized agency oiling the wheels of commerce in return for a cut of the profits, Valentin has a more scathing attitude. 'The Mafia does not help you work,' he asserts. 'It's a living organism. It's there and you have to feed it. When you are in business you have to feed either the Mafia or the government or both.'

When licences are required for a particular reason, an import or export deal for example, businessmen trying to cut corners are forced into paying bribes and seeking help from the Mafia if they are to make a profit. It may be unsavoury, but doing business while keeping your hands clean in Russia is a rare exception to the unwritten rules of commerce.

Valentin's experience in the meat processing business is common in today's Russia. He knew the head of a local food products factory – his father had been friends with the man for many years. He approached him and suggested selling his meat products in Moscow. At first business resembled a slapstick comedy more than a well-planned operation. Valentin recalls turning up to take the first delivery of sausages to Moscow only to learn that the factory lorry had broken down. 'The director told me, "You find the truck, we'll give you the sausage." ' On another occasion Valentin was loading his truck with premium-quality *kolbasa* – cured sausage – from special stores to which only he had access, under an agreement with the factory director. Another wholesaler, seeing the quality of the *kolbasa*, immediately struck a deal with Valentin to buy the lot at a 30 per cent premium. 'He asked me, "Who are you? Aren't you the son of the director? What do you want for this *kolbasa*?" I made $2,000 in fifteen minutes and didn't even have to leave the factory yard,' Valentin says, laughing.

His army experience and the year spent shuttling between Moscow and Siberia had taught Valentin how to bend the rules, but the challenges of starting a business and making money in today's Russia leave him cynical about the prospects of creating a real European-level market.

A change of directors at the meat factory forced Valentin to look for other partners and eventually he found another factory with a good name among consumers going back to Soviet times willing to invest in modern processing and packaging methods. But fluctuating production runs and difficulties with distribution forced Valentin to forge alliances with officials and other businessmen. A company director with extensive experience of keeping both the government and Mafia sweet joined Valentin and became what he describes as his 'business godfather'.

Valentin and his partner built a business which today turns over more than $10 million annually, yielding profits of more than $250,000 – money largely reinvested in the business. The Mafia proper – the *vory v zakone* or other groups – rarely figures prominently in Valentin's life. But paying officials is a fact of business life, and is hardly even considered a corrupt activity in a country where government salaries are paid at a level which forces any state employee with a modicum of influence to extort bribes in the daily course of their duties.

'If you define the Mafia as authorities plus the criminal structures, then I don't know anybody in business today who has nothing to do with these people,' Valentin says, nervously fiddling with a packet of Western-brand cigarettes. 'I personally do not pay anybody off, but of course you can't do business without connections and if I do not make the people who issue licences for my business "interested" enough, I won't be able to do business much longer. It's not a case of paying off the Mafia, it's a case of paying money to ensure that you get your licences on time; that the quality inspection isn't delayed or going against you,' he says. No one speaks about such activities, despite the fact they are endemic within the bureaucratic business environment, he adds quickly.

So how much do businessmen have to pay to keep the apparatchiks happy and more serious problems off their backs? Valentin is reluctant to go into much detail but eventually volunteers that 'small bribes, $100 here and $100 there', usually suffice. 'But you can imagine how much these officials earn just by thinking about the numbers of people who have to go through their offices each day,' he says.

Payments to officials, themselves often locked into involuntary relationships with criminal organizations, keep the wheels of commerce oiled, but at a cost to efficiency, peace of mind and a truly democratic market. Valentin, who suffers from chronic stomach ulcers and other health problems partially as a result of the constant pressures the Russian business environment brings, says he is happy he does not have to deal directly with *byki* who might demand anywhere between 20 and 50 per cent of his monthly profits. He considers the $1,000 he spends each month on payments to government officials a small amount to ensure his place in the market, compared to his overall annual profit.

Valentin says that he does not pay money to a specific *krysha* because his business is subject to close bureaucratic attention and the bribes paid to officials secure the sort of protection Mafia groups afford to other, less strictly regulated fields. But whoever it is an entrepreneur or trader must pay in today's Russia, doing business requires a very different psychology from that many brought up in Soviet times were prepared for in 1991.

'I don't see myself as a "new Russian",' Valentin says in horror when the conversation turns to the ostentatious class of the newly wealthy. 'I don't go around bedecked in gold chains, talking into my mobile phone . . . Sure, I have a gold chain, but I don't like to wear it, or those chunky rings that are so popular with some.'

Joking aside, he understands just how far he has travelled from the days of his youth. 'Of course my attitudes have changed. In principle we are all new Russians, because we are living under new conditions. It's difficult to say whether my attitudes have become better or worse, but if I could go back to Soviet times with all the experience and knowledge I have today, it would seem an incredibly boring life. Today it's not possible for me to live without pressure. I would like to live a long life, but I doubt whether that is possible. At thirty-five I have heart problems already. I can never switch off. Life in business in Russia today means you can never relax; you never know what crisis might arise next.'

Valentin judges senior officials as the 'most influential Mafia' and says the coolest – *sami krytoi* – are the police or special forces. But despite paying some $12,000 a year to stay in business, such protection is of little use when it comes to solving certain problems: when deals go awry and Valentin ends up being owed large sums of money, he turns to neither his protectors nor the courts for help. 'If I lose money somehow it's my problem. What's the point in paying someone to get the money back for you? You may pay some guys a few thousand dollars and they'll take your money and walk away. When I have problems like this I simply accept it and try to learn from my mistake.'

8

Leaving Russia

Retired Soviet airforce colonel Vladimir Kariakin has had enough of life in Russia and is leaving with his wife and young daughter to set up a business in the Czech capital, Prague. At fifty-eight Vladimir, a tall, well-built man with a carefully maintained moustache, is abandoning the country of his birth at a time of life when many Russians are considering retirement. A technical manager for an oil-exporting company, Rosneftimpex, he enjoyed a relatively affluent lifestyle until the banking crisis of August 1998 sent the Russian economy into a nosedive.

Before the crisis his $3,000 monthly salary was more than enough to support his family, run two cars – a Russian made four-wheel drive Lada Niva and an imported Nissan saloon – enjoy weekends at a country dacha they were building and take foreign holidays. Life looked relatively promising and Vladimir had no thoughts of uprooting – after all he and his wife had just spent a lot of money redecorating and furnishing their spacious three-room flat in Moscow's southern suburbs.

The blow to the banking and finance system caused by the August crisis had an immediate effect on Vladimir: his salary was cut to $700 a month and perks – foreign travel, car and mobile phone – were taken away as the amount of business his company was doing suddenly slumped. Seeing no prospect of the economy improving in the near future, he began researching his options for emigration.

The decision to move to Prague, where Vladimir and his wife, Irena, plan to run a small guest house while investigating other business ventures, may prove wise for a man of his age, given Russia's grim statistics on health, wealth and mortality.

As Russia has struggled during the Yeltsin years to restructure its economy after seven decades of Soviet rule, a stream of reports has highlighted the effect the collapse of the national medical system, industrial safety practices and income levels has had on people's health. By the mid-1990s life expectancy had fallen to levels last seen in Russia in the 1960s. While women could expect to live to their early seventies, most Russian men were dying by the age of sixty or sixty-one. An epidemic of heart disease was a principal cause for increased death rates, but alcoholism and related accidents and poisonings were also key in producing health and mortality figures rivalled only by Third World countries. A baby born in Russia in 1995 had a one in four chance of dying in some kind of traumatic accident, compared to a one in thirty chance for a baby born in Britain. In 1997 registered deaths exceeded births in Russia by 700,000 and further decline in the 148 million population was predicted.

Alcoholism had reached epidemic proportions. The average Russian was estimated to be drinking as many as five bottle of vodka a week and in 1996 more than 35,000 people died from accidental alcoholic poisoning, 100 times the comparative US rate. But as disturbing as the figures are, Vladimir, like others who contemplate leaving Russia, is motivated less by the prospect of an early death than by an impoverished future.[1]

The economic crisis of August 1998, which saw the

value of the rouble fall fourfold against the dollar and wiped out the life savings of many Russians, precipitated a wave of pessimism about the future. Despite signs that the economic depression had bottomed out by mid-1999, the vast majority of Russians believed the economy remained in a desperate situation and was likely only to get worse. Young people and those in their thirties and forties were the most optimistic, particularly those living in Moscow or St Petersburg, according to pollsters, but most Russians remained stuck in low-paid jobs with poor prospects of immediate improvement.[2]

Fewer than 10 per cent of Russians, some 14 million people, earn more than $400 a month, according to a 1997 survey,[3] and of these more than 85 per cent live in big cities. A further 27 million people (20 per cent) earn between $300 and $400 a month. But the vast majority of Russians – 100 million – get by on incomes of between $50 and $300 a month, with a huge number, some 85 million, growing some of their own food on the ubiquitous allotment plots found all over the country.

Looking around them many Russians, particularly the young, well educated and motivated, see little or no prospect for attaining a decent lifestyle in a stable law-abiding society and seek a way out. In July 1999 the State Statistics Committee reported that some 52 million people received salaries lower than the official poverty level of 872 roubles, or $36 a month.[4] Although official figures in Russia tend to overestimate poverty, due to widespread tax avoidance, non-declaration of incomes and black market earnings, the effect on the size of the population in recent years is notable. In the first five months of 1999 the population fell by 346,000 people to around 146 million and deaths during the same period outstripped births by 396,000.[5] Russia's population decline would be far worse if it were not for the numbers of immigrants, mostly ethnic

Russians, coming into the country from other former Soviet republics.

Research scientists, particularly those in fields such as mathematics and cybernetics, where there is a worldwide demand for their skills, have left Russia in droves, causing such alarm among the scientific community that the Russian Academy of Sciences warned in 1998 that Russia's scientific potential had dramatically deteriorated since the end of the 1980s.

By the year 2000 as many as 30,000 Russian scientists will be working abroad, fleeing poverty level wages at home and the steadily declining and ageing research infrastructure, according to one leading physicist. Professor Sergei Yegerev of Moscow's Institute of Theoretical Physics.[6]

All these factors formed the larger environment within which Vladimir realized he had had enough. A career officer in the Soviet airforce, he reflects that 'deep inside I was always a dissident', and feels that this maverick spark within may have played a part in his decision to finally seek pastures new at such a relatively late stage of life.

For a Cold War warrior, Vladimir was never entirely committed to the ideology of his motherland – even if outwardly he performed his duties and pursued his career with energy and attention. Born into a military family – his father was promoted to general after the Great Patriotic War – Vladimir joined the Communist Party in his early twenties while still at military college in Riga, Latvia. His military education and inclination led him into key areas of Cold War work – strategic aircraft defence, ballistic missile operation and control and, later, aerial reconnaissance. His early years of service were devoted to a thorough study of the Soviet Union's nuclear missile defences. By his late twenties he was a senior lieutenant and regimental engineer for missile guidance control systems for the élite 'rocket troops', based deep in the forests of the Kaluga region, near Moscow.

Through his work and studies he was privy to the most secret aspects of Soviet defence strategies and installations, yet always felt a deep ambivalence within. 'Every Soviet person treats his motherland like a wife. On the one hand, he loves her and on the other he fears her. The regime of hate oppressed me but at the same time I was a normal member of the Communist Party and always spoke and acted in the expected way, although of course this constant sense of oppression made a person very tired,' Vladimir recalls.

A bright and fit man with a robust sense of humour and optimistic outlook, he remembers the effort it sometimes took to avoid falling into depression at the excesses of the Soviet system.

During a number of brief stays in military hospitals in the early 1960s he befriended several elderly patients, people in their sixties and seventies, who had spent time in Stalin's gulag camps. The stories they told directly challenged the ideology surrounding the young Vladimir. The details of the horrors these people had endured left a lasting impression on him and, although he never spoke of it, he decided that should he have the chance to go abroad he would not come back. 'It was a difficult and contradictory life. At once I both believed in the triumph of Communism and, following the authority of these people, understood that the system was evil.'

Vladimir never did get that opportunity to defect. His application to enrol in a military reconnaissance and intelligence academy early during his service career was turned down on health grounds. Vladimir recalls the reason given was related to his – perfectly good – eyesight and believes the enrolment board somehow sensed something not quite ideologically sound in him. 'I was a general's son and there had recently been a defection scandal involving the son of another general, so probably they were rather suspicious of me.'

Had anyone in authority learned of Vladimir's true, inner convictions, the consequences for him would have been serious. As an officer responsible for minutemen intercontinental ballistic missiles housed deep in concrete silos in a restricted area, his duties included seventy-two-hour duty shifts sitting at the control guidance systems for the missiles. If the nuclear balloon had ever gone up, his finger would have been one of the first to reach for the arming switch.

Thankfully the day never came, but Vladimir continued preparing for the ultimate confrontation between Communism and capitalism. His first wife's father was an airforce marshal and through his influence Vladimir eventually moved out of the rocket troops – where boredom in the underground bunkers had been his chief enemy. His next posting was to the Central Scientific Institute for Strategic Research, where his duties were the stuff of a James Bond novel. 'We were engaged in mathematical modelling and computer analysis of combat activities of strategic forces – desk-top war games. Depending on the activities of the American forces, we identified and targeted different objectives for our nuclear missiles – industrial sites, towns, cities, lines of communication,' he says. And what targets did he pinpoint in Britain? 'Oh, we had more than 1,000 missiles devoted to Great Britain. You don't need to worry about targets with such a small island, there would have been nothing left of your country,' he says cheerfully, with only the slightest trace of irony.

It's not that he ever bore any malice towards the British, Vladimir is quick to add. Like most Soviet citizens, his life was lived in the presence of unspoken, but understood, double standards. He had learned English with a private tutor in Riga, a woman from an old aristocratic Russian family who had been married to a graduate of London University, a Jewish lawyer. The Nazis had executed her husband during the wartime occupation of Riga, but the woman and her son had escaped. Her abiding love for English and all things British rubbed off on Vladimir, who – like many Soviet military men – never really saw the British as enemies.

The one foreign posting the Soviet forces gave Vladimir offered little chance for defection. His technical skills and computer analyses were needed in East Germany, where he spent five years in the late 1970s heading a computer software department at Wunsdorf, the headquarters of the Soviet forces there. Vladimir later studied for a PhD, writing his doctoral thesis on the mathematical grounds for military intelligence and proposing a model for calculating exactly when a superpower confrontation would move from crisis to conflict. The casual, cavalier attitude the Communist leadership took to its citizens is demonstrated by the response that Vladimir got when he sought permission to defend his thesis before a Politburo committee. The head of his military institute told him that the Soviet leaders were so well informed and in touch with the world geopolitical balance that they 'could see years ahead and had no need for such mathematical planning'. For a career military officer who by that time was deputy head of mathematical calculations for the airforce, it was a definite snub.

Vladimir felt the brush-off deeply and, as glasnost loosened the constraints on the Soviet people, he took advantage of an opportunity to provide political and economic analysis to American businessmen. He wrote a series of articles commissioned through a Russian friend, the son of a famous aviator who had flown non-stop from Moscow to the North Pole via Alaska and who had connections in America. But Vladimir's 'surreal' analysis in the late 1980s that a bumptious former provincial party first secretary by the name of Yeltsin was the one to watch drew only incredulity and the Americans soon lost interest.

The struggle between Yeltsin and Gorbachev and the growing promise that a new economic order would emerge in the Soviet Union gave Vladimir grounds for confidence, as he approached retirement from the airforce at the age of fifty, that his post-military career would be bright. More than thirty years of loyal service to the Soviet military machine formally came to an end one Friday in late August 1991. His first weekend as a civilian was spent with his family at his dacha outside Moscow where, on the Sunday, television channels broadcasting Tchaikovsky's 'Swan Lake' and radio news off the air signalled a crisis. Vladimir wasn't one of those thousands who rallied round Boris Yeltsin and manned the barricades, but a profound depression descended on him at the prospect that the putsch might be successful.

'I decided that the attempt to oust Gorbachev was the end of all my plans; the end of my life. All my plans for life after the military were connected with his reforms and the emergence of a new economic system. There was a definite threat that we were about to return firmly to the past. There, in my dacha as a civilian, already a free person, I felt a deep sense of sadness as I turned on the television only to find "Swan Lake",' he says.

Although the collapse of the attempted coup brought an end to those fears, Vladimir remains equivocal about the eventual end of the Soviet Union, saying, 'of course, it was a pity'. His sentiments, echoed by many Russians who had no particular fidelity to Communism, reflects more nostalgia for a country which spanned many nations and maintained, however tenuous, a sense of greatness and significance in the world.

But enthusiasm for earning a living as a free man soon swept aside any doubts he felt and Vladimir plunged with customary vigour into the bizarre new world of the free market. He took a job with a Spanish businessman who told him he was involved in the computer business. Although he had years of experience in computer software development Vladimir's job was that of driver and bodyguard to the Spaniard's wife, for which he earned $60 a month – then a considerable sum.

'I had a Volga but little money, so sometimes after I had taken the lady home I would go to the airport or railway stations and pick up passengers. It was a very dangerous occupation, but I would come home with my pockets stuffed with paper money,' Vladimir recalls.

The job did not last long. It soon became apparent that the Spaniard's real business was 'buying and selling girls' and when Vladimir pressed for more money he was sacked. Although his wealthy brother-in-law came to the rescue – offering him a job exploiting his computer and analytical skills in the oil import-export business – Vladimir considers that the promise of the Yeltsin era has been squandered and wasted in true Russian fashion.

'When perestroika broke out all the country believed [in its promise] and had some kind of romantic hopes about the prospects for the country. They believed that the revolution will happen and everything will be different. Every person will be allowed to and will be able to earn as much money as he wants. Every person will be able to work where he wants, be free to go abroad and meet whom he wants. This romantic feeling continued for quite a while, but gradually it turned out that the capitalism people were planning to build with the help of the United States and Europe, this capitalism was exactly that which the world saw 100 years ago – the senile variant of capitalism,' Vladimir remarks with his characteristic irony.

As the changes begun under Gorbachev were let loose in the new post-Soviet era, Vladimir – along with many Russians – observed the cynicism with which so many party apparatchiks and place-men divided up the country's wealth and power between them. In his 1990 autobiography Boris Yeltsin had commented upon the skill with which the Soviet state had rewarded its loyal servants through a system of perks and preferential services which ensured that 40,000 members of the *apparat* enjoyed the benefits of what party ideology called 'full Communism'.[7]

It was just these well-fed, perfectly groomed types who so swiftly took advantage of the anarchy of the early Yeltsin period to grab a piece of the action in the great fire-sale that followed the death of the Soviet Union. Vladimir's brother-in-law, without whom he would not have found his temporarily well-paid position in Rosneftimpex, was a former Komsomol leader in the merchant navy and a Latvian Communist Party official who used his connections to set up in the oil business as soon as Russian law allowed it.

The rush for wealth was a natural phenomenon of a society plunged into social and economic turmoil, but Vladimir found his ambivalence towards Mother Russia growing as time went by. The corruption – unchecked frauds, manufactured crises – has left a bad taste. Stories that Kremlin cabinet positions can be bought for $40 million or that senior politicians have diverted huge sums from the budget into private Swiss bank accounts may be apocryphal, but they are widely believed. Figures on capital flight, estimated to total more than $150 billion during the Yeltsin era and currently standing at around

$17 billion a year, when Russia is going cap in hand to the international community for budget loans, makes a nonsense of government excuses for austerity measures.

'Consider the number of Russian youngsters who are studying in Britain,' Vladimir says, drawing on a story his brother-in-law, who was based in London, related. 'If there are 50,000 children of the Russian élite at private schools paying an average of $20,000 a year for tuition, that means $1 billion a year is being spent in Britain alone. Multiply that by all those in America, France or Switzerland . . . and we're begging the World Bank for a loan of $4 billion!'

The way the great mass of Russian people have been cheated since 1991 leaves Vladimir with a deep sense of disquiet. From the hyper-inflation of Yegor Gaidar's economic shock tactics of the early 1990s to the criminal pyramid savings scams and currency devaluations, the Russian people have been robbed time after time. 'Here it is impossible to function normally. If you start earning some kind of money, finally you are either robbed by the state or by bandits – you can count the number of times the state has robbed us, it's shame heaped upon shame.'

His relative success, securing a well-paid position as a technical manager and oil industry analyst, put Vladimir into an élite category within the new Russia and, although he disliked many of the trends and atmosphere of lawlessness, he and his family did not seriously consider emigrating. His wife, Irena, and their twelve-year-old daughter, Ksenyia, were settled and happy, and during the second half of the 1990s Vladimir built a new dacha on a pleasant forested plot just half an hour's drive from their Moscow apartment.

But the financial crisis of August 1998, precipitated both by the world economic situation and by the Russian government's decision to default on international bond payments, was the last straw. 'Coming from the perspective of economic and political life in Russia, I believe that now if there is a chance it is necessary to leave and settle in another country. I'm worried about my daughter's future. She will have to study, and despite the fact that here in Russia we have a very good education system, abroad she will have more opportunities.'

September 1998 was a depressing month for many among that slim band of Russians who had managed to create a middle-class lifestyle as redundancies, salary cuts and the flight of thousands of Western executives from Moscow signalled an end to the good times of the previous two years. Vladimir was told he could keep his company car if he bought it for $6,000 and his salary was drastically cut. A conversation with a friend, a lawyer for the Russian bank Menatep, threw a switch inside his head. 'He made a remark questioning what sort of a country we were creating where today or tomorrow people might start killing each other, and I decided the time had come to act,' Vladimir says. 'I saw that this crisis really put paid to my personal prospects. If I were twenty years younger I might have seen the situation differently, but I didn't want to hang on only to be told at some point in the future – go, it's time for you to take a rest.'

A lifetime's habit of methodically analysing situations helped him as he carefully sifted through the prospects and demands of emigration to different countries. Canada, America, Australia and New Zealand were all rejected as too costly. Greece, Cyprus, Hungary, Bulgaria and Poland were not convenient. Finally he settled on the Czech Republic, partially because linguistically it presented less of a challenge than other countries with its Slavic tongue, but mainly because a relatively small investment of several thousand dollars could buy the necessary business registration that would allow the family to settle there.

Managing a small 'pension' in a suburb of Prague will give Vladimir a toe-hold as he finds his feet in a new country. There's a sizeable Russian population in the city and it is a popular shopping and holiday destination for those Russians with money to spare. Rental income from the family apartment in Moscow will go a small way to offsetting initial costs and Vladimir hopes to sell his newly built dacha for whatever he can get. In partnership with his brother-in-law – one of the winners in the new Russia – he will investigate other business opportunities in a country he considers stable and civilized enough not to disrupt his hopes as Russia has.

'I had not planned to leave Russia before August 1998, but looking at the situation – at the helplessness, greed and egoism of the country's leadership – the future seemed worse and worse. The transformation of Boris Yeltsin from a leader of democracy to a person pathologically ill with the lust for power does not leave any promising prospects,' Vladimir concludes. 'Russia has always been a subject of experiments in world history to demonstrate what should not be done, how the world should not live and little has changed in that respect.'

Leaving Russia is not easy, but coming back can be harder. Research biologist Alexei Stepanov left Russia for America a couple of years after the August putsch, when it became clear that the declining support for science evident during the Gorbachev years would only accelerate under Yeltsin's *laissez-faire* regime.

When he returned in 1995 after two years on a research grant at the US National Institute of Health in Maryland, he and his family found the culture shock of coming home as great as that which they had experienced in America. Today Alexei divides his time between Moscow, where he is medical manager for the Russian office of American pharmaceutical firm Eli Lilly, and his home in Saratov, an old Tsarist city on the banks of the river Volga in central Russia that escaped the worst excesses of Stalin's architectural vandalism. Now he has the luxury of looking back over his life during the Yeltsin years from the position of a well-paid executive, but he recognizes that life on his return could easily have not turned out so well. His decision to return to Russia surprised many colleagues in the scientific community, who had assumed that he would seek further grant-aided projects and forge a new life in the West. Fleeing the West after already having gained a foothold on the escape ladder does not fit the pattern most Russians associate with those who leave. But, as Alexei found, leaving the country of one's birth, whatever the economic and social ills, is not simple.

A rugged-looking man of forty-four who bears a passing resemblance to Boris Yeltsin's former national security secretary General Alexander Lebed, Alexei's reasons for leaving Russia were scientific rather than economic. Alexei, who had been head of a scientific school at a microbiology research institute in Saratov before taking up the offer of a research fellowship, had enjoyed a high-profile career in a key research area, anthrax and plague viruses. But by the early 1990s evidence that the days of privilege and full funding were numbered at the All-Union Russian Anti-Plague Research Institute, 'MICROB', prompted him to start looking around for other opportunities.

As the Soviet Union crumbled and new economic vistas opened in a Russia where suddenly anything was possible, he decided to combine his scientific work with business. In partnership with some research colleagues from Moscow he set up a veterinary products business. The venture thrived and he and his colleagues prospered. But the environment in which business was done in Russia made him increasingly uncomfortable. 'It was not a very healthy atmosphere at that time. There was a lot of drinking involved in business meetings and as the business began to develop we were forced into contact with those people in Saratov who controlled business – the Mafia. I did not want to work with such people and decided to choose science over commerce,' Alexei says.

The opportunity to work at the National Institute of Health came about as a result of the close contacts Alexei had fostered with American colleagues working in the same field over the previous few years. A career scientist and Communist Party member, Alexei had taken advantage of the Gorbachev reforms to make contact with the leading American anthrax researchers.

In Soviet times Saratov was a closed city, with access restricted not only to foreigners but to Soviet citizens from outside the area as well because of the large number of military installations and factories in the region. Some of the research projects undertaken at Alexei's institute had security relevance, either as part of secret Soviet biological warfare programmes or as antidotes in case the West was working on similar weapons. So, when in 1988 Alexei decided to write to the leading American authority on anthrax, Professor Thorne of Massachusetts University, it was done more in the spirit of a dare than anything else.

'I was interested in obtaining access to up-to-date scientific literature from any sources – my level of English was quite good – but still was rather surprised when I received a reply to my letter inviting me to visit the States. I had never been abroad and certainly understood that getting permission would not be that simple,' he recalls.

Sitting in his air-conditioned office in a modern European-standard building overlooking Moscow's Garden Ring Road, Alexei smiles at the memory of the hoops he had to jump through to get his passport and visa to visit America for the first time. 'There were a number of barriers I had to cross. I needed specific permission from my institute and I had to go to the Ministry of Health in Moscow to speak with people right up to minister level. Even though I had the support of the local Saratov administration and the district party committee, it was not a straightforward process.'

He continued to exchange typewritten letters – he did not have a computer at that time – with Professor Thorne as he underwent a series of 'deep, searching interviews' where his motives for wishing to go to America were examined in minute detail. His first attempt to leave for America was frustrated by the Ministry of Foreign Affairs, which at the last moment unexpectedly refused to issue his foreign travel passport. The telegram he sent his American colleague, who had been expecting his imminent arrival, took nearly a month to get there. 'Several weeks after I sent the telegram I received a phone call from the professor and so was able to explain to him what had happened.'

Alexei reapplied for his passport and, by now experienced in the ways of the bureaucrats, finally made it to the States six months later. From his correspondence and other sources he knew he could expect a level of scientific research that could also be found in Russia. His home institute was directly funded by the Ministry of Health and was, by Russian standards, well equipped and staffed. But his immediate impression of America was certainly one of affluence and order. 'My first impression was that America had a different smell to Russia, something nice,' he says with a grin. 'If you are familiar with domestic Russian airports and railway stations you will know what I am talking about. Landing at John F. Kennedy Airport in New York I noticed not so much a different smell as an absence of any smells.'

Regular visits to America, funded by an international

exchange programme, followed as the grip of old ideas in the Soviet Union loosened with the progress of glasnost. Alexei's visits, where he conducted joint research experiments and lectured to students, continued to excite interest among his American colleagues. Contact with Soviet citizens was still something rare in the States at that time and Alexei was often quizzed on the military applications to which much Soviet science was put. 'Americans at the institutes I visited would often drop by to the lab where I was working just to see what this Russian bear looked like,' he jokes.

The collapse of the Soviet Union left little impression on Alexei, who then as now was always more interested in his scientific work than in political developments. On the day of the putsch he was at his dacha outside Saratov when he heard the news on the radio. He drove into the centre of the Volga riverside city, saw that people were going about their business as usual and drove back, thinking nothing more of it.

The new era was one of mixed messages. His veterinary concerns prospered even as his scientific work faltered. 'Business was something new and exciting for me, but as investment began to decrease in science I knew I had to make a choice. Offers from America were beginning to come in and eventually I realized I had to decide between business and science.'

Political events played no part in the family's decision to leave Russia, Alexei says. The attitude was, if anything, casual. 'We thought here's an opportunity, let's give it a go.' But arriving in America was a culture shock. 'My daughter, who was then thirteen years old, found it very easy and assimilated rapidly, but my wife, who did not speak English, felt completely lost and left after six months to go back to Saratov,' Alexei says. She returned within a few months and with his support took an inten-

sive language course before finding work as a fitting-room assistant in a department store.

Alexei enjoyed his research work at the National Institute of Health, where he continued his studies into anthrax as part of a global vaccine project, but decided to return to Russia before the three-year term of his visiting fellowship expired. His annual salary of $35,000 was enough for the family to live on, but faced with the prospect of having to pay that much each year in college tuition fees when his daughter eventually went to university, Alexei decided it was time to return to Russia. He had graduated from Saratov Medical University and knew his daughter would get a good education there.

A cable television service which relayed the Russian evening news every day had enabled him to keep in close contact with developments at home, so he was expecting to find a higher level of crime and corruption. But nothing could have prepared the family for what he describes as the even bigger shock they got on returning than when they had left Russia. 'We didn't realize that things had changed so rapidly. Relations between people had become almost entirely money-oriented. It was strange. We encountered a completely different environment from that which we had found in the States,' says Alexei, recalling that America had seemed similar to him to the Russia of the 1960s. 'We had only been away two years, but we returned to a country with a wild nature where if everybody was not exactly trying to kill each other, they certainly seemed to be trying to harm others.'

It was as if all the honourable social tenets of Communism had been discarded along with even the most basic human characteristics, long regarded as essentially Russian. Hospitality and good neighbourliness were rare commodities in a Russia driven by the scramble to privatize public property for private greed.

Alexei recalls his car – a Russian model – breaking down as he was driving along the highway near Saratov shortly after returning to Russia. The informal rules of the road had always dictated that any driver who could help would stop and offer assistance. In Russia, with its vast distances, bad roads and often poorly maintained vehicles, it had long been a social compact that made sense to all drivers. 'I waved a car down to ask for help and the first question the driver asked was, "Do you have money?" ' Alexei says, adding, 'It was as if the order we had known in Soviet times had completely disappeared.'

It was ironic that after years of Soviet propaganda about the evils of the greedy, selfish capitalists beyond the country's borders, Russia now seemed to have succumbed to the same disease. Alexei had returned in 'naïve belief' that, on resuming his post as a laboratory director at the anti-plague institute in Saratov, he would be able to raise the necessary grants from within Russia and abroad to continue his work. What he found plunged him into depression. Ministry of Health financing, for what had been an élite research institute, had disappeared. His monthly salary was just enough to pay for the cost of petrol for twice-weekly trips to his dacha. And raising grants of more than a paltry few thousand dollars – even with some support from American colleagues – was a hopeless task.

Living off money the family had saved during their stay in America, Alexei toyed with the idea of going back into business again. 'Initially I was quite optimistic and it took about a year for the truth to sink in,' he says, recalling the resistance he met from former business partners when he discussed doing business the American way – legally and with proper accounting systems. The commercial freedom that had allowed his business to prosper in the early 1990s was no longer evident. His partners had not been able to retain their position in the veterinary field and by

the time Alexei came back in 1995 most business niches were filled.

Daily life in Russia was an unending parade of difficulties, he recalls. 'That was another real shock. In our two years away we had become used to the convenience of life in the States. You took care of your job there and other parts of your life were taken care of. Here, for example, even to do something as simple as paying the phone bill you have to take cash and go somewhere. Over there you simply filled out your personal cheque and returned it along with the bill counterfoil in the envelope provided. In Russia a huge amount of time and energy had to be expended just on daily life.'

Beginning to understand that he had returned to life as a member of the Russian *nouveaux pauvres* rather than *nouveaux riches* was, not surprisingly, a depressing experience for a man who had always been aggressively career-minded. 'Many people today in Russia are depressed, only they do not realize it. They use vodka instead of Prozac to relieve their symptoms,' Alexei remarks.

Inevitably his thoughts turned to going back to America or finding a job outside of science. It was on the day Alexei resigned from his job at the anti-plague institute after a row with his director, over the hopelessness of running a research programme on entirely inadequate finances, that his luck turned. 'I had had enough and quit on the spot. When I came home I opened the pages of the local newspaper, *Saratovsky Vesti* [*Saratov News*], and was surprised to see an advertisement there in English – quite unusual in a provincial newspaper – asking for applications for pharmaceutical sales people.'

Two months later Alexei was appointed the regional sales manager for the Volga region and southern Russia for Eli Lilly's Russian office, just at the time his savings from the American fellowship were running out. For two

years he built up the sales network, supplying insulin, antibiotics, anti-depressants and cardiology drugs to hospitals and retailers before he was promoted to the head-office job in Moscow, where he is involved in trials of new drugs for the Russian market.

The job with Eli Lilly gives Alexei a measure of security and income enjoyed by few Russians and the company's reputation for investing in its employees offers good prospects for future promotion at home or abroad. But Alexei still laments the loss of his research career and considers that the collapse of the Soviet Union and chaos of the Yeltsin years destroyed any chances that scientific work in the country will ever return to its former level.

Alexei knows he is fortunate to have found a fulfilling and rewarding position in a benign environment – so many in Russia today are subject to immense criminal or corrupt pressures if they want to earn a decent living. When he thinks about Russia compared with his experiences of the West, he naturally divides the country from those who govern it. 'This country is great – I really love it and am happy here. But, of course, I don't like the political organization. I'm not quite sure how to express this, but it seems to me that these dramatic changes in Russia always bring some specific types of people to power.'

He sees hope in the growing understanding, particularly among young people, that hard work and application are the only ways to earning a good living. And he believes that all those Russians who have left the country during recent years want nothing more than to be able to come home to the country of their birth. But when pressed about how he sees the future he is more pessimistic. 'I don't think Russia will improve in my lifetime. I hope my daughter will see better times, although I'm rather keen that after getting her medical degree she should pursue a scientific career in Britain or America.'

Epilogue

Drawing conclusions about Russia is always a process fraught with difficulty. Churchill's famous phrase that Russia is a riddle, wrapped in a mystery inside an enigma remains as true today as half a century ago. Russia has always defied understanding, as much by the Russians themselves as by the outside world. The Russian poet Fyodor Tutchev said Russia cannot be understood by the mind, Russia can only be believed in. When I first broached the subject of his inclusion in my book, one of my interviewees remarked that I had given myself an impossible task in hoping to understand Russia. Then he wished me luck and said he looked forward to seeing Russia through the eyes of an Englishman. With these considerations in mind, I will attempt a closure on the experiences, observations and stories related here.

Boris Yeltsin remained at the end of the 1990s, as at the beginning, the key figure in the Russian political landscape. Written off dozens of times by his critics as an ill, impotent figurehead, he continues to surprise by his ability to spring back on to centre stage, pitching the political arena once again into chaos with his casual removals and appointments of prime ministers. The last three years of the 1990s saw no fewer than five changes of prime minister by an increasingly capricious president. Yeltsin's motives for creating an atmosphere of chronic political

instability are apparently connected to his fear that a future Kremlin administration will hold him and his family accountable for the rampant corruption and dividing up of the spoils evident in the years following the fall of Communism. Yeltsin may once have railed against corruption – his autobiography, published in 1990, is full of democratic indignation at the excesses of the party bureaucrats – but a decade at the top apparently did little to quench his thirst for power for its own sake.

The effect of the constant game of political musical chairs on ordinary Russians has been to leave most cynically resigned to the absurdity of Russia's democratic charades. The Kremlin long ago became a circus performance for most Russians and today they barely bother to watch the daily antics there. When Yeltsin sacked Prime Minister Sergei Stepashin in August 1999 to replace him with political unknown, Vladimir Putin, the head of the Federal Security Service, a successor body to the KGB, Russians barely batted an eyelid. 'Yeltsin's crazy,' was the most common response when I asked their opinion of the reshuffle. Politics remains a distant and dirty game to most Russians. What demands their attention and absorbs their energy is the economy.

Making a living in Russia has never been easy, but today mere survival is a challenge for millions. The people interviewed in this book are arguably drawn from the most privileged of Russian citizens. Moscow residents enjoy a higher standard of living and access to better services and medical care than most Russians. Yet the day-to-day struggle to make ends meet demands most of the attention of the majority of even these relatively well-off people.

The United Nations Development Programme report on human development in Russia 1998 makes for sobering reading, listing the growing socioeconomic inequality in

the country; the poor use and distribution of resources; the catastrophically high mortality rate for Russian men; the appalling legacy of environmental pollution left from the Soviet era. It concludes: 'In Russia the point is not to raise the level of human development but to conserve it and, what is more, to prevent an irreversible collapse in human potential.'

Perhaps the only safe conclusion one can draw about Russia after a century of turmoil is that the country and its people enter the twenty-first century with a huge task ahead. The challenge the Russian people face is to create a country that strikes a balance between its collective and Communist past and the individualism of its present and future.

Notes

1 From Failed Coup to Crony Capitalism

1. Excerpts from TASS version of text, *Daily Telegraph*, 20 August 1991.
2. *Today*, 20 April 1991.
3. Jonathan Steele, *Guardian*, 20 August 1991.
4. *Today*, 20 April 1991.
5. Mark Galeotti, 'The Mafiya and the New Russia', *Australian Journal of Politics and History*, Vol. 44, no. 4, September 1998.
6. Figures from Moscow market researchers ComCon2.

2 The Beautiful and the Damned

1. For a detailed analysis of the Chechen war and the history of Chechnya's people and their conflicts with Russia, see Anatol Lieven, *Chechnya: Tombstone of Russian Power*, Yale University Press, New Haven and London, 1998.

3 Winners

1. Matt Biven and Jonas Bernstein. 'The Russia You Never Knew', Johnson's Russia List, no, 3066, February 1999.
2. Ibid.

4 Losers

1. Vasily Filipovich and Raisa Alexeyovna, *Your Fate: How to Tear the Vicious Circle of Bureaucracy*, Prioi Publishing House, Moscow, 1996.
2. Yuli Daniel, *'This is Moscow Speaking' and Other Stories*, translated by Max Hayward, Collier Books, New York, 1970.

6 Harbours in the Storm

1. The apartment block bombings of September 1999 in Moscow and elsewhere in Russia in which 300 people died, set off a wave of panic with many Muscovites moving out of the city to the safety of their country dachas. The ensuing renewed Russian war against Chechnya was continuing to draw widespread public support in December 1999.

7 Mafia

1. Irina Khakamada, *The Russian Journal*, Vol. 2, no. 8, 22–8 March 1998.
2. Mark Galeotti, ' "Who is the boss, us or the law?" Corruption and Russia's Rulers', *Blat and Corruption in Russia*, eds. S. Lovell, A. Ledeneva and A. Rogatcherskii, Macmillan, London, 1999.

8 Leaving Russia

1. Nicholas Eberstadt, 'Russia: Too Sick to Matter?', *Policy Review*, 95, June–July 1999.
2. *Moscow Times*, 29 May 1999.
3. 'Inside Russia', The Russian Market Research Company, 1997.
4. Associated Press, 30 July 1999.
5. Ibid.

6. *Moscow News*, 3–9 December 1998.
7. Boris Yeltsin, *Against the Grain*, Jonathan Cape, London, 1990. pp.128–9.

Select Bibliography

Binyon, Michael, *Life in Russia*, Panther Books, London, 1985

Clark, Bruce, *An Empire's New Clothes*, Vintage, London, 1995

Cockburn, Patrick, *Getting Russia Wrong,* Verso, London, 1989

Daniel, Yuli, *'This is Moscow Speaking' and Other Stories*, Collier Books, New York, 1970

Goldman, Marshall, *Lost Opportunity*, W.W. Norton, New York, 1994

Kagarlitsky, Boris, *Farewell Perestroika*, Verso, London and New York, 1990

Kampfner, John, *Inside Yeltsin's Russia*, Cassell, London, 1994

Lieven, Anatol, *Chechnya, Tombstone of Russian Power*, Yale University Press, New Haven and London, 1998

Parker, Tony, *Russian Voices*, Picador, London 1992

Roxburgh, Angus, *The Second Russian Revolution*, BBC Books, London, 1991

Remnick, David, *Lenin's Tomb*, Viking, London, 1993

Steele, Jonathan, *Eternal Russia*, Faber and Faber, London, 1994

Wilson, Andrew and Bachkatov, Nina, *Russia Revised*, André Deutsch, London, 1992

Yeltsin, Boris, *Against the Grain*, Jonathan Cape, London, 1990

Yergin, Daniel and Gustafson, Thane, *Russia 2010 and What It Means for the World*, Nicholas Brealey, London, 1994